GET FIT
FOR LIFE

My Journey With Fitness, Health, and Aging

JACK LOWE

With the Collaboration of Andrew Gordon

All proceeds from the sale of this book
benefit the Fit for Life Foundation, a registered, independent
foundation based in Liechtenstein, which supports healthy
aging worldwide.

www.fitforlife.foundation

CONTENTS

FOREWORD

Longevity is among society's foremost preoccupations today. Yet, shouldn't we be thinking more carefully about how we are going to live those additional years? What happens after retirement? What does the future hold in store for us past the age of seventy? To what degree can our actions today make a difference to our health tomorrow? These questions and more need to be taken seriously as average life expectancy continues to rise.

No matter what your age is, whether you are pushing forty or seventy, there is reason to be concerned with the health implications of growing older. We ought to know what we are heading for, how to manage it and, when possible, how to fend off, or, delay the largely avoidable pitfalls that tend to occur with age.

While no amount of preparation can prevent the occurrence of sickness, infirmity, or death, many of the ailments that are most likely to affect us can nevertheless be offset, or sometimes even avoided, by maintaining our physical fitness and mental resilience as we grow older. Contrary to what many seem to think, it is possible to age well.

This book does not provide a comprehensive solution to all the problems that arise with age. What it does do, however, is encourage all those who feel dissatisfied with their current physical condition and want to get healthy for the long term. This book makes a case for the virtues of exercise, mobility, and a more active lifestyle.

My perspective is that of a lifelong practitioner rather than a certified expert. I am not selling a system or a method. That said, the claims I make—though sometimes counterintuitive— should be relatively uncontroversial and are easily verifiable. The scientific evidence overwhelmingly attests to the health benefits of an active lifestyle. It has worked for me, and I share my experience mainly to help spread the word.

Several important topics, such as diet and mental health, are not given as much attention as they deserve. Much more would be required to do both these subjects justice, and I intend to address them in more depth in the future as they are essential to any wholistic approach to healthy living.

This book fits into a larger project my family and I are launching called the Fit For Life Foundation. Born out of my desire to help promote innovative solutions for successful aging, the Foundation's mission is threefold: raising awareness about the importance of fitness for life-long health, promoting solutions for life-long fitness, and reducing the need for—and cost of—long-term residential care.

As we will see, our health is, to a large degree, dependent upon our lifestyle. As such, most of us are in a position to wrestle control back over our physical fitness and a number of other factors that determine our general wellbeing. Hopefully, this book will provide readers with ideas, tools, and a little shove in the right direction. The time to get moving again is *now*. It is never too late until it is.

Introduction
MOBILITY IS PRECIOUS

Seven years ago, everything changed. Without any forewarning, as I was walking in town with my wife, my left leg buckled and I fell to the ground and could not get up. When I tried to stand, my leg would not budge. Using my arms, I tried to pull myself up into a crouching position, but I could not. I was completely immobilized, and my mind reeled with adrenaline and panic. Had I done something wrong, made a false movement? This situation was so frightening to me precisely because it felt so out of my control. I had no idea what was happening. The suddenness of this event and lack of any warning or rational explanation brought on a deep and vivid anxiety.

My wife helped me drag myself to a bench. We sat there for a time, and as the minutes passed and feeling did not return to my leg, I imagined the worst. I had spent my whole life doing sports. This was my pleasure, my relaxation, my way of keeping my brain alive and doing the things I really wanted to do. Staying in good physical shape has never been an objective for me, it has always been much more: it has been my lifeline, a powerful source of energy and drive. Almost immediately I thought, *je suis foutu*, I'm done for. Would I ever be able to walk again? Could someone fix this? I was seventy-two and the sudden prospect of not being able to walk terrified me.

After about a week, countless phone calls, appointments, a number of opinions, and a great deal of insistence on my part, I was provided with the diagnosis. During an acute spinal stenosis flare-up, arthritic material gathers in the spinal column and compresses the nerves. There is only a relatively short window of time during which doctors can operate to remove the arthritic material before permanent nerve damage begins to occur. The longer we waited before going forward with the surgery, the higher the risk would be of this damage becoming permanent. I was told it was only a matter of weeks before I might lose all the nerves traveling from my spine down into my left leg. Although there was a significant risk involved, it was clear to me this risk was worth taking. A neurosurgeon scheduled the operation for the next day.

When everything is going well, we tend to take our bodies for granted. Why wouldn't we? Too often, it is only when something is taken away from us that we begin to appreciate its real value. We don't walk around in our daily lives thankful for our legs, our knees, our hips, or our spines, and yet we probably should, for how sorely we miss them when we lose our mobility due to illness or injury. As long as your body will carry you, you can do anything and go anywhere. Your mobility may well be your most precious asset and resource.

Waking up from the surgery, I was told to stay lying down and horizontal for at least eight hours. Despite the fact that I couldn't yet feel my leg, I felt fine. After a good night's sleep, the neurosurgeon asked me if I was willing to try to stand. I slowly got out of bed with someone helping me and was flooded with relief when I found I could stand on my own without pain. Within two days of the operation, I was in the hospital's rehabilitation center. The only downside to the operation was that the sole of my left foot felt like a lifeless lump on the end of my leg. Since I had lost all feeling, I had to train myself to take proper steps that wouldn't damage the nerves or bones in my feet. This basically meant relearning how to walk.

Losing my mobility altogether would have been a disaster. It threatened to take away what I had come to rely upon as my source of strength, vitality, and stability: my ability to move around. Luckily, I left the hospital once again able to walk. Although I had some residual nerve damage which required that I monitor and manage my way of walking and exercising to avoid repeat injury, a process that continues to this day, my instinct was to accept the new state of my abilities and to take control over the things which I could change. Despite the few drawbacks, it felt miraculous. Training to make full use of my newfound mobility then became my highest priority.

In retrospect, this event and the ensuing treatment was a turning point in my life. It kickstarted a still-ongoing series of actions and processes of which this book is part and parcel. Before 2013, I rarely stopped to think about the health benefits of anything I was doing. I simply enjoyed physical activity because I could and because I wanted to. The onset of spinal stenosis completely threw me off balance, upset my routines, and fundamentally shook my anchors.

I was, and still am, determined to keep my mobility for as long as possible. But I have had to approach the problem differently to take into account my age and be more realistic about the options available to me. The truth is, I was lucky. My problem could have been worse, and for many people, there is no escaping the ailments that have befallen them with age. But luck is only one side of the coin. There is never any shortage of ways to squander a good opportunity, or a lucky break. I was never one to let the winds of chance be the only force in charge and have always done my best both to make my luck when possible and, as in this case, work hard to take full advantage of it.

What struck me most as I was recovering from surgery was the prejudice linked to my age. It seems to be a common belief that after a certain point you become a victim of your body and there's no longer anything you can do about it. Offhand comments and remarks revealed that many people think a decline in health is an inevitable product of aging. Some thought I wouldn't come back from this because I was in my seventies, others suggested that these setbacks are inevitable, that acceptance and resignation are the only option. "I thought you would end up a paraplegic at your age," one person told me. "Not a chance that is going to happen to me," was my response. I was adamant. One of my anesthesiologists even came to visit me at the gym during a rehabilitation session to say that all the physical fitness work I was doing was crazy and wouldn't make a difference—that it would never keep another stenosis away because "they always come back." In my mind though, there was no question about what I had to do: accident or no accident, I was going to make full use of whatever capabilities I had left. In my mind, the threat of relapse did nothing to change the equation.

So I dug in. There was a learning curve, of course: exercising to compensate for an injury is a delicate affair, particularly as you age. Nevertheless, with the help of my physiotherapist I educated myself on the right exercises to do and redesigned my workout routine to meet my rehabilitation needs. As I worked away at the task of rebuilding my fitness, I realized that I was trying hard to avoid what many people simply accepted as a matter of fate. I became increasingly aware that the inactivity I was trying hard not to slide into was a widespread problem. As I grappled with this question, I began to consider the broader implications of so many people worldwide stuck within, or steadily edging towards, an inactive and sedentary lifestyle that has devastating consequences on both their physical and mental health. This also got me thinking about the healthcare systems that have to bear the increasing burden of an ever-aging population. The scale of this problem is staggering and continues to preoccupy me to this day.

As I grew fit again, regained my strength, and was able to resume an active lifestyle pretty much as before, two things in particular began to dawn on me. First, that a surprising number of people seem not to share my desire to stay fit into old age. Second, that the widespread preconceptions and biases about old age are not only misguided, but harmful. They have a strangely normative force such that people's behaviors are shaped in advance with expectations dramatically lowered about their own potential. The only upside to this is that we have set the bar so low as a society that any effort to raise it is bound to produce what will at first appear to be nearly miraculous results.

I resolved that I would take steps to do my part in addressing this situation. I have always been a man of action, a doer, and based on a lifetime of experience as a fervent amateur athlete, I feel that I am in a good position to contribute to the conversation we should be having about old age. I want to help us reimagine the way we age and do away with the dusty old stereotypes. They say that sixty is the new forty, and they're not wrong. The bottom line is that there's no reason for anyone to stop trying until it's over. There are many things that we all can do to live healthier, more active lives. It is within our reach. Our bodies are meant to be out there doing what they do best, and while we in our later life may not have the same youthful shine of the younger generations, there is no reason for us to sit back and wait for the lights to go out.

Our mobility is precious, but it requires maintenance. As we grow older, it becomes more and more challenging to stay in shape and keep ourselves healthy. But we are only as mobile as we train to be. Although the process of staying active is challenging, the fact remains: the less we do, the greater the risk of losing our mobility. This loss, if and when it occurs, comes at a tremendous cost. It means relying on others to get things done for us and gradually losing much—or all—of our autonomy and independence. Without a well-functioning body, we cannot work, shop, clean, cook, bathe, or do any of the other essential activities that we need to do to care for ourselves. For as long as we stay active, our bodies rise to meet the challenge. It is only when we begin to purposefully slow down that the decline in our faculties takes place.

The good news is that the human body can bounce back from nearly anything. This means that the chances are in your favor. It's never too late to learn how to use your body more, and how to use your body better. If you feel stuck in a slump or low on energy, if you suffer from pain or weakness, if you have reduced lung capacity from too much inactivity or from smoking, or if you are so tight and tied up that you can't reach your toes, know that this can change and that you are among those who have the most to gain from getting active again. I am here to say that getting active again is a worthwhile challenge, one which we need to rise to and meet every day that we are alive. All we need is the desire, imagination, and drive to do so.

We need to change the way we think about exercise and fitness. It is not just a hobby on par with stamp collecting or bird watching. It is not just a pastime, an extracurricular activity, or a fad—it is an activity that is essential to our survival, as important as eating and sleeping. For too long we have allowed physical activity to sink down in our order of priorities. We need to fight for our health and reintegrate physical activity into our daily lives, for we cannot do without it. To a large degree, the challenges and declines that most people associate with aging can be remedied and prevented. For this to work, however, you need a clear-eyed vision of both of the obstacles you're facing, and the condition in which you're facing them.

Beyond enabling our fundamental independence, mobility is also a pleasure—there are so many adventures to live for and age is no reason to quit. Your imagination is the limit. Find and cultivate your dreams, your motivations, your objectives, no matter how ambitious. Be creative, have fun, and try things. Even if you only make it halfway to the goals you hope to achieve, the time and effort will be well spent, and the journey will be worth it.

In the following chapters, we will explore some of the main topics related to the pursuit of a healthy and active lifestyle. This book is for anyone looking to live such a lifestyle, with all the positive benefits it entails. It is for anyone who wants to age without having to feel old, for those who aren't fit but who are thinking about it. It is for those who are somewhat concerned about their health and those who are thinking of neither health nor fitness, but probably should be. This book is for anyone who is already exercising and wants to do more, for anyone who dreams in secret about doing this or that activity without believing it to be possible (it is!), and it is for those who feel tired no matter their age and who deserve a second wind. In a nutshell, this book is for anyone ready and willing to improve their quality of life by working on their fitness and general level of health. And if that resonates with you, then here is my advice: *get out there and go for it.*

1

LIFESTYLE PREVENTS DISEASE

Living longer does not mean living better. Today, life expectancies are on the rise thanks to medical and pharmaceutical innovation, and yet the quality of life for those later years does not seem to be improving. It is an ironic and tragic state of affairs that just as we are learning to prolong human life with medical expertise, we are also seeing a severe reduction in the quality of these later years. Current predictions suggest that the added time is likely to be riddled with disease and disability. This premature deterioration of people's health should be a matter of concern to anyone paying attention, particularly since it seems by all accounts to be largely preventable. The elephant in the room is that *our lifestyles are killing us*, and we're only really starting to take notice of this because of how very, very slowly it is happening. It is time we take control of our lives and focus on extending our *healthspan*—or the part of a person's life during which they are generally in good health—not just our lifespan. Prevention *is* possible, but any attempt to bring about better health will have to integrate the essential question of lifestyle and the personal choices we make that relate to it.

THE RISE OF NON-COMMUNICABLE DISEASES

According to the 2019 UN World Population Prospects, people over sixty-five are the fastest-growing age group globally. By 2050, one in six people worldwide will be over sixty-five, with that number closer to one in four in Europe and North America. The number of people age eighty or over is set to triple from 143 million in 2019 to 426 million in 2050. And as another indicator of our increasing lifespan, 2018 was the first year ever when there were more people alive aged sixty-five or over than children under five years of age. Statistically speaking, we are living longer lives because of advances in medicine. It's hard to overstate how far we have come: from the infectious diseases that have either been eradicated or brought under control, to the plummeting rates of child mortality and neonatal disorders, we are living in one of the most positive environments for human health ever. Projected lifespans are lengthening, and this has the potential to change the story of humanity for the better.

Alongside these improvements, however, are a battery of health conditions that continue to plague our societies. They are not new, but their incidence is on the rise. Cardiovascular disease, stroke, type 2 diabetes, high blood pressure, all types of cancers, chronic respiratory disorders such as asthma and allergies, dementia, Alzheimer's disease, Parkinson's disease, musculoskeletal disorders such as osteoporosis, arthritis, and sarcopenia, frailty, loss of autonomy, loss of hearing, depression, and the list goes on. These are only a select few of the most prominent conditions with far-reaching, devastating consequences for public health. All of these and more fall under the somewhat expansive category of *non-communicable diseases*. Non-communicable diseases, or NCDs for short, are chronic, slow-progressing and non-infectious health conditions. They are not contracted accidentally from an outside source, though external factors may play a role, and are heavily influenced by lifestyle. These diseases crowd the list of major health risks today, and they make up the greatest part of the global disease burden.

In 2016, based on WHO figures, 71% of global mortality was attributed to NCDs, also sometimes referred to as chronic diseases. The four most common of these—cancer, cardiovascular disease, chronic respiratory disease, and diabetes—made up 80% of total deaths worldwide. This amounts to about 40.5 million lives lost. Just over half of these were among people aged seventy and over, but 15 million deaths occurred in populations aged between thirty and sixty-nine years. It's important to note that the vast majority of these premature deaths, around 85%, occur in the developing world. This does not mean that people in the developed world are necessarily much healthier, but that they are able to better manage the diseases due to a variety of factors such as better living conditions, access to healthcare, and so on.

We all imagine our lives with a certain amount of fantasy. It's a very human thing to do. We tend to remember the good things over the bad, and we tend to be optimistic and hopeful about the future. This is our capacity to see the glass half full rather than half empty, to have faith in the midst of adversity. These are all important elements of what makes humans so resilient. It is often true, however, that our greatest strengths are also sources of great weakness. Hopefulness and unfounded optimism may be doing us a disservice by blinding us to what is really happening and allowing us to overlook or ignore small warning signs that foretell life-changing problems ahead. Medicine may be able to save our lives and enhance our potential by freeing us from disease, but the quality of our health, for the most part, is related to our behaviors, choices, and lifestyle.

There is a song from the 1950s that proclaims a Hollywood dream which has been ingrained into our collective cultural consciousness: *I wanna live fast, die young, and leave a beautiful memory,* go the words. The reality is somewhat less cinematic. Apart from a few dead celebrities gone too soon and mythologized in their youth, most of us today will not live our life like a fairytale; instead we will go on to live long, unsung lives, with the extra years especially unlikely to be spent under good conditions or in very good shape. The way we imagine our life and where it is headed, tends to differ quite significantly from reality. But becoming aware of this gap could literally mean the difference between a long healthy life and one defined, or possibly even cut short, by sickness and ill health.

NCDS: AN EPIDEMIC

According to figures cited by the United States' Centers for Disease Control and Prevention, at least 60% of Americans are living with a diagnosed chronic condition, and the number of those living with multiple conditions is close behind at roughly 40%. In a staggering testament to the cost this is generating, these diseases account for 90% of the country's annual health care expenditures. In Switzerland, where I live, the problem is not quite as dire, and yet approximately one-quarter of the population suffers from an NCD, according to official figures.

These diseases rose to prominence among elderly populations in the Western world, but over the last few decades they have reached epidemic proportions among the broader population. Younger generations are also getting sick and suffering from problems we once thought were inevitably linked with old age. And it's worth pointing out that NCDs are not confined to rich countries; they are also spreading at alarming rates in the developing world. Between 1990 and 2017, a Global Burden of Disease Study carried out by the Institute for Health Metrics and Evaluation showed there was a 40% increase in the overall burden of NCDs worldwide. While the circumstances vary from country to country, this health crisis is global in scope and seems to be getting worse.

Cardiovascular diseases are the most deadly and widespread of NCDs. They account for nearly 18 million deaths every year, or nearly one-third of the total global mortality. Four-fifths of these deaths are due to heart attacks and strokes. Obesity, high blood pressure, high cholesterol, and diabetes are among the predominant factors leading to heart disease. Cancer is another front-runner among NCDs with close to 10 million deaths per year. And although cancer death rates have declined in many countries since the early 1990s due to technological innovation, better early detection, and more efficient treatments, the overall number of cases continues to rise alongside population growth and the problem is not going away any time soon.

The case of type 2 diabetes is a worrying one because of how rapidly it is spreading. In the late 1950s and early 1960s in the United States, the prevalence of the disease was roughly 1%. Today, that number has grown to around 10% of the country's population. Worldwide, it is estimated that a little under half a billion people suffer from diabetes today. If measures are not implemented to stem this advance, the number of cases is expected to grow to 700 million by 2045. The effects of the spread of type 2 diabetes include a reduction in quality of life for adults who develop the disease and a tragic reduction in the lifespan of the children who are contracting it at an increasingly young age.

There has been some debate since the 1980s about how to manage the healthcare costs for people requiring a marked increase in care during the final years of their life, and there has been disagreement about how significant this financial burden truly is. Regardless of the exact percentage of overall expenditure, it is significant and continues to grow. Furthermore, these cases are almost all linked to longer-term management of chronic, progressively worsening conditions that fall under the NCD umbrella. About 85% of all patients receiving palliative care for a life-threatening illness also suffer from one or more NCDs, with heart problems and cancer accounting for 72% of those diseases. In short, those populations requiring care at the end of their lives are overwhelmingly also subject to these preventable, lifestyle-related diseases.

If we try to attribute blame for this epidemic, we would have to assemble a long lineup of culprits. Some of these are environmental, genetic, or socioeconomic. Alongside these important factors, however, are all the lifestyle-related factors. While environmental and socioeconomic factors undoubtedly need to be tackled at the policy level, and by civil society, the causal chain of NCDs can be significantly disrupted by addressing the ways in which we live our lives and by making sustainable changes to the things we do on a day-to-day basis. To cite just a single example, the World Cancer Research Fund estimates that approximately 40% of all cancers cases could be avoided through changes to diet and physical activity. Prevention, in other words, can have a huge impact on the global disease burden.

Although important prevention initiatives are cropping up here and there, efforts to implement truly preventive measures on a broad scale are surprisingly lacking. While there is promising progress being made in diagnostic testing and monitoring capacities for high blood sugar, cholesterol, and high blood pressure, for example, there is a conspicuous lack of ambition when it comes to implementing ground-level preventive measures. Our main way of addressing these conditions continues to be essentially curative in its approach. In other words, we monitor and treat symptoms of these diseases instead of addressing their root causes. To be fair, this is not an easy project, not least because any solution needs to be tailored to each individual. But suffice it to say here that there is much more work to be done in this area.

HEALTH DEPENDS ON LIFESTYLE

What does it mean to live a life that is qualitatively *good* from the perspective of one's health? This question is one we should be trying to answer a bit more honestly, both as individuals and as a society. Too often, we tend to assume that health is an independent variable that somehow affects and afflicts us from outside our everyday actions. This lie we tell ourselves masks the truth of the matter. As if the way we live our lives were completely irrelevant to the maintenance of our health, as if our health were not intrinsically linked to our behaviors, environments, habits, and mindset. This misconception seems to have broad traction, and it is profoundly absurd.

We now know, without a doubt, that our health is, in very large part, a direct correlate of our lifestyle, and that nothing short of everything we do in our lives adds up to determine our bill of health. The sum total of our social behaviors and habits—our eating and sleeping patterns, work schedule, and so on—basically everything we do and, just as importantly, everything we don't do, has a cumulative effect that weighs very heavily on our wellbeing, or lack thereof. Developing an awareness of lifestyle and how exactly it impacts our body and health is something we all will have to come to terms with sooner or later. For better or worse, lifestyle is a primary factor determining whether or not we will develop an NCD.

From the food we eat and the drugs we consume to the quality of our sleep and the amount of exercise we get, modernity has changed our lives so that these have become "issues" we need to contend with. Modern society has brought a form of luxury that frees us from certain struggles to survive, and it provides us with enticing comforts that nevertheless come at a physiological cost. We now live highly moderated lifestyles, where our health is increasingly linked to the decisions we make, as opposed to external forces. We need to learn how to adapt and change our behaviors if we want to live healthier. No matter how you define the good life, I think it's a fair assessment to say that it could benefit from a good bill of health.

The notion that we should exercise and eat well to remain healthy has been around for pretty much as long as recorded history, and it has enjoyed renewed interest over the last few decades. But what does living a healthy lifestyle really mean? The differences in our experiences and needs are a serious obstacle to any one-size-fits-all solution. But if you consider that poor diet, excess weight, and a lack of physical activity are, along with smoking and excess alcohol consumption, among the main substantiated risk factors for developing an NCD, what this means, essentially, is that these conditions can largely be avoided by living differently. You really have to pause to let this sink in. It is easier said than done, of course, but it's one of those situations where small, seemingly non-medical changes to lifestyle could help you avoid disease and add years of healthy, active living to your life.

The real game changer here is the realization that NCDs arise as a result of lifestyle-related factors. The WHO estimates that insufficient physical activity is the fourth leading underlying cause of mortality, claiming over 3 million lives each year. Taking control of those factors that *are* within our reach can make a huge difference in the statistical likelihood of attaining a good outcome. The truth is that by living more active lives we can dramatically reduce the risks of contracting some of our most lethal and destructive diseases. And while the statistics are clear, anecdotal evidence abounds as well. Ask anyone who lives an active lifestyle how they feel on any given day and compare the answer to that of someone living a sedentary lifestyle. You could be either of these people. I'm willing to wager that the results of this little experiment will speak for themselves.

TOWARDS AN ACTIVE, HEALTHY LIFESTYLE

As we consider this issue, it seems to be a problem we can work on without too much controversy. Is there a magic pill? No, stemming the spread of lifestyle-related NCDs will require deep changes at all levels of society. Public policy, work culture, the economy, and individual lifestyle choices will all have to adapt to our growing awareness of this problem. Will it be easy to solve? Surely not. That said, there is the promising fact that the road ahead is obvious, at least in its broad strokes: if we want to improve our health, then we need to improve our lifestyles. This means eating well, getting enough sleep, and above all—

moving more, not less. With all of the seemingly insurmountable problems that exist in the world, from widespread poverty and inequality to an acceleration of climate change, here is one issue that by all accounts has a relatively straightforward solution. If we can all agree that we need to advocate for healthier, more active lifestyles, and educate and support people to make the necessary changes, we will see a net increase in the quality of people's lives.

While contending with the quality of these added years has implications at all levels, including public policy and medical care, it also entails a turn inward. We need to take a hard look at the ways we are deciding to spend our lives. We are now faced with a choice. We can either bury our heads in the sand and continue ignoring the signs all around us, submitting to the degenerative illnesses that are creeping in on our lives. Or, we can take matters into our own hands and begin working to cultivate active, healthy lifestyles to ensure that we remain able-bodied, alert, and mobile into old age. My vote is for the latter, hands down.

As I mentioned in the introduction, much of my own "healthy living" has been intuitive, and the practices I will share here are ones I developed over the course of a lifetime. I will address the issues of diet, sleep, and body weight, among a range of others, but the core of my focus will be physical activity. I have no intention of turning into a guru at this stage of my life, and I am sharing my stories and reflections not because I think they are the only way to go, but because I hope they will interest and inspire you. We are all different, and the best recipe for health is the one you make yourself.

Whether you are already active or trying to get back into it, more movement and exercise on a daily basis may be the singlegreatest factor in your efforts to preserve your health. One group of researchers from Duke University Medical Center, for example, set out to monitor the long-term effects of an eight-month-long exercise study. When the test subjects were interviewed and examined ten years later, they showed significant legacy health benefits. These included better preservation of cardiorespiratory fitness and significantly positive results for several other cardiometabolic measures such as waist circumference, arterial pressure, and insulin levels.

The reasoning is relatively straightforward. As human beings, our bodies are made for motion and sustained physical exertion and thrive when put through a regime of varied activity. Everything within us works better when we exercise—it's a fact. Even those organs and systems not directly involved will profit from the increased flow of oxygen, energy, and hormones that are set into motion by the effort. When we eschew exercise, however, our body slowly begins to break down, both metabolically and physiologically. This is exactly where we start increasing the likelihood of developing injuries and contracting diseases.

As long as we use our bodies, they continue to be able to function properly. It's when we begin to slack off that things start to go wrong. Our bodies enjoy the effort, it's what we're made for. Think of it this way: an active lifestyle means you are out there getting your fair share of physical activity, which itself requires that all of the body's integrated systems work together to meet the challenge. This is extremely positive. From your lungs breathing in fresh air and oxygen, to your heart and circulatory system pumping that oxygen to your cells and organs, the metabolic conversion of nutrients to energy, the activation and exertion of your musculoskeletal system to perform the activity, the release of beneficial endorphins in your brain that create feelings of elation and wellbeing, the release of excess heat and sweat through your skin, and more. Regular exercise has a galvanizing and fantastically beneficial effect on us as human beings.

Despite ample evidence that an active, healthy lifestyle contributes to preventing disease, it is not an absolute guarantee. Whether due to genetics or merely to chance, we have to assume that the risk of being struck down with misfortune remains a possibility, perhaps even a likely one. I have always been conscious of this fact, but have tried to use it as a motivating factor, a reason to take advantage of life to the fullest while I still can. There is no path to invincibility or immortality as human beings. And while I am writing here from the perspective of someone who has always upheld an active lifestyle, this has not prevented accidents or the occasional illness.

There are a number of ways to lead an active lifestyle; there is no exclusive system or set of rules that work for everybody. Just like those people who are naturally active, there are those who have a very good sense of what their bodies need, and they act accordingly. If you go looking, you will find a myriad of accounts and narratives, some not unlike this one, of people who have successfully designed, adapted, or changed their ways to improve overall health and activity levels. No matter where we are in our own lives, there's always room for improvement. It all begins with a spark of hope and the desire to do more, and to feel better as a result. In addition, we all have different needs at different times and need to take this into account.

Lack of physical activity and a generally unhealthy lifestyle have literally taken on the proportions of an epidemic in our day and age. They are a time bomb that has grown statistically more likely to throw our lives off course as we grow older. This is bad news, but it is not the end of the story. The progression of NCDs is a problem that can be fought and countered. There is still time. We still have a chance to influence the narrative and change the outcome.

Despite the doom and gloom, there are clear and concrete steps we can take to improve our bill of health. As we will see in further chapters of this book, small changes to the way we live our lives can go a long way. By all evidence, from the benefits of an hour-long daily workout routine, which we will discuss in chapter six, "A Workout Will Make Your Day," to the ways in which we can avoid the detrimental effects of too much sitting, which will be the subject of chapter eight, "Sitting Is The Enemy," to the importance of how much—and how well—we sleep, which we will discuss in chapter fourteen, "Sleep Is Sacred," we are not powerless in the face of these threats.

2

LIFE IS AN ADVENTURE

Living an active and healthy lifestyle will mean different things to different people. What doesn't change, however, is the potential for adventure that is unlocked by being active and healthy. Nobody wants to be sick, and so the prospect of growing old while continuing to be fully able-bodied should excite just about anyone. I want to get you interested in taking steps to bring more exercise into your life because it will increase your health, your fitness, and, importantly, your wellbeing. But beyond that it will also enable you to get out and experience life in a way that is impossible if you are unable to move. Mobility means adventure!

I have cultivated this sense of adventure for as long as I can remember. From the naive curiosity of my youth to traveling for business to every continent except Antarctica, from raising a family of three children with my wife, Claire-Lise—we are now grandparents to seven grandchildren—to summiting twenty-five high-altitude mountain peaks and much more, I have always felt a strong calling to explore the world and experience as much as I can of the wonder and excitement this life offers us.

WAYS TO TRAVEL

My desire to see the world started young. When I was in high school in my small town in California back in 1959, at the age of seventeen, I embarked on an exchange program to Turkey, where I spent three months. This experience changed my life and set the tone for many years to come. I traveled from London to Vienna to Istanbul through Holland, Germany, Austria and the Balkans on the Orient Express. From Istanbul I then continued via Ankara to Adana, a city located in the southeast corner of Turkey on the Seyhan River, beyond the Taurus Mountains. The stories I heard about this famous railway line had me sleeping with both eyes open. For a California boy like me with no experience of the world, this train journey was beyond description. The last leg alone—from Istanbul to Adana—lasted a full twenty-four hours. When I arrived, to my surprise, I was greeted by a delegation of over sixty people—all members of the extended Bugay family, who were to be my hosts. They were a well-to-do family, with deep roots in the area, and they all lived in the same six-story building in the center of town. Once a week, they would eat together on the rooftop—and what a party that was! Here I was, dropped in the middle of a vibrant world with few reference points, if any, to what I had known until then. It could have been a disaster, but I loved it.

After a few days with my hosts, my host father called me into his office and handed me a wad of Turkish banknotes. In French, the only language we had in common, which I had studied in high school, he said: "This is your allowance. It is what I give my sons each month. Use it to see Adana, buy presents for your mother and grandmother. And make some local friends." I didn't know what to say, so I thanked him and basically did as I was told. I had a great time. The local kids were happy to socialize, partly because I would teach them English words, and partly because, as the "rich boy," I would always pay for the coffees. Everything about being in Turkey fascinated me. In fact, it brought out the only real developed character trait which I was able to recognize at that time: curiosity. From the unfamiliar sounds of their language and my initial inability to follow conversations, to the food and its smells, the music, with its Eastern sonorities, and the rural and agricultural dimension of much of the life there—I was enthralled.

Adana was already a big city back then, buzzing with life. I remember walking through the markets, with their produce and spices—piles of turmeric and cumin, crates of potatoes and burlap sacks of rice, heaps of eggplants, stuffed bell peppers, and all manners of fresh fruits, vegetables, and butchered meats. I remember the *dolmush* taxis, composite vehicles made of old American cars that had been gutted and welded back together with up to three doors on each side and extra seats to fit more people in at one time. I was so impressed that I wrote a long, elaborate letter to my parents describing these unusual vehicles—years later, my parents visited Turkey and this was the first thing my father wanted to see. In 1959, the country was run by the military dictatorship that emerged in the wake of World War II, and I remember being struck by the presence of the army which patrolled the streets everywhere, while no police force was to be seen.

My host family, who were Muslims, were eager to take me to the city of Tarsus, famous among Christians for being the birthplace of Paul the Apostle. I was also able to visit Istanbul, where one of the family's cousins showed me around and took me out on the water. I stayed in a run-down hotel in the old town, close to the ancient port and within earshot of the great ships and their powerful fog horns. I remember the salty smell of the sea with its old wooden boats sloshing about in the historic harbor. All these experiences made a profound impression on me, for everything there was different and very little was familiar. My vision of the world underwent a dramatic shift: my eyes were open now to all I didn't know, and this sparked a desire for adventure which hasn't left me since. From that moment on, the question was not whether I would travel, for this became a certainty. I knew I could go anywhere and do anything. The questions became: where, when, and how. Would I have the energy? Would I have the courage? Could I create the opportunities?

I finished high school and began my studies at Stanford University immediately upon my return. After graduating with a bachelor's degree, I went straight into the Stanford MBA program, after which I was called into the military during the Vietnam War. I joined the Coast Guard to be able to stay in California and avoid Vietnam. As it happened, I was unexpectedly transferred to the Marine Corps Reserve which proceeded to put me through very demanding advanced infantry and commando training. This was a situation I thought I would never end up in. Twice we received the order to mobilize for transportation to the front in Vietnam, and I sat on these occasions with my unit at the airbase, bags packed, waiting for transport. For whatever reason, both times the order was eventually canceled and, in the end, we were never deployed. Sometimes, you just get lucky.

I had played sports at Stanford, but it was nothing like being trained by the U.S. Marines. This was where the heavy-duty physical activity started for me, and it set the bar very high. We were trained mainly to be able to defend ourselves, but these were tough times and we were at war. Many of the drills and exercises were extremely demanding, both mentally and physically, and we were pushed to the utmost limit day after day—their way of weeding out the weaker portion of the recruits. With the looming threat of eventually being deployed to the front, the idea was that we needed toughening up to withstand whatever happened, no matter how trying. If things went south during battle, you might end up in the wrong hands, and what then? This was the mentality that was drilled into us. We started off with ninety men in the company but that number quickly went down to sixty-five, and while many of us started out as smokers, there was not a single smoker by the end of it. Our physical training included long runs with twenty pound packs, crawling under a ceiling of machine gun fire, shooting old tanks with mortar shells, scuba diving for underwater demolition missions, parachuting into water, and more.

At the end of my service, I was honorably discharged and got my first job based in New York with an oil company that had all its operations overseas, mostly in Europe and the Far East. It was the job that paid the least of those available to me, but held the best prospects in my eyes because of the number of jobs they had available abroad. This was somewhat counterculture at the time, and when they eventually suggested the overseas assignments, as I knew they would, their apprehension turned to astonishment and approval when they realized how eager I was to accept. After a short stint in New York, I was sent to Australia, then Thailand, and finally was offered a position in Japan. It was at this time that I proposed marriage to Claire-Lise, and we moved to Japan as a family, where our first two children were born. I worked in Japan for two years as a crude oil salesman, long enough to learn the language and become familiar with the customs. While we lived in Japan, I was hired by McKinsey, an international and industry-leading consulting firm, to help open their first office in the Far East in Tokyo. I was the only foreigner in a team that was otherwise entirely made up of Japanese nationals. This was in 1968.

MAKING ENDS MEET

After several more years, my work with McKinsey eventually took our family from Japan to San Francisco, Paris, and Lisbon. But after almost a decade of working for large companies, it became clear to me that I could never be satisfied in this or any other corporate environment. I needed new challenges, new problems to solve, and I needed them on my own terms. In 1974, I started my first company when we moved to Switzerland. Claire-Lise had Swiss nationality and her parents lived in Geneva. In the middle of Central Europe, it was a perfect fit.

My first company sold Japanese casing pipe to companies drilling for oil in the North Sea, the Middle-East, and Iran. Travel takes up half your time in this business, and the work you have to do on location abroad is no picnic. I have had several businesses since then, and it is always the same story. The work has always been enjoyable to me, and I have thrived in this environment, but the responsibility and pressures that come with it are immense, especially in the initial phases of setting up a business when finance is in short supply and you have to do most of the work yourself. You have to be in good shape both mentally and physically, not only for the travel, the logistics, and the formalities, but also for the requirements of meetings and negotiations.

Over the years, I realized that my primary professional interest was in creating and building businesses, so it was normal for me to sell all or part of them once they were successfully up and running. I suppose this makes me something of a serial entrepreneur, and I feel certain that this drive also stems from the taste for adventure and change that has always pushed me forward. The important point to underscore here is that none of it would have been possible if I had not always been full of energy, which I largely attribute to an active lifestyle and copious regimen of exercise. This ensured I was always mobile, quick on my feet, and ready to react and get going at a moment's notice if I had to—and I often did.

In the early 1970s, I was on a business trip through the Middle East. I had made stops in Saudi Arabia, then Kuwait, and was in Abu Dhabi for two days. I was scheduled to meet my host, the purchasing manager of the national oil company, for a meeting at 8:30 a.m., but at 3:00 a.m. I awoke to the sound of fire alarms ringing and the smell of smoke seeping under the door of my hotel room. I looked out of my second-story window and was instructed by people outside to throw my suitcase and briefcase out and wait for the ladder. I did this and waited for what seemed like forever for the ladder, which was nowhere to be seen. To escape the smoke that was filling my room, I eventually had to climb outside the room and brace myself between the window's two walls. With smoke billowing out around me and nothing to do but wait, I stood perched on the sill for what seemed like another eternity until, finally, a truck arrived hauling a trailer with a ladder mounted on top of it. They lurched the thing into place and I was able to hop on and make my escape. I climbed swiftly down to ground level. I was in such a rush that I jumped the last six rungs out of impatience. I landed and rolled with the fall, got up, checked myself all over, and was OK. When asked where I wanted to stay the rest of the night, "Any place that doesn't catch fire," was my reply. What else could I say? That got a laugh. Someone from the hotel drove me to my host's residence, and he took me in at once. He worried that I would be too shaken or upset to enter into negotiation the next morning, but I thanked him for his concern and said I needed to fly out later that same day to Bahrain, so we should just go ahead with the meeting as planned. In the end, I got the supply contract, and caught my plane that evening. As we took off, I was still buzzing with adrenaline and felt as fit for life as I ever have.

I'm convinced that sports and exercise have made possible all the other things I have done in my life. Getting and staying in shape has allowed me the confidence and health necessary to push the envelope and take advantage of the adventures this world is full of. Some of these adventures we stumble upon by accident, yet it is often up to us to go out and find them. I would even say that it is our job to make them happen. Because when they do not, when life seems to dry up around you, when things get heavy and seem to lack meaning, you have to assume that there is a reason for this—that this in itself probably means something, and that you can probably do something about it. Speaking for myself, I have always taken this to be a sign I needed to shake things up, regroup, and try something else. When you get out there and put yourself in adventure's way, things have a tendency to sort themselves out once again. There is endless possibility for renewal, and it doesn't even need to be very much. The little things work just as well. An adventure can be any and everything from starting your own vegetable garden, to climbing the Mont Blanc, seeking out a new career or starting a new job, canoeing down the Lot River, or letting go of your child's hand as they take their first steps. Adventures are everywhere. Realizing this is like walking through the back of the wardrobe and finding a whole new universe hidden there, with the difference that this universe is where you've been living all along.

The world may be full of adventures, but it's a matter of perspective. You first must want to see it, then go towards it. You have to be open to the possibilities. In other words, life is largely what you make of it. The world is out there just waiting. Adventures can be stationary of course, like watching a good film, reading a gripping novel, or enjoying a delicious meal, but the range of experiences available to you when you are able-bodied vastly expands the boundaries of our human experience. Being able to seek adventure in fitness and health provides an incomparable sense of wellbeing and, as I argue in this book, a sense also of *achievement*. I have infinite admiration for culture, the pleasures and intellectual feats of the mind, but not at the expense of being able to enjoy life in a bodily, physical sense. The body and mind cannot be separated in my view—neglecting the one will prejudice the other. You have to be in shape to seize the day, no matter what you decide to do with it.

MOUNTAINS TO CLIMB

When it comes to physical activity, lots of people focus on just one sport. I have always tried as many as I could, mainly to see if I enjoyed them, and if did, whether I could master them. I was never a champion at anything, but I always gave it a go, and in some cases fell in love with the process. In many, I was quick to give up, and in some I was truly a lost cause. This was the case with golf, for example, which I took up for a stretch in Japan, as it was good for business. But I could never hit the ball straight, which was a constant source of frustration. I kept at it for a while, but despite its popularity with my Japanese friends and colleagues I eventually gave it up. I'm pretty sure my two-iron is still wrapped around a tree branch somewhere on the Tokyo Kokusai golf course, marking the finality of my retirement from the sport. That was the last round I ever played.

I tried a number of sports over the years including swimming, which was never my cup of tea, tennis, which I had to give up because of a back injury, and rally-car racing, which I enjoyed, but for family reasons gave up as well. All of these look difficult at first glance, especially for the uninitiated, but you never know if you don't give it a try. Like I said, I was never a champion, but always a contender. I wanted to try, so I did and had fun along the way. My advice for anyone looking to get active is to try stuff out. Try anything, try everything. Who cares? Give it a go. You don't need to excel, you just need to enjoy yourself and this will become your driver. Once you're over the initial hump of getting your body going again, you will start to have fun and feel great as a result. By putting yourself through the experience of learning a new sport or activity, you will feel more alive, and your body will swiftly begin to wake up. It's a magical feeling.

Some of these sports stuck with me as occasional or seasonal go-to's, including off-piste skiing, scuba diving, body surfing, and others. A few of them, however, became lifelong pursuits. This is the case of running, cycling, skiing, and mountain climbing. In hindsight, I believe they may have certain qualities and characteristics in common that suit my temperament particularly well. They require strength and technique, but also endurance and planning (when it comes to organizing expeditions at least), and they all can take you to any number of new and fascinating destinations. Whether I am traveling or not, I cannot stand to run on a treadmill for the simple reason that seeing the countryside or cityscapes I am running through is wholly part of the experience. The same goes for cycling, which for me has been a window into the world. And then there is mountain climbing, which is perhaps the most challenging and symbolically potent of all these.

I can't say that I have ever considered mountain climbing to be a spiritual endeavor, or that my interest in it had any metaphysical quality, but as I reflect upon it with hindsight I do think that in many ways it epitomizes our journeys and endeavors in life. Mountain climbing keeps you alert, anchored, aware of your surroundings, and it keeps your ego in check. It is an excellent barometer of the self, for it puts you squarely face to face with both your strengths and your weaknesses, and there is no pretending. You either have to continue upwards or turn around and go back down; there is very little in between, and either way you are moving onward. Understanding and respecting one's limits is therefore essential, and for me this has always meant surrounding myself with and following the advice of guides. Furthermore, climbing in these circumstances brings out our need to collaborate and band together in order to make it, and this is a powerful motivator, a good training ground for facing and dealing with other problems that arise in life.

Mountains hold a special place in my life, as they do in our collective imagination. They are keepers and markers of geological time on a scale that vastly outweighs and exceeds human history. Their imposing physical presence inspires a broad range of responses, from awe to fear. Although I was already an experienced skier and hiker, I was forty-three when I started summiting. I would not say that forty-three is old, but many would consider it too old to start high altitude climbing. At the time, Claire-Lise and I would take the kids skiing every year to Zermatt for ten days during their February school vacation, an absolutely beautiful place with great snow. We often skied off-piste in the side-country away from the groomed slopes, and when we did so, as an important safety precaution, we would usually hire a guide to map out a tour or show us the routes in person that weren't too difficult and, above all, had little to no avalanche danger. This gave us the opportunity to discover the less frequented slopes of the mountain and the untouched powder snow. During these trips, I would dream of making it to the top of the Matterhorn. Seeing it every day, I developed a fascination. It struck me as uniquely beautiful, a beacon among the Alps, a peak that was meant to be climbed.

One year, I pointed to the Matterhorn and, not without some bravado, asked my guide if he thought I could climb it. He took me seriously and, before I knew it, I was at a popular local rock for a two-day training session doing what in French we call *varappe*, that is rock-climbing upon a vertical rock face using hands, feet, and technical climbing gear. As I was already in decent shape, I was able to adapt to the physical part pretty easily, but I had no technique and that is what we had to work on. The golden rule is to make sure you have three solid holds out of four—two hands, two feet—at any one time when you reach for a new one. Apart from that, it's onwards and upwards. A few weeks later, still following my guide, I climbed the Matterhorn.

Now, climbing the Matterhorn today, and even back in the 1980s when I first did it, is not quite like it used to be. The barrier to entry is lower, mainly because the routes up are now better curated and you can rope into pitons that are fixed in advance and regularly maintained. Some particularly difficult passages even have ladders or cables. Nevertheless, the ascent does require some rock-climbing technique and, of course, since you are in a dangerous environment at high altitude, it is also a question of physical stamina and mental fortitude, not to mention resistance to altitude sickness.

The night before our ascent to the summit, we sheltered in a *cabane* at about 3,200 meters. The only truly dangerous part of the climb is a glacier you need to scale just before reaching the summit. This is where most of the accidents on the mountain take place, and there are still a few fatalities every year. It isn't quite vertical, but very steep nonetheless, and one needs to be properly roped and secured for most of the way up to the top. We had left long before dawn to avoid congestion on the way up. "What the hell am I doing here?" I thought to myself as we made our approach. I was extremely nervous, but I kept it together out of pride and stuck to the plan. The guide's only advice was, "Do as I say and nothing else." That was enough for me. I couldn't have done anything else, even if I wanted to. But my prior rock climbing training in Zermatt served me well, and under the instruction of my guide I made the ascent without incident.

Trailing behind us was a group of about thirty Japanese travelers whom we had met the night before. I had spent the evening translating for them, to the relief of their guides, who were doing their best to explain the procedures, dangers, and technicalities of the ascent. As predicted, given their number, they ran into technical difficulties on the glacier. My guide and I, having already summited, pitched in to help and were able to reposition ourselves to facilitate their way up the steepest section of the glacier. Without us, several of them would likely not have made it to the top and there may even have been accidents. This was my first taste of the camaraderie that is required in the face of difficulties when you're in a mountaineering setting and others need help. There is nothing quite like it. When we made it back after our successful attempt on the Matterhorn that evening, I was elated not only for having reached the summit, but for the richness of the experience, for all the hard work that had paid off. This was the first of many peaks for me, as for the next thirty years climbing became a regular fixture in my life.

I decided to quit the high-altitude climbs after my back surgery in 2013, at age seventy-two, but I continue to enjoy tackling smaller summits and hiking on challenging trails. There are many things I still would love to do. It would be great to hike the mountains of Iran, for example, and to explore all that they have to offer. Unfortunately, due to political circumstances, it would be hard to organize a proper trek there, at least outside of certain prescribed and regulated routes. As I write this, Claire-Lise and I are planning a twelve-day trek in Armenia. We've always wanted to see and, if possible, climb Mount Ararat, which rises up on Armenia's border with Turkey. It is a mountain of great beauty with a mythical aura and an ancient history; it is there that, as biblical legend has it, Noah first landed the Ark after the great flood. Mount Ararat is not a steep or technical climb, but it will be a long expedition and will require endurance. It's a challenge I know in my bones that I can take on, and I certainly won't let my age get in the way. They say you can move mountains when you put your mind to it. They also say that we all have our own mountains to climb. Only you know what yours are.

3
AGE IS RELATIVE

Growing old does not have to mean growing out of shape. In principle, there is no reason you couldn't stay fit until the day you die. Accidents and diseases do happen, but the effects of age are largely relative. To what, you ask? Lifestyle. Ultimately, there is no age limit for being in good shape and no retirement age from mobility, only a choice of whether we submit to or overcome whatever obstacles life throws in our path. As we grow older, our body continues to have needs, which we can meet for as long as we keep active, putting in the exercise that will allow our body to thrive and develop. These needs and abilities change, certainly, but they do not disappear. It is largely a question of adapting with the times, and continuing to achieve modest results one step at a time. The rewards are very real but they must be earned. Giving in to an inactive, sedentary life equates, in the long term, with giving up your mobility and, unfortunately, your health.

WE NEED TO CHANGE OUR THINKING ABOUT AGE

If we look back for a moment at the number of deaths caused worldwide by NCDs, just over half of all these deaths are among people aged seventy or over, but it is striking that younger generations are far from immune. Only about 4% of people who died from these diseases were under the age of thirty, and there is strong evidence suggesting that while age, on a superficial level, is clearly relevant in the progression of these diseases, it is not the cause in and of itself. In fact, age is not nearly as important as was once thought, insofar as *healthy aging is possible*. Conditions once thought to be exclusively age-related are being redefined to reflect this perspective. A good example of this phenomenon is type 2 diabetes, which accounts for the majority of all diabetes cases around the world and affected about 422 million globally in 2014, including roughly 10% of the population in the United States and Europe. This disease was formerly known as adult-onset diabetes, but the terminology was abandoned as more and more children are now developing the disease.

As we progress in our understanding of human physiology, aging, and lifestyle-related pathologies, it is becoming clear that we need to fundamentally change our outlook. What we will experience over the coming years is a paradigm shift. We can no longer simply blame aging for all the things that go wrong in our bodies. This is good news because it means that our chances of staying healthy will continue to increase. As researchers unlock the biological secrets of the human body, however, no scientific breakthrough will do away with our need to accompany these new technologies with regular exercise and healthy habits.

There are many ways of staying active and healthy, as we explore in this book, but giving up on all of them is synonymous with giving up on life. There is no advanced state of fitness that dispenses with the need to work on it in order to maintain it. When you see someone who is still physically capable, at any age, there is no mystery: it is largely due to that person's levels of activity. Although genetic makeup will have an influence on our bodies, people don't just stay magically fit or healthy, for this is overwhelmingly a result of lifestyle. Nothing comes of nothing, and it is only through regular commitment and work that any true physical transformation, however modest, can come about. Even a child needs to put in the effort to learn how to walk or the muscles will never develop. Movement and sustained physical effort are what we are made for, but when little or no effort is put in on a regular basis to maintain and develop one's level of fitness, then it is normal for the body to wither. This does not need to happen. You may be out of shape now, but you can change that.

Think of the mental image you have of "the elderly." How would you describe what you see? What was life like for those who were "old" when you were a kid? Has this changed? What is it like now? If you are already over the retirement age, how do you feel about the way you are perceived by society, generally speaking? Does this affect you and, if so, how? Would you want to change how you are perceived and, if so, how would you rather be perceived? Closer to home now, think about your friends, or your family. If you have children, how do you think they see you? And how about your grandchildren? Do these images square up, in your estimation, with how you would *like* them to think about you? Ask yourself also whether you are not prey to the prejudice that age is synonymous with decline. These questions may help you shift your perspective and see things as they could be. They may also help motivate you to achieve the level of fitness you desire for yourself.

I remember from my youth when my grandfather, who was a heavyset jolly "old" guy, died at age sixty-three. After that, my grandmother came to live with us so she could be looked after by my mother in what was then her ripe "old" age. She had her own house, which my father built for her behind our own, and would sometimes come and eat with us. But for most of the time, she would just sit. Virtually every time I went to her house to say hello or have a Coca-Cola, I would find her asleep in her easy chair. The last two or three years of her life, it was extremely difficult to wake her up. She was stuck in a state of listlessness and had become extremely inactive. I suspect she had no real idea of what to live for. She never went for walks, not even in the garden, and she did very little around the house. I can recall seeing her once or twice in the kitchen perhaps, but that's about it. She was seventy-four or seventy-five when she passed, which was definitely the norm in those days, but not only was she an "old" woman, she had been so for over fifteen years. Every time I think of my grandmother, I see her in that chair and she is asleep. It's a little sad for me to think of her in this way, yet this is the image of her I have carried with me throughout my life, and I suspect the same applies to many of my generation when they think about their elders.

I'm not trying to place blame or call anyone out, and I have no intention to be gratuitously judgmental, for this is a serious question. It's a question I have had in the back of my mind for years. The issue is not one of vanity, though I do care about my appearance, but rather it is a preoccupation with the fact that I am setting an example. Who we are, who we *think* we are, and who we *want* to be—these all have a deep impact on our family, our friends, and our community. The impressions we leave upon our children and grandchildren are as valuable as anything that is part of our generational legacy. Much of this book presents evidence, arguments, and opinions in a way that is relevant to the individual, with a strong and encouraging emphasis on the possibility of creating a better future for oneself. Nevertheless, it's important to bear in mind that we are also setting an example for the coming generations. What these generations feel when they look up to us—love, hate, pride, shame, pity, disgust, etc.—is really in large part up to us.

The scenario for old age which we need to resist and stop from taking root is that of a slow decline where life is reduced, at the very worst, to waiting and suffering, interrupted only by brief moments of respite, a situation in which survival is ensured only by cutting-edge advances in medical science and pharmacology. Most non-communicable diseases (NCDs) that are widespread among the elderly today—as well as the not-so-elderly—take a long time to appear, and do so gradually, as a result of a largely sedentary lifestyle. One somber effect of this, to put it somewhat crudely, is that these diseases take a long time to kill you. This is an alarming state of affairs. The upside to this slow burn of NCDs, however, is that it actually gives you time to act. A car accident happens in a matter of seconds, but the physiological disaster of an NCD happens over the course of a lifetime.

My hunch is that most people want to live as long as possible and as well as possible. Unfortunately, I also believe today that the "as long as possible" has largely overtaken the "as well as possible," if only subconsciously. Too many people forget what it is like to feel strong, and many don't know it's possible to regain lost ground in the fight against time and gravity. A simple web search will bring you in contact with the stories of many who have found creative and wildly varied ways of staying in shape, often well into their old age. There are people everywhere who have made it part of—if not their entire—life's work to stay active in all kinds of ways. Many cases have stood out for me, but one of my favorite examples is the story of the Swiss railway worker and mountain climber Marcel Remy. In 2018, at the age of ninety-four, he and his two sons climbed the Miroir de l'Argentine, a 450-meter limestone rock face above the town of Bex in the Vaud Alps.

Remy is a veteran of the Swiss Alps and has climbed this same route well over two hundred times by his own estimate, so often that he stopped counting. At his age, however, this is a truly incredible feat. There is a documentary available online, produced by the Swiss mountaineering company Mammut, where you can watch the weathered climber as he prepares for and successfully completes the climb, under the supervision of his sons, both of whom are professional climbers themselves. I admire his passion and the tremendous effort of this undertaking. I also admire the tenacity and resolve with which he completed the heavy training schedule imposed by his sons. Beyond the impressive nature of the feat itself, the amount of work necessary to prepare for such a climb, especially at age ninety-four, is tremendous. His views on the age question are unmistakable. "I can't figure out these young people who think someone my age shouldn't do it anymore. I just don't get it," he declares to the camera during an interview, genuinely perplexed.

While cases of extreme physical prowess like that of Marcel Remy are somewhat exceptional, more mundane examples abound of admirable people staying in fantastic shape well into what is considered old age. Not only is it much more common than you might think, but I would argue it should be the norm! Aging is a normal process, it is the natural way of all life. Although our bodies do decline and droop when we do not use them, they nevertheless remain ready for action at all times. People too often fall prey to the common delusion that declines are entirely due to age and that growing old is nothing but a long inexorable exhaustion. This assumption is false. There is no reason we could not bring back "as good as possible" in our aspirations for life. Age does affect our physiology, obviously, but perhaps not quite as unilaterally as you might imagine. You can slow down and mitigate the effects of age with an active lifestyle and enough exercise. If it seems extraordinary to see older men and women who keep themselves in shape, that is only because a minority are taking the time and putting in the effort to do it. If we put our backs into it, we could make it ordinary again.

STAYING ACTIVE IN SPITE OF AGE

As we get older, it is generally accepted that we slowly lose muscle mass, dexterity, balance, and thus overall strength and speed. This is due, at least in part, to factors out of our control such as a falling hormone levels and a natural decrease in the number and quality of the muscle fibers that make up the building blocks of our musculature. "Natural" aging also affects our body's ability to convert food into energy. Unfortunately, these facts too often become a self-affirming bias, leading people to believe that their fitness is doomed to decrease as they age.

This does not have to be true, however, for we have the power to seriously slow the "natural" process of aging and mitigate its effects on our body, health, and fitness. The important thing to remember is that the effects of remaining inactive are highly likely to be much worse than the effects of being active. Will you ever be twenty years old again? No way. But can you rebuild muscle mass by lifting weights or build your endurance by getting your blood pumping and pushing air through your lungs? Can you increase some of those lost hormone levels by working out? Absolutely, yes you can. Growing old changes us, but growing old without being active will wildly accelerate the process of aging. You too could be one of the people working hard to lead an active lifestyle into old age, if you're not already.

One excuse I often hear from people who don't exercise is that their health is too poor. They say that they can't take it, that they're afraid of overdoing it, and so on. The crazy thing is that this situation tends to replicate itself indefinitely: one week it's a cough, the next it's a sore ankle, seasonal allergies or a bad knee, and this goes on and on until it develops into a form of hypochondria masking a covert aversion for exercise. I respect people's decisions and do not pass judgement on those who *choose* to reject exercise. But for those who are dissatisfied with themselves and nevertheless continue to make excuses, I encourage you in all friendship to have a long hard look at what it is you really want. If your answer to that question involves getting into better shape, then I urge you to drop the excuses and to start working through or around whatever obstacle—accident, illness, genetics, or age—is preventing you from taking the first step. The window of opportunity is there, but it won't be there forever.

Another excuse I often hear when people quit physical activity or forever delay getting started is, *I don't have the time.* This is a tricky one to address, because I know there are a million and one good reasons to throw on the table. Everyone has important business in their lives. However, as someone who has managed seven companies, six of which I created myself, over the course of almost five decades without sacrificing either my family time or my workout sessions, I assure you—there is always a way. Yes, it may be a give and take: you may need to be more organized and efficient with your time, or you may need to take time away from something else in order to spend it exercising. That is true. Sacrifices have to be made. Either way, it's a choice. It's a question of priorities. And remember, if you choose a passive activity over an active one, that's absolutely fine, but don't fool yourself, it most likely is a choice.

Lifestyle, of course, cannot be reduced to how much exercise you get. It refers to everything you do, all the time. This includes your diet and weight management, daily occupations, intellectual interests, levels of curiosity and creativity, social life, family, and so on. My main focus is on exercise because it's a *huge* part of the equation, but that doesn't mean that all the rest doesn't count. I urge everyone to critically consider their lifestyle as holistically as possible. The body is an impossibly sophisticated machine that needs all sorts of nutrients, stimuli, and maintenance to keep it going. Nothing will be sufficient, however, unless you also put your body to *use*. Even if you forget everything else you read in this book, remember one thing: keep moving, as much as you can, as often as you can. That is the secret.

Our bodies respond to the situations we put them in. Get out there, pumping those legs and arms. Swim, run, walk, crawl, cycle, climb, squat, roll around on the ground, jump out of an airplane with a parachute, whatever floats your boat. Don't listen to the rumors about "overdoing it," prove them wrong. We are not destined to decrepitude. Don't let hearsay fool you, and make no mistake: you are only as old as you allow yourself to become. An active lifestyle will mean different things to different people, and what level of fitness you desire or require is a personal matter. Nevertheless, it all begins with staying mobile. This does not come easily, but it really is that simple.

I am conscious that an assessment of my own experience with sport comes in on the active end of the spectrum, but it is an account among others of how one can put one's energy to good use. You don't have to go pro to make it count. Many people are fanatical about sports, but how many try to achieve even a modest amateur level? I am willing to wager that number is nowhere near as high as it *could* be. Give it a try! The only competition I ever really engaged in was with myself or with friends, and although it was fierce at times, it was always playful and enjoyable. Over the years, I have constantly adapted my activities and regime of exercise. I have done so partly following my interests and changing desires, partly to adapt to and work around my professional and family obligations, but also in order to accommodate my advancing age. I am and always have been conscious of my limits, and have tried to push them as much as possible without being dangerous or detrimental to my health.

PUSHING THE LIMITS

Nowadays, the basic exercise routine I adopted in my seventies, which I discuss further in chapter five, has become a fixture of my life. I do it with gusto every morning before breakfast. The exercise I get from my fitness routine is absolutely essential for me. Not only is it *fun*, but it is *necessary* because it allows me to stay in good shape and to undertake more exciting trips and forays. In a sense, I think I have always imagined my daily exercise as a form of training. Like an athlete, I understand the necessity of building and maintaining physical capacity, and I value the power of a structured training program to meet and regularly exceed my objectives. You might say that I have always worked hard all year round to make sure I am fit enough to lead not only an active, but an adventurous life.

This has always been my modus operandi. My training habits have changed over the years, but not the basic awareness that I need to work hard to maintain my fitness so I can meet the objectives I set myself. It has been true for cycling, skiing, and mountain climbing, insofar as my yearly climbing expedition to conquer a high-altitude summit came at the tail end of many shorter, tamer, and more approachable climbs and hikes that

I would carry out in preparation. I have always been very goal oriented in my physical activities. And a variety of sporting events were usually the desired outcome.

But it's important to realize that your approach could be, and is likely to be, something very different. In the end, it doesn't really matter what you're doing, just that you are doing it. For this reason, you may as well choose something you feel passionate, or at least curious about. Whether it is in the realm of the arts, architecture, music, engineering, sciences, what have you, there are ways of creating opportunity for an active lifestyle that will greatly benefit your health and help you invest in graceful aging. There are thousands of ways to get the ball rolling and many resources like online videos and how-to books that can help you plan and succeed as you do so. What matters is that you enjoy the process. It's all about the doing.

For me, as I say, this has always been about sports. And while I have had many pursuits across numerous sports, cycling, in particular, has always been a great love of mine. And it has long been one of the main motivating factors in my aerobic workout regime. For twenty-six years, I organized yearly cycling expeditions with a group of friends and acquaintances, and we took these trips very seriously. Training and getting ready for these was no easy feat. The trips were incredibly fun, and I look back with great fondness on the memories, but they were also very demanding. Yet this has always been my idea of a great vacation.

The way the bicycle tours worked was as follows. Eight to ten of us would travel to a new destination we had never been to before, where we would cycle a prearranged route, covering between 125 to 150 kilometers a day, on average, over seven days. In this way, we traveled about 1,000 kilometers a week. We replicated the experience on roads in twenty-two countries over twenty-six years. These trips were incredibly enriching, and nothing in my life has allowed me to discover so much countryside in such pleasant company. I developed fantastic lifelong friendships, and all with the invigorating effects of an intense, prolonged physical workout that requires you to give everything you have to see it through.

The group was just a bunch of guys, but they knew how to handle themselves and the bar was set pretty high. Most of them were impressive athletes in one way or another. The fear of falling behind and not being able to keep up with the group was a powerful motivating factor that kept me on my bicycle all year round, both indoors and out, making sure that I was in shape for our tours. In the final months of preparation prior to departure, my training program included over 2,000 kilometers of cycling: 150 kilometers a week for one month, then 200 kilometers a week for the second month, and 250 kilometers a week for the final month.

One year, we traveled to the Dolomites, in the Italian Alps, and we had with us Eddie Borysewicz, a legend in the cycling world. He was brought along by Thomas Weisel, a long-time friend and business partner of mine, whose investment bank at the time had taken over sponsorship of Eddie's professional cycling team. Eddie had been the U.S. Olympic team coach from 1976 to 1986 and at the time was the creator and coach of what became known as the U.S. Postal Service cycling team.

Having Eddie with us was a source of pride, but it also made us fear how weak we were as cyclists in comparison with the Olympic athletes he was used to training. We were keen not to disappoint him, so we decided to make our itineraries longer than what was originally planned. As I mentioned, we would normally cycle between 125 and 150 kilometers a day on these trips, which frankly is already ambitious for people in our age group—we were all at least in our fifties at the time—but we decided that since our new coach was with us we would try to impress him, and so we pushed that number up a notch. We figured this would be a stretch, but the challenge itself was motivation and a contributing factor to our success.

The Dolomites are both stunningly beautiful and incredibly challenging for cyclists. The roads through the French Alps, while also very beautiful, are usually long and slow to ascend until they peak and head down again. You might do two of such climbs in a day. The Dolomites are a different story. They are beautifully rounded, rolling, almost flat-topped hills, with small dips and valleys in between them. They don't look like anything else in Europe that I know of. The roads can't get around this endless rise and fall, and I have never recorded so much elevation traveled—over 25,000 vertical meters in a week—as I did cycling through the Dolomites.

One day as we set out, pumped up for the ride ahead, we forgot to make copies of our itinerary as we usually did. This was a problem because these copies allowed individuals, or small groups within the group, to break off and move at their own pace, not delaying the rest for punctures, bathroom stops, and so on. But it was a lovely day with no rain, very few cars, and we had all looked at the itinerary over breakfast so we decided to move ahead anyway. What could go wrong?

We had a pleasant day of it, moving more or less as a group until, roughly on kilometer 125, two of us somehow lost track of where we were going because of a flat tire which took ten minutes to fix. Ten minutes is a long time on a bicycle though, and the rest of the group was nowhere to be seen. We knew the names of all the places we were supposed to travel through, as per the itinerary, but had no maps to confirm the route. With not much else to do, we continued cycling, keeping a lookout for the main intersections and villages we were supposed to hit. The first intersection came as expected and we followed the signs, no problem. Then, nothing. We cycled on. Still nothing. We kept on riding, but there were no more intersections. Covering large distances on a bicycle, or by any method that requires physical exertion, is something you train for. It is a test of endurance, and one derives great pleasure from passing these tests. Getting lost on the back end of an already-extended itinerary and not knowing whether forwards or backwards is the right way to be going is about as severe a test of one's endurance as can be imagined. With no choice but to go on, drawing deep in our reserves of energy, we kept on cycling, mired in doubt.

This went on for what seemed like forever, until, with nightfall looming, we finally made it to a village and were able to inquire at a small inn. This put us on the right track and, not out of the woods quite yet, we set off again in the right direction, but this time with a map. We had veered off-course, and had to loop back around through the interminable ups and downs of the alpine terrain. By the time we made it to the hotel that night at 11:30 p.m., everyone else had already eaten and gone to bed, and we had ridden over 250 kilometers! My co-cyclist and I were completely exhausted. I went to see Eddie, the coach, to say I probably couldn't ride the next day because I was so tired. His response surprised me in a way and, in addition to the obvious—*always bring a map*—I learned a valuable lesson that night.

WHAT IS OLD AGE, ANYWAY?

Eddie wasn't worried in the slightest. We talked at the table as I devoured leftovers in the dining room. The main thing he said, laughing, but with a serious look in his eye, was: "Now you know that you can ride 250 kilometers in a day, and that's all you need to know." He gave me a short sports massage, slapped me on the back, and I was off to bed. I woke up the next morning feeling very stiff, but otherwise pretty much as fresh as I ever have before a day of riding on one of these trips. Was it the massage, the motivational speech, the extra kilometers, the hormones liberated by the effort, the good night's sleep, my pride? Probably all of the above. But I learned that when we are prepared, we really can go the proverbial extra mile. Our bodies are capable of more than we realize.

This lesson has accompanied me over the years. Our body gives back and responds to all the work we put into it. It's like making deposits into a bank of physical resourcefulness. If we build our body up conscientiously, carefully, and sustainably over time, it can take the strain and effort we put it through, including the occasional burst of exceptionally intense activity. All the time training and preparing, all the daily workouts, the walks, the shorts runs, the squatting down and jumping up, everything—it all adds up and pays off when you are put to the test, as I was that day in the Dolomites. At the end of the trip a few days later, as we sat elated around the table at our destination in St. Moritz, Switzerland, coach Eddie raised his glass for a toast and, jokingly, declared: "I never knew that old guys could ride like that."

Now, I was in my mid-fifties during this episode, so you may not think that it quite qualifies as an "old age" story, but that's precisely it. What is old age, anyway? I have known people who were "old" at forty-five, and others that were still "young" at ninety-five, despite the wrinkles. It's not just a question of physique or fitness, it's something innate, an unmistakable feeling one gets in the presence of someone who is alive and leading an active life, with desires and dreams, no matter how humble. I have known people with artistic temperaments who were always active in their pursuits even though they never left the house, people with simple passions for their modest but very intricate and thoughtful routines, businessmen who couldn't stay in one place for more than five minutes and paced through whatever room they were in with so much passion that they never needed to go to the gym. *Il faut de tout pour faire un monde,* as we say in French—it takes all sorts.

Since I turned seventy, and especially since the operation to deal with my spinal stenosis, I have been learning to manage my expectations. Soon, I will be eighty and, yes, this does mean I am somewhat slower. I don't ride my bicycle as fast or as far, I'm more careful on my skis, I no longer do any high-altitude mountain climbing, and at my doctor's insistence I agreed somewhat reluctantly to give up running, a decision I stuck to for seven years and have only recently reversed because I felt strong enough to do so. I take satisfaction in my exercise because it enables me to stay in shape. Within the boundaries of reason, and the knowledge of my limitations, I basically still aim to do as much as I can. I continue to cycle, to ski, and to spend time hiking in the mountains or trekking abroad, and this brings me a lot of pleasure.

Even though we must learn with age to adapt our expectations, our bodies are amazing and, when taken care of, will consistently surprise us with their ability to continue performing and even exceeding these expectations. Whatever limitations or obstacles we face, correctly gauging the depth of our resources will make the difference between a thriving life and the encroaching paralysis of inactivity and immobility. The story of old age that tells of withering away and inevitable decline is in large part an unfortunate and unhelpful myth. As long as we are still breathing, it is very much possible for us old guys and gals to build up our level of fitness. We write our own stories. Don't underestimate what those old bones of yours can get up to. It may not be easy, but you can do it.

4

ACTIVITY IS EVERYWHERE

An active lifestyle is exactly what it sounds like. It is not something that you can own or buy or consume. It means living your life in a way that welcomes, and even seeks out, activity and exercise in some form or other. And the keyword here is life: an active *life*style is *lived*. It is the process itself, the doing, that is important. Even though you can tick the exercise box in your routine on any given day, it's only one check mark among many, and it all begins again when the sun rises. In other words, physical activity is synonymous with life, and that's just the way it is. Our bodies require movement to function—lots of it. Rather than think of this as a chore or a burden, why not reimagine this requirement as an opportunity, a chance to get out and to explore, to find adventure and a new lease on life. While we all enjoy a lazy day here and there, the need to get moving again will always be right around the corner. It is a biological imperative.

EVERYDAY OPPORTUNITIES

Most of us probably need to rethink what it means to lead an active lifestyle in terms of all the occupations with which we fill our days. Even if you already feel like you're already putting in some time to exercise on a regular basis, you might ask yourself what the overall picture of your life looks like. For while it is certainly positive to undertake scheduled exercise in any form, whether these are floor exercises in the privacy of your home, an aerobics class at your local gym, jogging, or something else, the rest of your physical—and *not-so-physical*—activities are also part of the equation. Thirty minutes of active movement several times a week is not enough. You need this every day, and as much of it as you can fit in. Don't get me wrong, I'm not trying to set the bar so high that no one can make the cut, but we do need to reconsider what it means to *be active* in a general, holistic sense. We underestimate the important role our physical condition plays in creating a meaningful and lasting connection between ourselves and the outside world. Our mobility is like a bridge that allows us to get out and experience new things, at once a training grounds for the self and the means by which we can truly explore the world.

Sometimes you need to do a little pushing for things to go the way you want them to, but where there is a will, there is a way. When I took my first job, the oil company I worked for was housed in an eleven- or twelve-story building on Madison Avenue, in New York City. I had been there for a few months and decided that I wanted to walk up the stairs on my way to the office for exercise. The stairs being locked, I went to the building concierge to ask him for the key. His answer was negative. "The stairs are off limits," he said. I insisted but he didn't budge and stuck to his line that it was impossible without authorization from above. At the time, as part of my management training, I was working as the personal assistant to the president of the company. We had a good relationship and so I decided he was the best person to go to to sort this whole situation out. I explained I wanted to gain access to the stairs so I could walk up to the office and get some exercise on my way to and from work. "You do that?" he exclaimed, amused. He was happy enough to help though, so he took a piece of paper with the company letterhead and, with a touch of sarcasm, wrote out a note to the building owners, melodramatically requesting safe passage for "one of his key employees who is in fantastic shape and expects to stay that way." A week later, he called me into his office and read out the response. The building owners had written back in astonishment saying that no one had ever asked for anything like this in the history of the building. They were so impressed, however, and found it to be such a good idea, that they included four extra keys just in case anyone else wanted to work on their physical fitness.

It's not always that easy, however. Years later, in the late 1980s and early 1990s when I started a private equity fund in Geneva, we had a considerably large team and I struggled to find appropriate office space until, finally, I discovered a place that worked for us on the fifth floor of an old but very decent and sunlit building on what is usually referred to as the *rive droite*, or right bank of the Rhône that flows through Lake Geneva. Rare for the time, the building had an underground parking lot and I was able to get a spot in the third basement, three floors down. This meant eight floors up. Since my days in New York, I had always made a point of taking the stairs, but these were usually just a few floors, and I was no longer young. Eight floors every morning and evening is a different beast when you're in your mid-fifties. Nevertheless, I resolved to climb them every day, and with a few exceptions, I did. Let me tell you, I have never been in such good shape as I was during those five years in that office! Those eight floors were a workout and a half, and greatly contributed to keeping me active throughout the day. Needless to say, I am a big believer in the health virtues of climbing stairs.

OK, so I'll grant you that this may not always be the most convenient solution. You may have your reasons for not exerting yourself "unnecessarily." You might not always be in a position to work up a sweat, or spend twice as long to cover the distance on that particular day. So be it. Take the bus if you have to, don't walk if you don't want to. Take the elevator, not the stairs. But at least realize that the opportunity is there. It's an opportunity to get those legs moving and let your body register the exercise. And remember that this option is always there, for those days when you're not short on time. I am writing from the assumption that you are reading this because you want to get into shape. Given this fact, my advice is straightforward: start making a habit of weighing these kinds of small decisions as they arise, take the time to spot them and think about how you could factor in the exercise you could be gaining for free every day.

PHYSICAL ACTIVITY IS NEAT

In the late 1990s and early 2000s, researchers led by Dr. James Levine, a professor of medicine at the Mayo Clinic in Minnesota, carried out a series of experiments in obesity research, designed to measure various factors in weight gain. Participants were fed high-calorie diets and instructed not to change their routine. What the researchers noticed was that some of the participants were gaining weight while others saw no change. The significant variations in metabolic responses that they observed prompted them to go further. In an effort to understand this discrepancy, they devised what is now known as the "magic underwear" experiment. All of this was before the more recent explosion of tracking technology, and their methods were rather ingenious. The participants were asked to wear a special pair of underwear that tracked their every move and body position, day and night, over a period of eight weeks. What they found was surprising, and included a number of observations that have contributed to a fundamental change in what we know about the effects of inactivity. It's worth noting that all participants were chosen for the experiment because they had lifestyles with near-average activity levels—none of them were into sports or went to the gym. Chief among the results of this study was the fact that those who gained a lot of weight sat for over two hours longer every day than their leaner counterparts. Sitting was thus singled out as a main culprit of weight gain and obesity.

More specifically, however, those participants who remained lean would naturally increase the amount they moved throughout the day while simultaneously declaring that they did not change their habits. As part of the conclusions from this research, Dr. Levine coined a term that has since become quite popular: Non-Exercise Activity Thermogenesis, or NEAT. This refers to all the activity-driven energy consumption that happens outside of actual exercise—all those little movements that we do throughout the day, many of which are often subconscious. Your body burns significant amounts of calories with these not-so-insignificant movements: from chewing gum to tapping your foot under the desk, these things have an impact on your level of energy consumption, which in turn has an influence on your overall health.

So in addition to whatever workout you choose to implement, if this is indeed your course of action, this means that you can adopt a frame of mind that recognizes the benefit of any form of non-exercise activity you can think of. Allow yourself to think creatively about how to get *non-exercise exercise*, so to speak, through activities that have nothing to do with sport. I have found that home life in itself offers a lot of opportunities for such kinds of physical exercise. In the garden, the basement, the kitchen, the living or laundry rooms, wherever you are, there are ways of moving around more. Pace while you read the paper or a magazine. Stand up and move when you answer the telephone. Do squats while you fold your laundry. Stretch out when you're putting away the dishes. Be creative, because anything goes. Anything that gets you using your muscles and making an effort will wake your body up and have a positive effect. The same goes for anything that gets you working up a sweat or breathing a little harder than usual.

WE ARE WHAT WE DO

When I was a young boy, living on a small farm, I remember working on weekends to bag apples at our neighbor's apple farm. His name was Art Langford, and he sold his produce from a roadside stand: apples, of course, apple sauce, apple jams, and apple cider which he made from a jerry-rigged juicer. I would watch Art and his father closely, and lucky for me they enjoyed having me around. They were kind, jolly, hardworking men with a good sense of humor, and they lived in an old adobe house dating back to when the Spanish missionaries settled in California in the 1700s. Like most people in the rural community I grew up in, at a time where there were still many small-time hard-working farmers about, they seemed to hold a wealth of wisdom on how to live a good life. This image is one that has stayed with me throughout my life. They were short, stout men who dressed in bib overalls and wore old battered Stetson hats all stained from perspiration. Their hands were strong and gnarled and there was always a line of dirt visible under their fingernails, even when they washed their hands, which in those days only happened before a meal. Both men were comfortably overweight, but instead of flab, their round stomachs were firm. I remember asking Art one day how he managed to keep his stomach so hard. He looked at me and said: "Jacky, when you work hard, your stomach stays hard. But when you work hard, your stomach also needs to stay fed."

Most people who still worked on their farms in those days knew little about the modern science of physical activity or nutrition beyond the good sense and wisdom that had been passed down to them through the generations, but that seemed to be enough. They had no need for planned exercise or diet plans and always seemed to radiate strength and health. Men like Art and his father were out on their farms every day of the week, including weekends. And while many probably ate or drank too much, they ate good food. You can figure this pretty easily, because much of what they ate was home-grown and came from their own backyard. The Langfords raised their own chickens for eggs and meat, and they used the money from the apples to get everything else they needed from other local farmers. Theirs were full lives with a strong sense of equilibrium. Art and his father both lived into their nineties, and they never quit working on the farm. Right up until the end, they continued to be independent, mobile, and in full control of all their mental faculties.

Imagine, as a thought experiment, that your relationship to your body is that of a sculptor to his or her work of art. Everything you do is geared towards shaping the object you are trying to create. Your tools are the movements you make your body do. Depending on how sophisticated, intense, diversified, or sustained these movements are, your body will adapt as a result and show evidence of these adaptations. Now think of the things you spend the majority of your time doing. If your body were to permanently retain the postures and poses you have it perform most often, what would these be? What would you look like? Remember that every hour of every day counts: all the time spent sleeping, walking, showering, eating, sitting, and so on. Hopefully this is a pleasant thought. If not, what would you change? The point here is not to cultivate greater vanity—though for some people this can be a strong incentive for change—but rather to develop an awareness of the relation between our appearance, our health, and our everyday actions.

This thought experiment is simplistic, of course, for our bodies are not objects and thankfully do not become fixed in any one posture or state. But the activities we fill our lives with are a form of conditioning. Even the mundane task of putting on your morning kettle or coffee pot is one that requires significant coordination and muscle strength, and if you don't believe me, think about which arm you usually do it with, then switch. If you're right handed, try using your left hand, and vice versa if you're left handed. Try the same experiment for brushing your teeth, or for buttoning your shirt. What you will find is that your regular habits and routines are a form of exercise which, although it goes mostly unnoticed, train and condition your body to perform certain tasks. If you are not able to brush your teeth with your left hand, or find it hard to lift the kettle with your left arm, try doing it for a month and your ability will improve. The task itself, in this case trying to brush your teeth with your "other" hand, is not an easy one.

This is where the commitment comes in and determination is needed. Just keep in mind the example of trying to brush your teeth with the other hand: it is hard to do this with the same ease and efficiency as the hand you've used for most of your life, but it is not impossible. Think about the training you have and what is needed to compensate. You may never get as good with your left hand as you are with your right, but you can diminish the skill gap with practice. All those who want to build up their physical form face the same problem. It feels and seems impossible when you're standing at the bottom of that hill, but the truth is you just need to get going and make what progress you can wherever and whenever you can. It's so simple that it's almost laughable. The saying that *we are what we eat* holds true, but also, by all evidence, *we are what we do*. Our body becomes what we make it do on a regular basis. We are constantly adapting to the environment around us and our behavior within it. The body develops according to the way it is guided. Understand this, and a world of possibilities opens up.

STAYING ACTIVE

I want to suggest two complementary notions which roughly mirror the nature-nurture debate, as applied to fitness. Both notions are important to integrate independently, and in relation to one another. On the one hand, none of us are able to choose our genes, nor are we able to control fate. This means we are all predisposed to certain medical conditions or weaknesses which will shape what we are able—or unable—to physically *do* throughout our lives. We also know that accidents happen. I have had plenty of them over the years, and most of us will be more or less impacted at some point in time, too. This is the first notion: there will always be things that are out of our control. In other words, we play with the cards that are dealt to us.

On the other hand, *life as we live it* changes our body's composition and influences its development. To put it bluntly, you might say that we all get the body we deserve. Bearing in mind the variables that can be attributed to accidents, genetics, and so on, this means that whatever we put our body through will shape the way it functions and feels. This includes the foods and substances we ingest, the activities we undertake and also, importantly, the activities we forego. When we do not sleep for a night, or two, there are consequences. The same goes for any sort of activity you undertake: jumping, sitting, jogging for an hour, running for seven hours, yoga, Pilates, Zumba, meditation, Jiu-Jitsu or Tai chi. All these activities have an effect, but they do not have the same effect.

Nowadays, I have found, the tendency seems to be that many of the things which people spend their time on should be labeled as "passivities" rather than "activities." Let's not shy away from stating certain facts. Whether you are at the office, at home, reading a book, sitting at the computer, or in front of the television, all this time during which you are allowing yourself to remain "inactive," in a passive state, your body is taking a hit. And while you may without a doubt be developing useful intellectual skills, building your knowledge, or getting important work done, this does not change the fact that your body is being forced into a form of metabolic torpor, and suffering as a result. Think about it: this happens day after day after day. You are basically ignoring and depriving yourself of a primal need to move. I also read and watch a bit of television myself, of course, and I'm not trying to say you shouldn't ever do either of these things at all, but you *should* be aware of the facts. We cannot escape the physical impact that our behaviors and actions have upon our bodies.

Most physical activities include something of all the four main exercise types which we will explore in the following chapters. These are: aerobics, resistance, stretching, and balance. While we usually talk about lifting weights, going for a run, and lying face down on the floor in a yoga pose when referring to these categories, we can also take the approach that all of the above are readily available in everyday forms of exercise. Imagine the task at hand is simply to make your bed. You will have to stretch out across the mattress to reach the corners which you will then pull back in order to fit the sheet, a form of exercise which requires significant balance, flexibility, and strength. If, in order to do so, you also had to walk up a flight of stairs from the laundry room, then you will also have included an aerobic element in this regular household chore. Hitting the gym is one option, and can be a good idea if that's what you enjoy, but start taking everyday activities seriously and you will also find a good deal of workout potential there too.

Keep this principle in mind and you will begin to see opportunities to improve your fitness everywhere. It's not all about running marathons. If you can't make it up the stairs without getting out of breath, make that your objective. If what you want deep down is to look better and feel better about your outward appearance, then accept that and run with it. Whatever works. Whatever gets you going. Take your time, and go slowly if you have to, especially if you've already reached a certain age, but go at it again. Walk up those stairs two, three, four times, do it several times a day, whenever the opportunity presents itself. You will find that the difficulty progressively decreases, and you may well soon feel comfortable and breathe normally doing it. It may take a week, or a month, or several months, but you will see progress. I guarantee it. This is not just my opinion, it is a fact.

Consider that there is a whole range of *active* alternatives you could be engaging in during your leisure time that are just as entertaining, educational, and incomparably healthier. You could listen to an audiobook or a podcast while you go for a walk, or put a treadmill or a training bicycle in front of the television and move while you watch, even if only at a low intensity. And for all those necessary, productive *passivities* you choose to hold on to, you can break them up to reduce uninterrupted sedentary time by taking short, intermittent breaks. These can be as simple as walking around the house, doing a few stretches, maybe even some more demanding exercises if you feel like it. As for your work environment, there are a number of solutions you could adopt there too. You might consider getting a standing desk, and alternating between sitting and standing throughout your workday. You can fix yourself the objective of taking regular stretching breaks, or maybe you decide to stand up every time the phone rings, just as a way to break up the sitting. You could take this one step further and join the latest "walk and talk" trend. I've adopted this, and I now take business calls on the move so I can get in some exercise whenever I am on the phone. Depending on the length of the call, I may even leave the house or office to cover more distance.

FINDING THINGS TO DO

Gardening is a big activity at my house. My wife and I have a vegetable garden with southern exposure where we grow lettuce, tomatoes, cucumbers, zucchini, pumpkins, green beans, berries, and so on. This is a great source of exercise, for gardening has the advantage of involving many movements. You have to prepare the earth with a shovel and chop it up with a hoe to prepare it for compost and for planting; then you get down on your knees to make holes and prepare for planting seeds. You have to pound in stakes with a large heavy hammer and tie up the plants as they grow. And then there is the weeding—lots of weeding—which requires you to bend down and get your hands dirty. You also have to water the plants on a regular basis, and continually rake around them to ensure the earth is porous enough to feed the roots. Finally, after all of the above, picking the vegetables or fruits also requires lots of bending over, rummaging around on all fours, probably a fair share of lifting, and even some balancing on top of ladders. This is, of course, primarily a summertime exercise, and it requires the garden itself for it to work, but if you can manage to set it up, it is a great way to stay physically active, not to mention that it will provide you with a supply of fresh produce.

Engaging in other kinds of handiwork around the house can also be a worthy workout. I'm not particularly gifted at it, but I give it a go nonetheless and have undertaken some fun and useful projects over the years. Probably my proudest achievement was to convert part of my basement into a proper wine cellar. This involved several projects. First, insulating the hot-water pipes so they didn't bring unwanted heat. Second, building shelving units solid enough to hold the weight of the wine bottles and securing them to the wall. And third, organizing the wines according to geographic origin, grape variety, and vintage, though I admit this was mostly my wife Claire-Lise's idea—she is a trained librarian. When selecting the evening's bottle, there's nothing quite as fun as having your own oenological classification system, complete with region, appellation, vintage, grape variety, producer, tasting notes, and ratings.

I also wanted to have an exterior shed to house gardening tools, materials, and outdoor furniture. The shed itself was prefabricated, but the project was a handful and took several days because the floor's precast concrete slabs and gravel had to be put in, holes had to be dug in the ground for stability, and the walls and ceiling had to be mounted. There was a lot of messing around with screws, drills, and extension cords, not to mention climbing up and down ladders and balancing on a roof while using power tools, and so on. I didn't do all the work myself, of course, but I was totally bushed by the end of it and felt like every single muscle in my body had been used to the maximum. This kind of exercise is simple but fulfilling, and the results of your labor are right there in the garden for you to enjoy, rain or shine.

Children or grandchildren, if you have them, can be relied on to keep you busy. Keeping up with them in the first place is hard enough, and keeping ahead of them is even more of a challenge. We have seven grandchildren, and for years it was our honor to be the babysitters of preference. During these times, my career as a football—or soccer—player saw a brief but enjoyable revival, and my wife and I were always on the move, participating in their discovery of all sorts of activities and games, from swimming, skiing, and badminton to swinging and trapeze tricks. There were board games, occasionally, but the outdoors seems to have been their thing, and we were always in high demand. After a day with the grandkids, if you let them lead you back into action, you are as ready as ever for a good night's sleep.

These are just some of the everyday activities that have stood out in my life, but the possibilities are endless, and whatever you decide upon will do just as well. Be imaginative and be opportunistic! There are as many ways of bringing physical exercise into your life as there are ways of moving your body and working up a sweat. Regularly going to the gym may be one way of getting the exercise you need, but it is not the only or even necessarily the best way. An active lifestyle can only truly be defined holistically. We are all equipped with our fair share of dexterity, strength, and flexibility, but we only get as much as we work for. Start thinking of the exercise value available in daily tasks, chores, and commutes, and a whole new world will open up. Everything counts, whether it is shopping, cooking, cleaning the house, working in the garden, or anything thing else that involves *moving around.*

A MODEST PROPOSAL

All I am arguing for is a small shift in consciousness, one which acknowledges the human need to move and be active. Once this shift occurs, you carry your strongest asset around with you wherever you go: an inventive ability to find exercise anywhere. Try asking yourself how you might feel if, let's say, you were faced with the decision of choosing the stairs over the elevator, or walking up a hill rather than taking the bus. What is your emotional response? How do you feel at the prospect of making this decision? If it sounds terrible and rubs you the wrong way, if you strongly feel that it's definitely not worth the effort, then let's just say you might want to reconsider your position. Every day we are still mobile is an endless source of free miniature workout opportunities. And these small things add up. It has become a cliché by now, but that doesn't make it less true: taking the stairs on a regular basis rather than waiting for the elevator is the responsible thing to do because it *will* do you a lot of good. This is a modest, accessible proposal. Once you bring it onboard, it becomes second nature.

Spend less time sitting, and if you really must stay in one place, then stand if you can, and know that, in a pinch, even fidgeting burns calories and helps the blood flow. Every little bit counts. Be more conscientious about moving around and performing what little activities you can throughout the day to get your body moving. Try to integrate a mindset that values light to moderate exercise, movement for its own sake. And try to find pleasure in it too. Align all the above with your interests for maximum effect and engagement. Start to behave in accordance with the real impact these choices will have upon your level of fitness, your mood, and your life in general. It won't be long before you start to see and feel the results.

An active lifestyle can't really be faked, and your body is the only one keeping score. Every time we put our bodies—and minds—to use, there is an effect. The sum of these effects is the state of our bodies in the present moment, right now. We need not aspire to become elite athletes in order to qualify as active individuals, and our bodies can be well maintained through an infinite number of ordinary or extraordinary tasks that we may not even think of as exercise. Plus there are thousands of fun ways to get a little more exercise here and there. If you can learn to take advantage of these opportunities, you'll stay ten steps ahead of the aging curve.

5
EXERCISE IS INDISPENSABLE

Exercise does not wear us out, lack of exercise does. Think of it, if you will, as a "good" tired versus a "bad" tired feeling. Physical exertion is a crucial, indispensable part of what makes us tick. When we exercise, our body is building itself up to deal with life's trials, burdens, and exhaustions, but it is also getting fit for the pleasures life has to offer. When we don't exercise, our body does not get a chance to build itself up and is slowly worn down over time until, gradually, it can no longer cope and starts to wither and break down. This process, however, does not take place overnight. It happens progressively, often imperceptibly, over a lifetime.

We all know, deep down, that moving makes us feel better, despite some of the discomfort and heavy breathing that sometimes come with it. If one refuses to recognize this fact, one has either forgotten or is in serious denial. Keeping our bodies more or less optimally functional, whether we like it or not, is essential to living a full and healthy life. It can be a challenge because we're pretty much on our own when it comes to doing this, and there is no *bona fide* user manual. However, you don't need to run marathons to get into shape. Getting in the equivalent of roughly half an hour a day of exercise is a good start and, as we will see later in the chapter, this will go a long way to helping you climb that fitness ladder. We have to piece this puzzle together by ourselves, but a word of advice or a helping hand at the right time can make a difference, and it is in this very spirit that this chapter is intended. My hope is that it will inspire and encourage you.

In the long term, regular physical activity will help your body get better at regulating itself. Think of the body as a smart machine that is always trying to optimize its own processes and overall functioning. If you never put your body through the metabolic experience of exercise, it will not be ready and will not know how to respond efficiently on the extraordinary occasion where you exert yourself more than usual. Think heavy breathing, buckling knees, and spaghetti arms. Your body will do its best to try to cope, but there is no getting around the period of adaptation and training required to become more accustomed to exercise. When, on the other hand, you regularly put your body through physical exertion, the response to exercise is radically different. In this case, your body is already primed and ready to go. Regular exercise maintains your body in a state of readiness that can be felt at the level of your lungs, your heart, your muscles, your flexibility, and your range of motion. It will also change the way you metabolize what you eat, and it is even very likely to improve your mood.

SO, WHAT IS EXERCISE EXACTLY?

There are any number of answers to this question. On a fundamental level, however, exercise is anything that gets your body moving. Technically, unless you spend your days in bed without moving a muscle, you are "exercising" all the time, if only at low levels. So when people extol the virtues of exercise, as I am doing here, it is largely a matter of diversity, intensity, and regularity that separates what they are referring to from all those activities we perform in the course of a typical day. I see exercise as a spectrum of physical activity, from wiggling your toes all the way up to running a marathon. You could argue, and some do, that exercise ought to refer to structured physical activity, but I understand these terms to be somewhat synonymous. If I am referring specifically to a structured exercise routine, I use the term "workout," or "workout routine."

As we saw in the previous chapter, "Activity Is Everywhere," opportunities for casual exercise are everywhere, and they add up. We should seek these opportunities out, seize them when they arise, and make them happen when they do not. In addition, however, I highly recommend a structured workout, much like the one I do. If you are looking to build your fitness in a holistic way, you might want to aim towards developing a full-body workout that covers all the bases and gets the various muscle groups working. I go through the main things to look out for in the next chapter, "A Workout Will Make Your Day."

Fitness experts generally distinguish four categories, or types, of exercise: aerobics, resistance, stretching, and balance. Each of these types is directly related to a physiological attribute that they work to improve. Aerobics improve endurance, resistance builds strength, stretching increases flexibility, and balance maintains your ability to move freely and steadily without falling. It gets more complicated of course, but these four areas of activity should allow you to better grasp the overall picture of what it means to be active. Depending on who you ask, you could break it down even further to include things like hand-eye coordination, agility, or breathing. While these are important skills to develop, they can also be considered as subsets of the four main types of exercise mentioned above, and are likely to improve alongside them.

Our bodies are sophisticated machines that require constant maintenance, and these four types of exercise do just that. Aerobic exercise gets you breathing hard, working air through your lungs to your heart, which then supplies the rest of your body with the oxygenated blood it needs to perform the physical activities you're engaged in. This type of exercise is also referred to as cardiovascular training, or cardio for short. Strength training, as its name implies, is what puts your muscles to use, keeping them strong and healthy by pulling and pushing against whatever weight or resistance you are using. Strong muscles mean the ability to move around, and it also means better support for your skeleton and vital organs. Flexibility training conditions your body to make use of its full spectrum of mobility by loosening up joints, articulations, tendons, and muscles to improve range of motion and the capacity to perform basic and complex movements in a safe and controlled way. Balance training targets our innate capacity to manage and move our own body weight. Whether standing up, sitting down, or moving around, it is balance that keeps us from toppling over.

DO I NEED EXERCISE?

Yes, everyone does. We all need exercise because our bodies need it. This is as true for a toddler as it is for an adult, albeit for different reasons. That said, you must bear in mind any weaknesses, health conditions, or injuries you may have, for these will influence *how* you should get your exercise, *how much* of it you should get, and so on.

Everything about starting to exercise again is a good idea, and this is true at any age. The questions we should really be asking ourselves are ones like: Can I touch my toes? Can I comfortably tie my shoelaces while bending over with my legs straight? Can I sit cross-legged? How long can I jog—or power walk—for and at what pace? Can I lift my own body weight? How long can I hold a plank? Can I perform a deep squat? Can I sit comfortably in that squatting position? For how long? How many push-ups can I do? How many pull-ups? How often do I do sprints, or some other high-intensity workout? Could I be playing any team or individual sports?

You may be gawking at these questions, and that's OK, but they should be within the norm for anyone leading a truly active lifestyle. The point is not to create gym-freaks, but to encourage people to explore the full functionality available to us as human beings. Even if you don't regularly do push-ups, trying to do one should not seem like an impossible feat. Spandex and dumbbells aside, all these movements and exercises are directly linked to physiologically essential, functional movements which the human body has evolved to perform over the course of millennia in order to survive—hunt and gather food, escape predators, build shelters, and care for the young.

In reality, the questions that probably make more sense to ask, especially when addressing an older audience, may be more along the lines of: Can you walk up a flight of stairs without getting out of breath? Can you do this in one go without taking a break? How long can you walk at a leisurely pace before getting tired or out of breath? What if you make that a brisk pace? Can you run to catch a bus without tasting copper, becoming nauseous, and getting severely out of breath? Do you have enough strength to open a jar unassisted? Can you get up out of a chair without using your arms? Can you cut your own toenails? Can you bend over and pick something up without holding on to something with your arms for balance? Can you reach your arms above your head to lift a small weight, for example, to take a small stack of plates out of a kitchen cupboard?

If you have answered no to any of these questions, that should flip a warning switch in your brain. The main NCDs mentioned in the previous chapters are only part of the picture. Generalized weakness, frailty, and the loss of muscle mass are problems of epidemic proportions among older people today. In addition, poor cardiorespiratory capacity, greatly reduced balance, and restricted flexibility and range of motion are extremely common in all age groups.

Fortunately for us, there's a pattern to these conditions: they overwhelmingly correlate with inactivity. These are all problems that *can* be addressed with relative ease and a little everyday *uhmpf*. Their symptoms are the result of, or at the very least exacerbated by, the accumulated lack of exercise in one's day-to-day activities. In other words, these problems are due to lifestyle and can therefore be remedied or prevented by sustainably increasing physical activity. Let's have a quick look at the main problems associated with a lack of each type of exercise.

Lack of strength training

Over the age of thirty, muscle mass tends to decrease steadily at a rate of approximately 3–8% per decade. Although this loss of muscle mass is normally observed with age, it is particularly associated with inactivity. In its more acute forms, this condition is known as sarcopenia, which in the original Greek literally means "poverty of flesh." It is both a symptom of inactivity and a significant risk factor for developing NCDs, and, as you can readily imagine, it represents a significant hindrance to any kind of normal lifestyle. If you cannot lift yourself out of a chair unassisted, what else are you unable to do? Building muscle mass does not get any easier with age, but it continues to be possible, and very beneficial. Your musculature keeps you bones and organs in place, and is literally what allows you to continue moving.

Lack of aerobic training

While we need all four types of exercise, regular aerobic exercise in the form of vigorous walking, running, cycling, swimming, jumping, or anything else that gets you breathing hard, is the best thing you can do to maintain a baseline level of health. When you're breathing harder than usual and your heart is pumping at a higher intensity, it means your body is working hard to meet the demands of the effort. This is not a problem: it's what should be happening on a regular basis. When you do not put your body through regular cardiovascular exercise, your lung capacity diminishes and you risk developing chronic respiratory and circulation problems, as well as a whole host of the NCD-related issues we have already discussed. Lung capacity can be monitored by measuring what is called your "VO2max," literally your volume (V) of dioxygen (O2), or the amount of oxygen you can inhale within a minute. Your VO2max is a very good predictor of aerobic fitness and projected healthspan—the higher it is, the better.

Lack of flexibility training

Flexibility training improves our ability to stretch and move each of our joints, tendons, and muscles within their range of motion. When your daily movements are restricted due to inactivity and a sedentary lifestyle, you are not using your body the way it is designed to function. As a result, what we see over time is a shortening of the muscles that greatly reduces your capacity to perform a broad range of essential movements. This tends to manifest in the hips, the knees, the ankles, the shoulders, or the spine as a stiffness or even soreness. It often may be more pronounced in the morning, or after a long period of sitting or inactivity. Lack of flexibility is likely to have a negative impact on physical ability and to increase the chance of injury.

Lack of balance training

Balance is essential because it correlates with control and coordination. Balancing mobilizes not only your muscles and skeleton, but your sense of space as well. Our sense of balance tends to diminish naturally with age, but, again, the degree to which this happens will vary greatly depending on your lifestyle. Poor balance is one of the major causes of falls and injury in older adults, and these accidents are very often exacerbated by sarcopenia or frailty. The better your balance, the less likely you are to stumble or fall over. The stronger and more flexible you are, the less likely you are to suffer serious injury if you do. It's important to note however, that poor balance could be due to other factors, such as deteriorating vision or ear—and inner ear—problems. If you experience any of these symptoms, or a sensation of vertigo when you move your head, then you should probably seek medical help.

WHAT ARE THE BENEFITS OF EXERCISE?

Experience tells us that *it feels good* to get regular exercise. We feel it in our muscles and in our bones. The exertion is not only a source of physical wellbeing, but of mental and social wellbeing as well. We feel it in our mood, our attention span, our sharpness of mind, our general emotional state, and in the way we interact with others. Exercise has healing and preventative qualities that everyone can feel and benefit from. We are hardwired for it. These health benefits, and their relation to physical activity, are something that we ought to relearn to appreciate.

Scientifically, we are still far from fully understanding all the benefits that exercise has to offer. Research continues to regularly provide fascinating insights, but we are still piecing together the many facets of *how* exactly exercise is good for us. What's clear beyond reasonable doubt, however, is that the more we learn about the beneficial metabolic effects of leading an active lifestyle, the more the small, seemingly obvious fact that *exercise is good for us* is confirmed. So much so, in fact, that it boggles the mind.

Almost any condition you can think about is made better by exercise, which has a complex and beneficial effect on the human body at the *systemic level*. There are so many positive effects that it's hard to know where to start, but to prove a point, here is a quick, non-exhaustive list of some of these benefits. Intelligent exercise performed well and regularly over time will: boost and balance your metabolism and energy levels, increase your strength, strengthen your bones, prevent osteoporosis and fractures, improve the quality of your circulation, your heart, your brain function, your sleep, your breathing, your mood, self-confidence and wellbeing, and your sex drive and performance. It will help you control your weight, enhance your immune system, lower your susceptibility to non-communicable diseases and statistically decrease your chances of premature death, etc. And this is one serious "et cetera" because the list goes on and on.

The effects of exercise range from a lowering of the chances of having a stroke or contracting cancer, to increasing testosterone and insulin efficiency. Exercise impacts everything from the density of your bones to the wrinkles in your skin. Generally speaking, on a metabolic level, our body undergoes a whole range of immediate changes and adaptations as soon as we begin to engage in physical activity. These depend on type and duration of the exercise. In a nutshell, however, we can say that: heart rate begins to rise, breathing intensifies accordingly, blood flow is redirected to those muscles that are working and need the oxygen, the brain gets a boost due to increased blood flow, our digestive system slows down, and a whole host of proteins and hormones are secreted with varying effects on energy consumption and the registering of pain. Even our cells and DNA are affected by this changed state. Let's briefly take a closer look at some of the major positive effects that exercise has on our bodies.

On a cellular level, research has shown that exercise slows the aging of cells. It also improves the body's ability to clean up dead or dying cells. Much of this happens through improvement and proliferation of our mitochondria throughout our body. Mitochondria are organelles that function as energy-creating factories in our cells and play a key role in maintaining the health of the cell throughout its life cycle. They use oxygen to convert food into energy in the form of adenosine triphosphate, or ATP. It seems that regular aerobic exercise increases the number of mitochondria in our muscle tissues, which is good news because this essentially correlates with an increase in physical capacity. In addition, exercise increases levels of "mitophagy," the process whereby old or damaged mitochondria are cleared away, enabling cells to function more efficiently and leading to healthier muscles and bones. Furthermore, exercise has even been shown to change the way our DNA behaves, influencing how genes receive information from the body during a process called methylation, wherein clusters of atoms attach to the outside of the gene and make it more or less able to communicate, potentially affecting a variety of genes implicated in NCDs.

On a hormonal level, exercise stimulates the production and regulation of a whole range of hormones. Most notably, our body releases endogenous opioids such as endorphins to help deal with pain, stress, and the heightened metabolic demands of physical exertion. These help to boost one's sense of wellbeing, and can even cause a feeling of euphoria, which regular runners sometimes experience as a kind of "high." Exercise is also known to help regulate cortisol, commonly referred to as the stress hormone, though this benefit tends to be erased at very high levels of endurance training. In any case, the combined effect of these and other hormones tends to reduce anxiety, stress, and feelings of depression. Furthermore, the increase in human growth hormone associated with high-intensity effort is known to be very helpful in building strength and muscle mass, increasing bone density, focus, and performance, in addition to boosting libido and overall metabolic functioning. Other hormones that get a boost during exercise include: testosterone and estrogen, our sexual hormones; insulin and glucagon, which are crucial to managing blood sugar; and a whole range of other signaling proteins with complex names referred to by acronyms such as BDNF, TSH, FGF19 or FGF21. These have a wide range of beneficial effects on our metabolism.

On a cardiovascular level, the heart pumps blood via our arteries to the body's muscles, organs, and tissues. When we exercise, our muscles require more oxygen, so the lungs and heart must pump harder to keep up, and our circulatory system speeds up as well. To use a crude image, getting your heart beating fast is a little like the cardiac equivalent of pumping iron. The heart, being a muscle, becomes more efficient from the extra work. This slows the natural decrease in ventricular function. Our bodies have a natural tendency to overcompensate, meaning that when under stress the heart will pump harder, just to be sure, and when going back into a resting state it will generally try to slow down beyond its previous normal rate. Over time, aerobic exercise thus has the effect of slightly lowering one's resting heart rate. It's also worth mentioning that arterial health is an important cardiovascular component. Far from being just a form of bodily plumbing, our arteries are actively involved in maintaining a healthy metabolism. Research shows that the heightened blood flow that accompanies exercise strengthens the lining of our arteries and increases the network of capillaries.

On a pulmonary level, exercise increases the amount of air we take into our lungs with each breath, as well as the overall rate of breathing. The rate of increase depends on the intensity of the effort. Over time, our lungs adapt to the effort we put our bodies through and we see an increase in lung capacity and lung function, measurable in terms of VO2, as we have seen. When our lungs are "fit" they can move air in and out faster and more efficiently, thus increasing oxygenation of our blood and cells, meaning more energy and a greater ability to move. Intense exercise that gets you breathing hard will have the most benefits here, though you always need to work up to it. Same as with the heart, the more we work our lungs, the better we get at breathing hard. It might be added that living with a pulmonary disease does not necessarily preclude aerobically challenging exercise. Furthermore, the breathing we do during exercise is vital to supply the body with energy, as it ensures a steady production of ATP. Breathing hard gets the oxygen we need to our cells, where ATP is created so our muscles can keep burning energy.

On a musculoskeletal level, exercise stimulates blood flow, growth, development of strength, and much more. Our bones and muscles are the scaffolding around which the rest of the body is built, enabling us to move around in the world. Our musculoskeletal system is at the epicenter of our mobility, our health, and general sense of wellbeing. The more you move and use your muscles, the more they grow. More movement equals less loss of muscle mass and lower risk of sarcopenia––it's a simple equation. The more we take care of our muscles, the more they take care of us. This is a strong reason for keeping them as healthy as we can. The same goes for our bones. The stress and strain of physical exertion encourages bone tissue to create more cells, which helps to preserve bone density. Among the conditions that tend to occur with age is a pathological shrinking of bone density over time. This condition is known as osteoporosis and it can be a serious problem. The bones become fragile, brittle, and thus increasingly prone to fracture. Strength training with weights and high intensity exercise will be the most efficacious at preserving bone health because they load the most weight onto our bones, and thus make them work the hardest. Lower-impact forms of exercise such as swimming, walking, or yoga, while good for flexibility, balance, strength, or aerobic fitness, will not have as much of an effect on your bones. According to the International Osteoporosis Foundation, one-third of women over fifty are projected to experience an osteoporotic fracture compared with only one-fifth of men in the same age group. This disproportionate incidence between genders is due, in part, to differences in bone structure and the decrease in estrogen experienced by women after menopause.

At the level of the brain, the increase in blood flow associated with exercise also has powerful effects, stimulating the creation of new cells and neurons, positively influencing concentration, focus, memory, and mood. In the short term, exercise brings with it a sensation of alertness or of being more "awake." This feeling has a tendency to translate into sharper focus after exercise. As already mentioned in the discussion of hormones above, the chemical processes triggered in the brain by exercise have very tangible effects on one's mood, raising spirits and keeping at bay the chemical deficiencies associated with depression. One study published in *The Lancet* in 2018 looked at the data from 1.2 million respondents to a United States Centers for Disease Control and Prevention survey. The researchers observed a 43.2% reduction in days of poor mental health among participants that exercised regularly, and although certain types of exercise appeared to boost mood more than others, all types were associated with a lower mental health burden. It has also been shown, as reported by Harvard Health Publishing, that by improving memory and thinking abilities, exercise is a key factor in the preservation of mental acuity into old age. With regards to exercise's effect on brain diseases, researchers remain cautious, but hopeful. According to a review by the Alzheimer's Society UK of eleven different prospective studies, regular moderate exercise considerably improves memory and thinking, and reduces the risk of developing dementia and Alzheimer's by 30% and 45%, respectively.

As this non-exhaustive list attests, exercise is fundamental to any healthy lifestyle. It is inherently linked to what makes our bodies function properly. There is no process in your body that does not profit from regular exercise. Along with a good diet and ample amounts of sleep, it is the best thing you can add to your routine for a healthy lifestyle.

Two things are important to remember. First, a lifestyle with adequate amounts of exercise has a preventative effect against NCDs. That does not mean that exercise will immunize you against disease, but statistically speaking it boosts your health in so many ways that your chances of getting sick will be seriously reduced. Second, not only does exercise have preventative effects, it may also improve your ability to cope with the symptoms of any disease you may already be suffering from.

One paper that reviewed the research on this topic in the *International Journal of Clinical Practice*, for example, lists around two dozen physical and mental health conditions that are improved and prevented to some degree by physical activity. These include many of the main NCDs, such as heart disease, several types of cancer, stroke, type 2 diabetes, and the list goes on. In other words, even if you are suffering from a debilitating or life-threatening condition, the right amount of exercise and regular activity may greatly increase your wellbeing and improve your ability to fight disease. If this is the case, talk to your physician about making exercise an integral part of your treatment plan. Ask him or her to become part of your team and help you to invest sustainably in your health.

HOW MUCH EXERCISE IS ENOUGH?

This is a difficult question to answer, but you are best positioned to answer it for yourself. Through newspapers, scientific studies, and social media, we are often reminded that many people are not sufficiently active, but how active is active enough? This is of course a relative concept, but the guidelines for exercise set by the World Health Organization (WHO) are modest: 150 minutes a week of moderate-intensity physical activity (less than half an hour a day), with a suggestion to increase this to 300 minutes for extra health benefits; 75 minutes a week of vigorous physical activity; and muscle-strengthening activity involving major muscle groups at least two times a week.

If you are thinking these recommendations are aimed at young adults, you would be wrong. Whether you are eighteen or eighty-one, the recommendations are the same. By all accounts, however, the average person is far from reaching these levels of activity. Still according to WHO figures, the percentage of adults engaging in regular physical activity is abysmal, with 60% to 85% of the population failing to meet recommended activity levels. Among children and adolescents, only a small percentage (less than 14% in some demographics) are getting enough exercise. At cause is the increasingly sedentary lifestyle that the vast majority of the world population now leads. For most people, therefore, the answer to how much exercise is enough exercise is simple: *more, more, more!*

You may be pleased to hear that those getting the least exercise stand to gain the most from increasing their physical activity. This means that if you're a couch potato, you will be able to benefit significantly more from starting to exercise than someone who is already active and increases his or her levels. According to a 2015 study published in the *American Journal of Medicine*, the benefits we draw from physical activity depend on a number of factors, including how active we already are, the intensity of the exercise, and so on. When plotted onto a graph, the benefits of exercise appear to follow a bell curve, rising rapidly with the initial efforts, then evening out, and falling again after a certain point. This suggests, on the one hand, that more is not always better, that too much exercise may start to erase some of the previous health gains. That said, it's important to understand that "too much exercise" really only refers to extremely high levels of intensive exercise—say, if you're running regular marathons or ironman competitions multiple times a year. But for most people within the norm, and particularly for those leading largely inactive and sedentary lifestyles, the message is clear—get going, and do as much as you can. More, in this case, is definitely better.

Although 150 minutes of moderate activity a week is not that much, it requires a qualification which is conspicuously absent from this otherwise important guideline: the human body needs regular movement throughout the day. This means that grouping all exercise into 30-minute sessions, five times a week, will not be enough to counteract an otherwise sedentary lifestyle. While structured exercise sessions are essential, they should be complemented by as much movement and activity as possible. We will return to the question of sedentarism in more depth in chapter nine, but for now it is important to note that too much sitting will erase any health benefits from short sessions like those outlined by these guidelines. So get your 150 minutes of structured exercise a week, and then some.

A regular and sustained exercise regime can save your life. The idea here is not to try to convert you into a sports fanatic, but to highlight the need that every human body has for physical exercise. Too much exercise could be bad for your health, so listen to your body, but too little exercise will lead you to a certain cardiovascular, muscular, and metabolic decline, as well as a very strong likelihood of disease, and a shorter lifespan. Your mobility is the key to your independence, and, as your age progresses, if you want to lead an active lifestyle and continue being able to move around at will—without crutches, cane, or wheelchair—then exercise is the answer. It is perhaps the most underwhelming of all health tips, the most anticlimactic secret of all, but that's how it is. You have to work for it, and it doesn't get any easier with age, but it is possible. It's been done. You can do it too. The real question you should be asking yourself is not whether or not to exercise, but what kind of exercise do you want to be doing?

There are more and less efficient ways of getting your exercise, and you will always be able to improve, no matter what your level of fitness is. Ultimately, if what you want is good, well-rounded physical fitness, then you probably should design a full-body workout that includes cardio, resistance, flexibility, and balance training. You can also do all the other stuff you want to do on top of that, but a regular full-body workout plan will allow you to cover all your bases. This is hard to improvise, and requires some research and planning. You need to understand what you're going for and develop a routine accordingly. The next section of this book aims to provide some tips and tools to get started. An active lifestyle requires effort and commitment, but there are many ways of getting the exercise you need, and how you do so is up to you. Whatever your strategy though, doing something is always better than doing nothing, no matter how little or how much you decide to do.

6

A WORKOUT WILL
MAKE YOUR DAY

Working out on a daily basis will change your life. You don't have to pump iron, but you do need to get your body going. Remember what they say about the apple? Well, apples *are* good for you, but a workout a day is your best bet to actually keep the doctor away. My advice? Figure out a list of essential exercises you can do on most days of the week, get going first thing in the morning and get it out of the way. It gets your blood pumping, helps to loosen any accumulated tensions, primes your muscles, focuses your mind, and if you happen to be going for weight loss, it's the ideal time too. This is what I do. I get up and work out every morning as a matter of choice, and although it's not easy to get going because my old body *does* complain, I do it anyway.

What you will not find in this book is a detailed list of exercises you should do daily. These will very much depend on your specific needs and health status. However, if you go to the Fit For Life Foundation's website at www.fitforlife.foundation, we will be curating online resources with links to professional trainers that provide full-body workouts and instructional videos. It is also worth thinking about finding a fitness coach, physiotherapist, or sports doctor to work with. While there are many resources that will allow you to devise your own workout, having a knowledgeable expert to talk to is invaluable. I definitely recommend this. It is a worthwhile investment, and can save you a tremendous amount of time and, potentially, help you to avoid a good deal of trial and error along the way.

Also bear in mind that whatever you choose to do, it doesn't have to be a solo affair. Everybody needs exercise, and there's no reason it shouldn't be a social event. If you don't like to exercise alone, you can join a class or organize a group of friends or colleagues to join you at home, in the local park, or at the gym. This has the added advantage of giving you some social time, which is a great mood booster. Also, the stimulation you get from the group will help keep you going when the going gets tough. We will return to this topic in more detail in chapter fifteen, "Together Is Better."

That said, I want to share some knowledge on what to look for and what to include when you are putting together a workout yourself. The following pages should be of some help to orient you in your journey back into fitness and an overall active lifestyle.

WHAT IS A STRUCTURED WORKOUT, AND WHY DO I NEED IT?

An active lifestyle requires you to be mobile, and mobility begins with you and your body. A structured workout is a set of specific exercises and activities that you carry out on a regular basis, making it part of your routine in order to maintain and improve your basic fitness. The four main types of exercise introduced in the previous chapter are the building blocks for any such routine. Aerobic endurance, strength, flexibility, and balance are the foundations of any healthy mobility. No matter where you are starting from, whether you are inactive and sedentary or already active but looking to fill in the gaps in your fitness, a structured workout should provide you with the means for covering all of these bases.

As we move around in the world, going about our normal business, we use our muscles selectively and this creates problems. We only develop musculature, cardiovascular health, and flexibility according to the levels at which our daily tasks require them. For better or for worse, most of us barely need to lift a finger for anything anymore. Unfortunately, this has repercussions. The levels at which life requires us to use our bodies is vastly inferior to the true capacity we have as human beings, even old human beings. When we do not make full use of our musculoskeletal capabilities, our body slowly becomes lazy, and this is where the problems start. One weakness leads to another, and left unchecked can trigger a cascade of other problems. Strong muscles compensate for weaker ones, then get tired. This, in turn, leads to further compensations by other muscles, more discomfort, muscle fatigue, and finally, injuries. A nagging problem in your knee that you leave unaddressed leads to a sore hip, this spreads to the other hip and your lower back, and before you know it you have generalized back pain because your posture is affected. Then a shoulder starts to ache, and pretty soon, everything hurts all over and you are miserable. It's important to understand that the human body is an integrated system. In other words, everything is connected.

A structured workout means that you can prevent and, where necessary, address the imbalances created by everyday life. Bear in mind that muscular imbalances also arise out of any repetitive activity, not merely a lack thereof. Sitting all day, every day, is the worst thing you can do—as we will see in chapter eight, "Sitting Is The Enemy"—but it's not the only thing that will cause problems. Think of professional tennis players, for example, who have to make up for the discrepancy in musculature between both arms, one of which is swinging a racket for half of their waking life. You can also look at the case of fencers, who notoriously suffer from the fact that they always lunge with the same leg, creating the problematic situation of having one leg with a very strong thigh, and the other with a very strong calf muscle. We don't have to stay within the realm of sports either, any profession you can think of will include some form of activity with the potential for creating imbalances. Warehouse workers who lift heavy packages all day might develop strong muscles, but if they don't get any cardiovascular exercise, they may never work their lungs, thus developing cardiorespiratory deficiencies, and so on. A workout should be designed with the idea of lifting the general level of fitness, strength, flexibility, and balance across the board to a baseline proficiency. We're not talking about anything wild here, just the fact that you should feel good enough to move around to the full extent that your body was designed for.

A full workout will enable you to build a good level of overall strength, target all the main muscle groups, and readjust any muscular imbalances you have. It will help you organize aerobic sessions to build your pulmonary capacity and cardiovascular health. It will also allow you to work in flexibility training and balance exercises, and help you understand the good times for doing these—in short, *when* you should be doing *what*. The trick of putting together a workout is knowing what to do, in what order, and finding the right time to do so.

THE FOUR TYPES OF EXERCISE WE ALL NEED

In the four sections below, I break down some of the key aspects that are useful to know about the four main types of exercise. You can find more information online, in local fitness centers, or in manuals and guides written by practitioners. Several sources for further reading are also provided at the end of this book.

1. Cardiovascular training (aerobics)

As its name implies, aerobic training gets you breathing hard and stimulates your heart and lungs to pump blood and oxygen through your veins and into the cells throughout your body. Aerobics is the key to cardiovascular health, and therefore to health overall. Get to know your body and take it in stages. Walking, jogging, running, cycling, and swimming, are all good solutions to get your heart rate up and going. While there are physiological aspects to take into account when you take up these activities, such as the effect of running on your joints, and so on, your body is perfectly capable of adapting to these stresses. Any downsides, unless you have a permanent condition or serious injury in need of attention, pale in comparison to the cumulative effect over time of poor aerobic fitness.

The intensity of the exercise will determine the outcome here. We can distinguish between light, moderate, and vigorous forms of exercise, and the key indicator for this, generally speaking, is the level of your breathing. This makes the scale highly variable and dependent upon one's personal fitness. Realizing that the intensity of an exercise is largely dependent upon your level of fitness is crucial because you are your own barometer. Just because someone can jog up and down a flight of steps without getting out of breath doesn't mean that you can too. Similarly, just because you once were able to do so, doesn't mean you are still able to do so today. But just because you can't hit those stairs when you read this doesn't mean you won't be able to a few months from now. This is why regular training is so important—it allows you to maintain, regain, and ultimately improve your fitness.

The following forms of aerobic exercise are all valuable in their own right and ought to be worked into one's lifestyle on a regular basis:

Light exercise is considered to be any form of movement where you're moving but not pushing yourself. Your breathing isn't affected and you probably don't feel too much strain on your muscles (although you could be working on flexibility, among other things). This is everything you do from light housework to leisurely strolling in the park or doing a bit of shopping. Light exercise is good for you because you're moving and your metabolism is therefore in an active state, even if you're not getting the kind of health benefits you do from moderate or vigorous exercise, where the real changes come about.

Moderate exercise is aerobic activity that raises your pulse enough so that you become aware of your breathing and it eventually becomes harder, but not impossible, to speak and hold a conversation. Brisk walking, slow jogging, or moderate cycling typically fall into this category. When I refer, generally speaking, to exercise in this book, most of the time I am referring to forms of moderate, aerobically challenging exercise. The reason for this simply has to do with the fact that light exercise, while it is not negligible, has the least to offer in terms of health benefits, whereas vigorous exercise requires a certain amount of structure, time, and sustained effort to work up to. Moderate exercise, in contrast, can usually be done without having to think too much about it because it won't put too much strain on your body. As a general rule––and especially if you are out of shape––you should get as much moderate exercise as you can.

Vigorous exercise territory is entered as soon as your breathing becomes heavy and your pulse begins to be significantly elevated. Typically, this will involve running, intense cycling, or anything that similarly strains your cardiorespiratory capacity. You should be aware, however, that lesser forms of exercise will count as vigorous if you are severely out of shape. Despite its challenges and the discomfort it may initially cause, as well as the fact that it may seem daunting, integrating forms of vigorous exercise into your schedule is absolutely essential and highly recommended. Bouts of vigorous exercise will be key in improving your endurance and resistance. They will enable you to truly push your boundaries and lead your body to improve. Be aware, however, that of all three levels of exercise, you are most likely to injure yourself during vigorous exercise. This should not be a deterrent, but do always proceed with caution. Increase the intensity very progressively and listen to your personal barometer: your body.

Once again, these levels of intensity are entirely *relative* to your own physical condition. It's important to keep this in mind because being realistic about one's own current levels of fitness is the only way to truly progress and see any real gains. Regular activity should raise your aerobic capacity pretty quickly, and you may be surprised at how quickly you see improvements.

2. Resistance training (strength)

Maintaining muscle strength is basically a battle against gravity that we all have to fight for the duration of our lives. There's no mystery as to which side will prevail in the end, and so the real question is: how much can we hold on to, and for how long?

When we talk of strength training, it usually involves lifting weights, or your own body weight, to build your muscle capacity. The rule of thumb is pretty simple: when you exercise, you use your muscles, and using your muscles automatically strengthens them. Pushing or pulling is the way this goes, not just with your arms, but with your whole body in a variety of ways. Building muscle is important for a number of reasons, chiefly because it allows you to carry the weight of your own body as you move through the world. We tend to take this for granted; but the more time we spend sitting or lying down, the less we train to carry our own weight, and the harder it gets.

Our muscles react very differently to different forms of exercise. When we compare primarily aerobic activities like jogging or swimming with more focused kinds of resistance training, such as lifting weights in the gym or lifting your own body weight, what we find is that they have very different effects on the body, including on the way they influence muscle development. Resistance training with weights will create muscles with greater mass that are more efficient for powerful contractions and lifting heavy loads, whereas aerobic activities will tend to create leaner muscles that are more efficient for the kind of repetitive, small-load muscle contractions that occur when we walk or run, for example. In short, *function determines form.*

There are many ways to build strength, and many different kinds of strength to build. Again, I recommend aiming for function and mobility. To achieve these goals, a training program should target all our main muscle groups. These are your arms, shoulders, back, chest, abdominals, thighs, and calves. Whether it is through activities that require you to mobilize your whole body, or through specific exercises that isolate an individual muscle, you will want to get all these muscle groups working in one way or another.

Everybody has different physical characteristics and varying levels of aptitude, but behind every *good* workout program, you are likely to find the same starting point: strength comes from your core. Your core is constituted by the muscle groups that connect your lower and upper body, and is concentrated around your hips, pelvis, abdomen, and lower back. This is a good place to start with any workout, because your core is where all movements come from and go through. Your core provides you with the stability and support you need to perform all other movements. One good way to strengthen these muscles is to try Pilates or yoga. Both of these disciplines have a large number of techniques and exercises that build core strength, albeit in different ways. Regardless of the practice, however, I recommend finding some good floor exercises that get you rolling around and strengthening the muscles in your stomach, back, and buttocks.

Yoga and Pilates are good for strength, but they are also great for working on flexibility and balance. From a fitness, cost, and time standpoint, these activities are a great compromise for anyone who wants to engage in relatively efficient exercise that covers most needs without being too intense. For someone with back problems like myself, and most other older people, these disciplines provide numerous exercises that cover basic needs. Yoga exercises are particularly good for flexibility and mobility, while Pilates is particularly suited to helping you protect and strengthen the core-stabilizing muscle groups around your waist which diminishes the likelihood of injury in general, and back aches in particular. All you need is a floor mat and loose-fitting clothes. In today's world, there are versions of these disciplines that have been developed for all ages and all levels of fitness.

3. Flexibility training (stretching)

Working on your flexibility has a range of benefits. It will help reduce the stiffness you feel from the shortening of muscles over time and, as you build strength, it will allow you to slowly stretch your muscles towards their full range of motion. Regular flexibility training is an essential part of any workout.

In a nutshell, there are two types of stretching exercises: dynamic and static. *Dynamic stretches* involve entering the stretch with your muscles activated and in control. These types of exercises can be incorporated in a workout or a warmup, and they involve a form of natural resistance, thus also building strength. *Static stretches*, on the other hand, involve entering a position that pulls a certain set of muscles and tendons into a stretch, but without them being active. Remember to breathe deeply and perform all movements as smoothly as you can, avoiding choppy or jerky movements.

There are different schools when it comes to best practice. Some say you shouldn't stretch before intensive exercise, and others strongly disagree. The same goes for the value of stretching *after* a workout. I say, experiment for yourself. Keep in mind, however, that you want your muscles to be primed during exercise, though not necessarily fully stretched out. There is also some debate about stretching after exercise, and as to how much is appropriate. Speaking for myself, while I always warm up before exercise, I don't do much stretching other than during my morning workout which includes stretches to cover all main muscle groups.

However you decide to plan your flexibility training, stretching is an essential part of any workout and simply needs to be done. In addition to being the perfect accompaniment to your strength and endurance training sessions, it is likely to improve your posture over time, and will greatly help in preventing injury by keeping your body nice and limber, ready to absorb the shock of a false movement, or to bounce back from an unexpected impact.

4. Balance training

Our sense of balance is our inherent awareness of our body in space. It is the system that allows us to keep track of movements in relation to gravity, and it prevents us from falling over. As such it is crucial throughout our lifetime. Balance is reliant on several elements, including our eyes, for visual cues, our inner ear, which functions both as a tracking system and as a level, and our sense of touch, through anything we may be holding on to or standing upon, such as the ground under our feet. The musculoskeletal system is also involved since it performs the movements in question, as well as any corrective action required to maintain balance.

There is often a correlation made between age and loss of balance. Part of this is just the wear and tear of what we consider normal aging. And yet, consistent with the message concerning exercise, balance can be worked on and improved. The rule, once again, is straightforward: the more you do, the better. Try standing on one foot for sixty seconds or more while looking straight ahead. This exercise alone, performed on a daily basis, can make a big difference over time. Yoga and Pilates are also excellent sources of further exercises to train balance.

Do note, however, that if you have severe vertigo or balance issues, this may be more than just a sign of age. You may be experiencing issues with your vestibular system, or the organs in your inner ear, and there are measures you can take to address these issues. Talk to your doctor about your concerns. He or she will be able to suggest therapeutic solutions that may include corrective or rehabilitative exercises.

HOW TO STRUCTURE A WORKOUT

When designing a workout program, you need to find an organizing principle according to which you can make decisions about what to include. While I say a few words on this below, ultimately you will need to explore what works for you, aiming to cover all four types of exercise we have just seen.

The human body is a very complex and sophisticated machine within which everything is interconnected. We all have our own history and characteristics, which include, but are not limited to: body type, fitness level, medical antecedents, injuries, strengths, and weaknesses. Taking these into account is an important element in any workout routine, but once again, it is important to understand that no matter what your strengths and limitations are, they can be worked around or worked into your training.

The first question you should ask yourself when creating a workout routine is: "What are my objectives?" My suggestion here is simple. The goal I advocate is to achieve a baseline level of mobility and functional movement which is synonymous with overall general fitness. Anyone wanting to lead an active lifestyle should aim for a full body workout that gets you into good enough shape so you can move around independently and perform most of the basic functional movements our bodies are designed for.

The main movements I would include in this category are: walking, running, squatting, lunging, pushing, pulling, rotating, and jumping. Most of these will seem somewhat bland, and they are, yet there is a strong chance you have not performed a portion of them for a while. It's time to start rediscovering them. Take it slow to begin with because it is very easy to overdo it. If it seems like a long shot, don't worry—just remember it's possible to work up to it.

A well-rounded workout should get your heart pumping, raise your breathing rate, and include strength-building exercises to tone your muscles. It should also include stretches to relax and elongate the fibers in your muscles after you have used them, and it should allow you to improve your balance. You can develop a workout that you do everyday, or develop a weekly program, which may give you more room to cover all the elements you need to fit in. Once you accept the need to exercise every day and make this a reality, you can start planning to focus on different types of exercise on different days. Remember too that all the four types of exercise overlap, and most physical activities rely on all of them in some way.

People undertake a fitness program for many reasons, and all are valid. Depending on where you are fitness-wise right now, you may have specific objectives, like building endurance, flexibility, strength, or some combination of these. You may, for example, be looking to complete a 5-kilometer or 10-kilometer race, or a kilometer swim in the pool. You may want to perform a handstand, or you may simply decide you want to be able to touch your toes again, to stand up straight without having to feel pain, or to unlock the crippling tightness in your hips. Maybe you are one of the millions who suffer from chronic back pain, and you want to free yourself of this nightmare. These goals are typically the kinds of things you want to put at the center of your workouts because they are a source of motivation you can then build around. Whatever your objectives are, with the right amount of dedication it is possible to achieve them. I highly encourage you to try.

SOME PRINCIPLES FOR A GOOD WORKOUT

Regularity, repetition, awareness, and a careful monitoring of your condition as you exercise are of utmost importance, since you will not be able to transform your body overnight. You need to pace yourself, and learn to exercise in a sustainable manner. The ideal goal is for you to be able to perform some kind of exercise every single day of your life. This can't happen if you're injured, or if you're exhausted because you overdid it. Try to establish and become comfortable with a basic level of mobility through regular, preferably daily, moderate exercise. From there, in order to continue your progression, you can try to push yourself with regular, short sessions of vigorous exercise. Not too hard, not too fast, always in control. Find your limits, get to know them, and start pushing them as soon as you are comfortable.

Warming up. Before you get fully into your workout, you need to take the time to warm up. This will mean different things for different people, depending on your level of fitness, but you need to get your blood pumping and get yourself somewhat loosened and limbered up before you launch into the thick of your training. The first exercises therefore will always be warm-up exercises. You can slowly build up intensity after that, but it's important to start slow.

Exercise with control. Remember to keep control of your movements at all times. It's important that all your movements and every repetition of your exercises be carefully managed. Whether you are stretching or doing a more demanding strength exercise, do not push it beyond your limits or your range of movement. This is where injury happens. It's better to shoot for quality over quantity, which means doing less but doing it well. You will work up your endurance, strength, and overall capacity over time. Remember that careless and uncontrolled movements are the enemy of a good workout, and the injuries that result will set you back in the grand scheme of things.

Work on range of motion. Be conscious of the fact that you want to extend and maximize your range of motion. All our joints and body parts have a range within which they can move. You should understand, however, that the range you are able to cover is likely less than the one that could be available to you with training. This means working regularly on stretching and strength to be able to move into and out of these extended positions with control. Working to extend range of motion is central to avoiding injury and will significantly help improve overall performance.

Find and respect your limits—don't overdo it. My rule of thumb, which has always gotten the green light from my doctors, is *if it doesn't cause pain, you can do it*. So while you should always proceed with caution, you should not be overly cautious or paranoid either. Take care, but don't let caution be an excuse for laziness or for throwing in the towel. Finding and respecting your limits will ensure you make steady progress, and it will help you tune in to the incredible power your body holds. Solidify your gains and be patient—take things one step at a time.

Ideally, you want to keep a little energy in reserve so that you don't collapse when you are done exercising. You should be able to move around normally and go about your daily life without any problems. By not pushing yourself beyond your limit every time you work up a sweat, perform a strength exercise like a series of pushups, or stretch out your muscles, you will be ready to go again the next day. Respect this principle, and you will greatly reduce—and eventually get rid of—the stiffness and pain you feel after a workout.

Rehabilitate according to your abilities. It's hard to reach a certain age without taking a tumble here and there and accumulating a few scars. Whether by accident or illness, or by genetic predisposition, we all have our weaknesses. It's important to take these into account when you go about building and following your new workout schedule. Acknowledging weaknesses is an essential step that will heavily influence your workout, and in order to do so you must take the time to articulate as clearly as possible what your problems are. It's also the only way to choose the right corrective and rehabilitative exercises that fit your needs. Depending on the severity of your medical history, you may want to consult a healthcare professional, such as a sports doctor or a physiotherapist, for guidance.

WHAT *MY* WORKOUT LOOKS LIKE

Up until the age of fifty, I spent most of my exercise time on aerobic training, like biking and running, with some resistance training thrown in when it was apparent from my activities that I needed to build more strength, such as for mountain climbing. This shifted slightly when I began having back trouble, but all I did was include some exercises to flex my back and spine. I performed these on a semi-regular basis until my early seventies, at which time I had my spinal stenosis flare-up. This was the turning point when it became absolutely clear that I needed to implement a structured routine. I had been close to the brink, and my weaknesses were beginning to show. The path ahead became clear: shoring up against the tides of time was now my main fitness goal.

Because I was told by my surgeon that my narrow spine would soon fill up with arthritis again after the operation, which would require another intervention, I made it my mission to avoid this by all means through an unflinching commitment to regular exercise. There are a number of exercises that specifically target the maintenance of spinal mobility, and effectively protect against the build-up of arthritic material. I have been following these exercises for the past seven years, and in the two MRIs that I have had during this time, there has been no evidence of any buildup so far.

Every day when I wake up, I do feel old. My body feels stiff and heavy from sleep and the temptation to roll over, back into comfort, is appealing. But "feeling old" poses a problem for me, as does staying in my comfort zone. Within minutes, I go straight into my exercise routine, waking up my body with gradually intensifying exercises. In under an hour, I am able to shed this "old" feeling and get primed and ready to meet the day. This never gets any easier, but it does remain possible, and it remains necessary. By the time I'm through with my exercises and drinking a cup of coffee with my wife, I feel many years younger. As my father used to say, I feel *like a million bucks.*

My typical exercise routine for a week looks as follows:

Six days a week, I have a list of twenty-five different exercises that I do in just under an hour. I first get my blood pumping with some aerobically demanding exercises like leg raises. I then cover core strength with a series of exercises derived from yoga and Pilates. I include stretches to loosen up my legs, my arms, my neck, and my back; a few balance exercises like standing on one leg for a minute; as well as a few more demanding strength-building exercises like pushups and squats. Importantly, I also include a number of exercises to compensate for my back and shoulder injuries. I perform these twenty-five exercises swiftly and without taking a break, which means that I generally begin to sweat and breathe heavily, which gives the workout an aerobic element as well.

Three times a week, I do one hour of light weight lifting at home. This is mostly for upper body and leg strength, and in order to compensate for the shoulder injury which I suffered. My objective here is not to have big muscles, but rather to make sure that all my muscle groups are active on a regular basis so that I can manage the strain of all my other activities and avoid injuries. These activities could be anything from everyday lifting—groceries, household items, and so on—to more sporadic and physically demanding sports, such as skiing. I am in the process of slowly but steadily increasing the load of my weights in order to rebuild the muscle mass, in so far as that is possible, that I lost during my shoulder rehabilitation and due to the process of aging.

Three times a week, I get aerobic exercise either by cycling for two hours, or running for an hour (usually if it rains or if I am in a rush). These are true staples of my workout routine. While most of this is at a normal, moderate pace, about one third is high intensity. This is how I get my vigorous exercise, in the form of sprints while I am cycling. I go as fast as I can for short bursts of several minutes, followed by recuperation times so I can catch my breath. These sprints are essential for pushing my limits and building endurance. Remember that the WHO recommends that everyone get at least 75 minutes of intensive exercise like this every week.

I also keep in mind the following principles to help me stay active:

- I make a point of staying active throughout the day, walking wherever I can, and getting in small amounts of movements and stretches whenever the opportunity presents itself.
- Whenever I can, weather permitting, I ride my bike to and from my office.
- I have a standup desk in my office, so I avoid sitting as much as I can.
- I take phone calls standing up and will either pace the room, or go for a walk if it is a long conversation.
- I organize regular trips with my wife, family, and friends. Whether it is for the afternoon or a long weekend, these often involve hiking or cycling for pleasure.

My morning routine is a source of strength, confidence, and internal wellbeing, as well as a means to an end. Every morning, I am able to loosen up, get centered, and become more in touch with my physical self before I meet the challenges of the day. While the most efficient way of achieving better fitness is to implement a structured workout that you integrate to your routine, any step in the right direction is progress. The crux of my appeal is that we should aim to maintain and develop as much functional movement as possible. Being able to perform according to our body's natural abilities should be the aim of any normal level of fitness.

Remember, you will only reap the benefits you manage to sow. Start doing at least 30 minutes a day, more if you can, and you will begin to feel results within weeks. I recommend a daily workout to everyone for the simple reason that it is the best way to ensure and preserve fundamental mobility, or its retrieval if it's already been lost. I can't stress this enough. You need to understand that working out will get you moving again in ways you wouldn't otherwise be able to. Don't be fooled by the cliché: old age does *not* breed weakness. A sedentary, inactive lifestyle does. Right up until the end, it is possible to dramatically increase your level of fitness. This will improve your health, make your life infinitely more enjoyable, and enable you to do all the things that you want to do and that your body is designed for. It is also very likely to increase your healthspan. You won't see results overnight, but if you stick with it, they *will* come.

7
MINDSET IS HALF THE BATTLE

Getting into shape is not a one-time transaction, it is a process. Think of it as a resolution that becomes a building block for the rest of your life. Fitness is not a product, it can neither be purchased nor faked, rather it is the ongoing effect of an active lifestyle. You don't have to dedicate your life to sport, or give up all the physically passive passions you may have, but if you're looking to get fit for life and you want the results, then you must accept that it will require effort, and that it will come with challenges. Whether you are building a workout, trying to stick to one, or simply looking to change your habits to integrate more exercise across the board, then finding ways to commit physically and mentally will be key to implementing any lasting changes. You have to get your mind right if you're going to see it through, because your mindset really is half the battle.

THE IMPORTANCE OF MINDSET

Giving in to adversity should not be an option. Whatever life throws your way, make it your job to overcome it. You can make this happen whether you are starting out, ramping up, or getting back into exercise. In order for this to work, however, and for your body to be able to make the journey, your mindset needs to be solid. The way you internalize and imagine *what* exercise is exactly, what it means for you, will be crucial in determining not only your ability to stick with it over time, but also your feelings about the process.

Your emotional response before, during, and after physical activity will define the experience. If your natural reaction to exercise, or the idea of exercise, is a negative one, then you might want to pay special attention to this particular point, because it could be the key to unlocking the potential of physical activity for you. Learning to develop a positive mindset about the things you do to stay fit and healthy will set you on the right path. If you look at active people and how they feel about life, you will notice how much they love the things they do. The effort therefore comes naturally for the most part.

Exercise shouldn't feel like a burden or a chore, it's what our bodies are designed to do. *Why* you are doing what you're doing is just as important as *what* you are doing in the first place, because a good answer to this question will create a real and powerful connection between you, your body, and your spirit. I believe that, even though there are clear trends, the road towards finding satisfaction in one's activities and, by extension, in one's life, is different for every individual. And so I urge you to take the time to ponder and explore this question.

While there is no doubt that regular exercise has tremendous benefits to health and wellbeing, this fact in and of itself is probably not what is going to ignite a secret love for, say, jogging. When you're breathing hard on your first run since the turn of the century, with the unmistakable taste of copper in your mouth, the conviction that you are contributing to your longevity and health may have trouble holding its own against the urge to give up and retreat into familiar comforts.

Somehow, you need to create that connection in your brain, find that *something* that gets you out there, creating and living your version of an active lifestyle. These difficult moments are the true battlegrounds of this war on inactivity. These are the times when you have to dig in and hold on. This is where you make progress, and change happens. Those first few hours turn into the first few days, which turn into the first few months, and so on, until you finally do manage to turn exercise into a habit you can no longer live without.

CLAWING BACK FROM INJURY

In 2019, at the age of seventy-seven, having come to terms with the challenges of managing my spinal stenosis and just as I was beginning to feel comfortable in my new routine, a cat sprang out into the road in front of me one day as I was cycling. I slammed on the brakes but was going too fast, so I went head over heels and crashed hard, falling heavily on my left side. My shoulder took the brunt of the damage, and all the ligaments were torn off the bone. My arm was shot, and I had to be operated on by an orthopedic surgeon specializing in shoulder reconstruction. Recuperation time was supposed to be about four months. The operation went well and I went into convalescence, eager to heal and regain the use of my arm and shoulder as soon as possible. Unfortunately, I caught a staphylococcus infection at the hospital after the initial operation. The infection only declared itself after a month had gone by, however, at which time I had to go back under the knife. This added at least three or four months to the whole process, and I lost more flexibility and muscle-mass than expected. I could see my flabby skin just hanging there where muscle had been. This was particularly the case on my arms, on the back of the shoulders, and on my thighs. For the second time in my seventies, I was faced with the need to rehabilitate and it weighed heavily on my morale.

This was one of the harder and more lengthy recuperations I've had to work through in my life, but I kept at it, doing whatever was within my reach. Not much was. My left arm was immobilized in a sling and I could only use my right hand and shoulder. This severely reduced my overall mobility, and basic, daily tasks became impossible. For months, sleeping was a nightmare and I could not even wash myself unassisted. From buckling my belt to tying my shoes, from lifting a glass to brushing my teeth and putting on a shirt, every task became extremely challenging, and I needed my wife's help for everything. Although I was grateful to be on the road to recuperation, in my own mind I felt completely useless and it was hard to keep the faith.

Exercising while your whole arm is immobilized and you're not allowed to move your shoulder is uncomfortable, awkward, and exhausting—and yet this is exactly what needs to happen. Maintaining some level of fitness and activity as you recover from injury is crucial. It keeps your body functioning at healthy levels, and bolsters the quality of your healing. Despite the difficulty, I powered through and kept at it, doing the best I could. The rehabilitation itself involved essential rebuilding of muscle mass. It also included specialized exercises that help improve the way the shoulder works. The process is delicate and involves progressively strengthening the shoulder's muscles and supporting structures while slowly reclaiming and regaining range of motion. The routine you follow is decided on by a physiotherapist who supervises the process, but you have to do the work on your own. Obviously, I can't stress enough how important it is to do what the physiotherapist tells you to do. Overdoing it can lead to unnecessary pain and the undoing of any progress you make. If you don't do the work, however, this can result in limited strength, limited range of motion, and what is sometimes called a "frozen" shoulder. Often, this then becomes a chronic problem that is extremely painful, possibly requiring further surgeries.

Everything contained here is an account of how to manage from one's own perspective, but it does not discount the role of healthcare professionals. As I write now, roughly nine months after the first intervention, I am still following the path of recovery, but my left shoulder is once again as functional as my right. I continue to do specific shoulder exercises, including more and more weight training to regain muscle mass, but I feel strong again, and I am able to lift objects and perform complex movements in awkward directions. Much to my delight, I am back on my bike again, taking long rides and keeping a vigilant lookout for any cats that might try to jump me. If it ever were to happen again, however, I have a feeling the cat might just get run over.

SETTING YOUR MIND RIGHT

Whether you are getting back into exercise after a period of inactivity, recovering from an injury, or launching out for the first time into an active lifestyle, here are some principles for the road ahead that will help you prepare for its challenges:

The need is evident, but desire is essential. You have to want it

This is how it begins—with desire. It is what will keep you going, and therefore it is crucial. It is no good telling anyone they need exercise if it rubs them the wrong way. Anyone who knows what's good for them will see that they *need* exercise. And while this should be motivation enough, realistically, it is not. And therefore you need to want it. Desire is the driver, but desire is also somewhat fickle. You absolutely have to find a way to want to do the things you need to do.

The aim here is to boost your level of fitness, reclaim your mobility, lead an active lifestyle, and open yourself up once more to the possibility of adventure, to redefining what "old age" looks like. Try to visualize what it is you could picture yourself doing differently. Dare to dream a little. Use your imagination, and make it specific. Ask yourself what you would like to be doing. Take some time to really let your ideas creep into uncharted territory, whatever the outcomes. Find out what others are doing or have done and get inspired, and if these people are close to you, why not do it with them? Remember, it's not just about exercise, but mobility. It's about all the new things you could be doing. The sky's the limit.

Is this desire within you already, or do you have to learn to cultivate it? Maybe it's something you've dreamed of for years, or maybe it's something you haven't thought of yet. Assume that anything is possible. Put yourself in the shoes of those with stories to tell. What stories would you want to tell your friends or your family a month from now, and how about five years from then? Perhaps, like me, you are drawn to your bicycle and the infinite possibilities of discovering new places by road. You could take up swimming again, in a lake, a river, the sea, or the ocean. Maybe you want to take up a new sport, or go on a walking tour in that city or exotic country you've always dreamed of visiting. Maybe you want to take advantage of the opportunity to explore the region where you live and all it has to offer, something which we often overlook.

Dreams don't have to be grandiose, but they are important because they will allow your imagination to feed your desire. Both of these together will carry you forward and ensure that you succeed no matter what path to exercise you choose. In order to get fit, or to get better at anything really, you have to want it, and you have to want it like mad.

Be ambitious in your targets, realistic in your approach

When it comes to setting goals and objectives for your physical development, don't be shy, and shoot high. Take it in stages, however. You need to take your current physical condition into consideration. Allowing yourself to dream and yearning to make it come true will propel you forward, but only by being fully aware of yourself and your situation can you keep moving and ultimately achieve these goals. You won't be able to run a marathon in a week if you haven't gone jogging for over twenty years. Chances are that with the right training program, however, it *will* be possible for you to run that marathon *someday*, even if it takes you a year or two of preparation.

Be as clear eyed as possible about your weaknesses. We all have them, it's normal. Developing an awareness of your weaknesses means, first of all, that you can work on them, reducing them where possible. Second, it will help you avoid injury or failure by not overdoing it.

Many people restarting exercise end up doing too much, too fast. We get excited, enthusiastic, and blow ourselves out in a sprint. When this happens, our body needs time to recover, and enthusiasm begins to dampen and fade. If this is a repeat scenario, it's very hard to make any progress because you spend most of your time in recuperation. Body and mind both lose out in the equation. What you want to do is pace yourself, find a speed that is manageable at your level of fitness and slowly build up.

That said, setting yourself unachievable targets is not necessarily a bad thing. In my own experience, whenever I have been discouraged in my sporting endeavors, I usually think back to the things I used to be able to do in my youth and set myself the goal of trying to get back to that level. I never quite manage this, but I occasionally come close and somehow this has a way of keeping me on my toes, striving for some form of excellence. Several weeks into my shoulder rehabilitation, for example, I tried to do a pushup and was unable to do even one. I felt terrible. In my former routine, I had been doing thirty every morning. When you're not able to do something, it can often feel like you never will be able to again, but this is wrong. One step at a time is the only way to go. I kept at it with unwavering determination. Nine months later, I am now doing thirty again. It wasn't easy by any means, but I clawed my way back.

Which brings us to the other side of the coin: do not sell yourself short. You're probably much more capable than you think. In terms of fitness, we all have the capacity to adapt to an increased regime of exercise and physical activity. I've said it before and will say it again: this is what our bodies are made for.

Be realistic about where you are in the process. Keep your wits about you and don't get carried away if and when you begin to enjoy yourself. It's easy to overdo it when you're in the thick of it. Knock off early if you have pain. As soon as the pain is gone, and you are able again, then you can get back in the saddle and go for 100%, but it's not worth blowing it and suffering setbacks due to unnecessary injuries.

Set clear objectives and make them real

You can't run a race if there's no finishing line. Once you've managed to get your imagination going and begin to have a pretty good idea of what it is you want to do, decide upon your fitness objectives. Set yourself some challenges, and this will structure your efforts. It is very important that these objectives be clear and unequivocal.

Make them real. Get them out there. The problem with keeping everything in your head is that you can easily allow your goals to slide or shift according to your whim of the moment. As ideas, your objectives remain fluid and malleable, easy to blow off or to neglect. Giving life to them—for example by telling people around you or keeping a written record—will make them real and keep you accountable.

You might consider using so-called "wearables," which are powerful tools available in shops everywhere. You can slip these electronic devices around your waist, your arm, or your wrist, just like watches. You can also download a whole range of applications on your smartphone via app stores. It is easier than ever to use these wearables to set goals, track them, and even share them with a circle of friends to stay accountable and have fun while you're at it. As we will see, you can even use these to monitor your progress.

I would suggest that you classify your objectives along two lines. Firstly, in terms of the activities you want to be doing, things you want to achieve, places you want to go, etc. Secondly, in terms of the physical changes, transformations, or adaptations you want to bring about in your own body. Understand that both of these types of objectives are co-dependent. As you are choosing them, you will want to think of the relationship between them and how they influence each other. For example, in order to run a 10-kilometer race, you will have to build up your running ability, and therefore your endurance, or cardiovascular fitness, as well as all the muscles involved in the activity.

With regards to the first type of objective, just go with your gut, get inspired and be creative. From yoga to croquet, from sailing to snorkeling, skydiving, or scavenging for mushrooms— all activities on Earth are available to you here. All you need to do is give it a try. The second type of objective, which concerns your physical fitness itself, may be harder to benchmark. You will have to educate yourself about your own body and its physical needs. As a general rule, these objectives will include some combination of improving strength, lung capacity, endurance, flexibility, and balance, as well as trying to ensure a general level of overall health. Furthermore, remember that all your fitness objectives will be bolstered by a healthy diet and sufficient amounts of sleep.

When deciding upon your activities, be precise. Join in with other amateurs for a 10-kilometer run, a 30-kilometer bike race, or a 2-kilometer fresh water swim. That's great. But, for example, don't just "decide" that you want to "go to the gym more often," without really understanding what it is you're going there to do. Without some substance to it, this is not really a decision. Joining a gym might be a first step, and getting to the gym twice a week might be a second step, but ultimately it's what you do while you are there and the precise fitness objectives you set yourself which will make the difference. If fitness in a gym setting is what you set your sights on, then maybe your long-term objective is to build overall strength, which you will achieve through a detailed workout plan that you either create yourself or with the help of a fitness instructor. Whatever it is that you come up with as objectives, accept them and own them. Make your decisions count.

Make a plan you can stick to

So you've decided what you want to do. That's great. If you can't decide, then just choose the easiest thing available and give it a go. Don't let yourself get stuck in the preparation phase.

Now ask yourself how it is going to happen. What resources do you need? What changes do you need to make? How will it affect your life? When will you make time? Do you need to shift anything around? This step is essential because it's where you lay the groundwork for your game plan, your overall strategy. There are three things to put down on paper: what you want to achieve; how you're going to do it; and when you're going to do it.

Here is where you will benefit from a good balance between realism and ambition. No matter whether your objective is humble or wildly ambitious, you will want to fix short- and medium-term goals, as this will allow you to recognize and *feel* the progress you make along the way, but you will also need to fix long-term goals that keep you regular and help push you to do better. Whether you aim to run a marathon, or simply to walk at a steady pace for a full hour without stopping—that's absolutely fine. You are where you are, and you have to work your way up from there. Establish a framework, and stick with it. As you steadily increase the length, load, or intensity of your activity, you will also see a steady increase in performance.

Making time is essential. Remember, you want to exercise as often as possible, even every day if you can. Many people, myself included, find that first thing in the morning is the perfect time of day because it is the time at which you are most likely to have complete control over your schedule. If you still work in an office, for example, you may not be able to absent yourself whenever you want to, or things may come up such as unexpected visits, phone calls, and meetings. This has been my experience even during semi-retirement. For many of us, first thing in the morning is the ideal time for a daily workout, but you could also consider your lunch breaks or the late-afternoon hours after work. In addition,

I like to take advantage of holes in my schedule to get outside to do something or go somewhere, essentially creating free time for myself within the restrictions of my day-to-day routine.

Get yourself a to-do list, a calendar, and get started!

Commit to the process and make it happen

Now that you know what to do, you have to get moving. Don't overthink the doing part, just start. Yes, those first steps are hard. And yes, it's also hard to *keep* going, because every day you have to begin again.

Building up a regimen of regular physical activity is a daunting challenge—but commitment is key. There will never be a shortage of reasons to quit and you *will* be tempted. There are infinite distractions and more than enough obstacles to make you lose your nerve or your courage: people and things will lure you away; work will demand your time and attention; you will have to push yourself physically, struggle to make time, work through new sensations of pain and muscle soreness, take time off for recuperation, perhaps even to heal injuries, fight off feelings of impending failure or lack of confidence; and the list goes on. This is especially true the longer you have spent away from exercise. Nevertheless, I urge you to be determined—*do not give up!* Make it your job to show up when you say you will. There are always significant odds to overcome, but you will never regret the effort you put in. Own those goals you've chosen for yourself, hold yourself to your schedule, and stick with the plan. Getting fit is a process and you will only see results over time.

The *process* is the point. Results will come, and while some will be easily noticeable, others will not be felt immediately. In fact, many of the most important benefits you are reaping may never be felt at all, simply because they are happening on a metabolic level. This is one area where I think many people make a mistake: they get too hung up on results and do not have the patience to play the long game. Strike a balance between objectives you can achieve in the short term and long-term goals that will keep you committed and enthusiastic. You must allow yourself to build up strength and endurance at your own pace and rhythm. Only push yourself within reason, but do what you have to in order to keep getting out there one day at a time.

And because there is no getting rid of the difficulties, you have to embrace them in order to overcome them. This, I believe, is the trick. You learn to love the "hard" part. If you are too focused on the results, the difficulties and challenges will be too much to handle because it will feel like you are doing all of this for nothing. Nothing could be further from the truth. If you learn to love the process, you are on the path to success.

Monitor your progress

Keep track of your efforts. Be thorough, and be honest in your monitoring. This will enable you to look back and have a clear-eyed view of what you have undertaken. It will enable you to record the ins and outs, the ups and downs, and see your journey in its entirety.

Monitoring yourself serves at least two main purposes. First, the ability to recognize your progress and maintain proper perspective is important for your sense of self-esteem and achievement. Second, it enables you to adapt your workout according to your changing needs, which will progress and evolve over time as you become more active, and increasingly fit.

You may notice as you train that your level of ability seems to fluctuate up and down depending on other factors in your life, including diet, sleep, stress, and so on. If you are looking to complete a ten kilometer run for example, you may find that some days you are more capable than others. You ought to be able to learn a few things about how external factors influence your performance, how your body responds to different levels of exercise, and what seem to be the better activities for you.

I tend to subscribe to the school of thought that advocates pushing limits, but doing so in a gentle way. You should be able to train again the next day, and should not have to recuperate for a week before starting up again. If the latter is something that happens to you, then you could probably benefit from doing a little less. Or maybe you could be doing less, but more often? Try different configurations out to see what your body responds to.

You can use a pen and paper to keep track of your efforts and progress or, if you're so inclined, there are lots of electronic tools in the form of apps or devices that exist nowadays. Either the wearables or the apps on your phone can then be used to measure a whole array of variables, such as types of exercise, activity durations, distances covered, steps taken, heart rate, and blood pressure. The data from individual workouts can be analyzed or printed out as graphs to identify long-term trends. If the technological and scientific dimension to exercise interests and helps motivate you, then you may as well take advantage of these tools in your efforts to get active.

And don't forget that getting others involved is a great idea. You may want to recruit the support of family and friends or colleagues, you could ask for the input of a professional coach, and you may even make new friends who are looking to get into the same kind of activity as you are. Try joining a class, or joining a club! A support network and exercise community will greatly help to keep you focused and accountable. It also makes it more fun.

Enjoy who you are, where you're at, and what you're capable of

Give yourself credit for your achievements. Meeting your short- and mid-term goals will boost your confidence and motivation as you progress. Whatever gains you accumulate, however small and insignificant they may seem, are an important part of the process and serve to positively reinforce your mindset. Be kind and forgiving to yourself, too, as you honor your commitments. Remember that winning in this current scenario only means doing your best. If you meet your objective, even better, but that's just a bonus. Allow yourself to be a beginner, to be weak, as this will allow you to develop better strength and fitness, and to make real progress. We all start from where we're standing, and recognizing this is a crucial step for getting good at anything.

Learn to find pleasure and take pride in the process. If you commit to getting those muscles working on a regular basis, your body will quickly begin to move in ways you may have forgotten. Exercising can be a lot of fun. There is pleasure in the small things, such as the rediscovery of lost muscles and sensations. This too can be an adventure of sorts. Activities you never before considered will feel different to you because you will approach them differently. You will begin to notice that taking out the trash, watering the plants, or buying a loaf of bread also impact your metabolism and are a source of wellbeing. Bending down will become easier, and you'll understand once and for all what they mean when they say, "lift using your knees not your back." You'll understand the value of stretching more intimately because it's when you start actually using your muscles that those stretches really begin to feel good.

From the satisfaction of meeting your fitness objectives down to the excitement of feeling your body come alive again, there is much to discover and find pleasure in. At best it is like reuniting with a long-lost friend, and I guarantee you will be surprised to see how much you could be doing (again) in time. Whether you want to reconnect with an activity you are familiar with or discover something new, there are many ways to bring excitement into your exercise routine. The more connected you become to your own body, the more you will be able to enjoy the activities you undertake, the places you are able to visit, the events you are able to attend and participate in.

Whether it is the sense of achievement you get from meeting your own objectives or the pride of receiving recognition from your peers for your progress, you can turn exercise into a great source of validation. On a deeper, physical level, you will start to enjoy the way you feel both during and after a workout. Running is a good example of this. Runners often enjoy the feeling of freedom they get from not needing anything other than a pair of running shoes to work out. Many, myself included, enjoy the way it clears their head of all the noise. As a morning runner, I have always particularly enjoyed the feeling of being alone on the streets before the rest of the world wakes up. I also enjoy the freshness that lingers after I am done.

Repeat this process as many times as you need to

It's important to point out that any effort to include regular exercise requires trial and error. It's OK to take it from the top again. The whole process is repeatable *ad infinitum*, or at least *ad finem*. The goal is to find something you like to do and want to continue doing on a regular basis for the foreseeable future.

The good news is that even a failed workout session––if failed means you didn't enjoy it and would not repeat it––is a success in the sense that you got some exercise in while learning that it might not be for you. Don't be afraid to try new things. You don't need to hit the bull's eye the first time around, or ever. Ask yourself what you might enjoy doing and give it a go. See if it sticks. If you find that you misjudged, try again.

We all give up at one time or another. The temptation is always there, and sometimes we give in to it. But the situation we then find ourselves in is one of needing to give it another go. Even if we find ourselves back at square one, we need to try again, and again: two, three, four times over. If this is part of the process, that's OK.

Peer pressure, medical advice, a second wind of some sort, some sudden shift in conscience, concern for your future life, whatever it takes—give it your best shot and if you fail, that's not the end of the world, just try again. We all have an innate capacity to make life-changing decisions, but the road to making that shift lies within. No one can take that responsibility for us.

If it helps, think of it as a game. No one ever got good at anything without repeated experimentation and formative failure. This notion of trial and error is essential, because it is only by trying again and again and again that we can develop the skills and physical fitness required to achieve our goals.

Be patient with yourself

I must admit that patience is rather contrary to my nature. I am one of those inherently impatient people who need to be doing things at all times and get frustrated if things move too slowly. My temperament is geared towards action, and I usually refuse to sit back and wait. In this case, however, being patient means staying active, and accepting the obstacles that lie before us. Changing our habits to live a more healthy and active lifestyle is no easy task, and patience will be a formidable ally in avoiding mistakes that might set us back.

At times, the slowness of the process can lead to frustration. Our minds may stubbornly refuse to acknowledge the gradual nature of change. And yet, we need to look beyond immediate rewards. We tend to think in terms of results, but ultimately it's the journey that matters, not the destination. Wherever you start from or arrive, the beginning and end are always outweighed by the middle, which is where all the living happens. We need to learn how to take it in stages and understand the timescale we're working with. I, for one, plan on staying fit for life for the foreseeable future. And so, I'm doing what I can to prepare for the long game by focusing on today.

8
SITTING IS THE ENEMY

The human body is designed for mobility, not immobility. We are made for movement. Prolonged immobility leads to illness, and if we allow ourselves, for an instant, to simplify the problem of general lack of fitness and increasingly poor cardiovascular health in our modern society, there is perhaps no greater culprit than sedentariness. Yes, there are many factors, and rarely can any health problem can be reduced to a single cause or culprit. Yet, sitting is high up on the list of risk factors that we all can avoid or at least mitigate. That's right, sitting. And it's no exaggeration to say that it is slowly killing us. The situation is so bad that scientists and activists throughout the world have begun referring to this problem as *sitting disease*.

RECOGNIZING A MAJOR HEALTH HAZARD

Imagine a health hazard warning on every chair, couch, and car seat—it seems absurd, but it is no joking matter. It is a biological fact that we are not meant to remain in a seated position for the long hours so many of us put in on a daily basis. Whether at work, in leisure, or in transportation, we are spending more and more time immobile and slowly ruining our bodies in the process. Sooner or later, our philosophies concerning what constitutes *normal* behavior on a day-to-day basis will need to be adapted to account for and correct the devastating effects of our sedentary habits.

One of the single most important changes we can make to our routines if we wish to improve our general level of fitness and lower our chances of contracting non-communicable diseases (NCDs) is to stand up and start sitting less, a lot less. One analysis by the Mayo Clinic of thirteen different studies on the dangers of sitting observes that people who sit for eight hours or more a day without physical activity had risks of dying similar to those created by obesity and smoking. If you consider that people throughout the world, on average, are sitting more, not less, this is extremely worrying. The long and short of it is: avoid sitting whenever you can. Stand up right now, if you can. Even if it means putting this book down for a while, consider getting up to go for a walk. If nothing else, try pacing around the room for a few minutes. Adopt a critical eye towards the time you spend sitting down and chances are that this alone will significantly increase not only your activity levels, but your longevity.

The problem, of course, is not that we shouldn't sit down at all. As with many things, it's the dose that makes the poison. The truth about sitting and how bad it is for one's health is something which, frankly, I discovered while writing this book. I had no idea of the true extent of the damage it is causing. As a businessman, I have spent a considerable part of my time in an office, much of it sitting at a desk or a conference table. Looking back at my past behavior, however, I realize that not only have I always scrupulously maintained a fitness regimen that meant I had already worked out by the time I made it to the office, but I was also always conscious of my body's dislike of being stuck in a chair.

"MANAGEMENT BY WALKING AROUND"

It's a lucky by-product of my restlessness perhaps that I have never been able to stay put for too long at one time. While I was never aware of the extent to which sitting is nefarious for our health, I have always sought out reasons to keep moving. Throughout my career, I was able to use this as a way of optimizing whatever desk work I had to do. I always tried to get through my to-do list as quickly as I could, or at least to get as far as possible within a limited time frame to avoid spending too many hours sitting at my desk. Around the necessarily sedentary elements of my schedule, I built a series of activities that would somehow contribute to getting my body moving and blood pumping, even if I was still working while doing so. I did this instinctively, however, not out of conscious concern for my health. In fact, for a long time I was convinced that my restlessness was due to nervousness and wasn't good for me. I'm not sure I would have chalked it up to the need for exercise, but it was a natural go-to nonetheless.

I have always felt as though there is something isolating about being stuck behind a desk. Certainly from a managerial perspective, it has very serious downsides. The relationships you make and nurture throughout life are, put simply, essential to everything you do. Maintaining a good network of partners, clients, colleagues, and employees has been one of my most central and necessary pursuits, an essential investment of time and attention. Doing so involves meeting people face-to-face, and these meetings often involve a fair amount of movement. I have always been in the habit of walking through the ranks, so to speak, in order to get to know the people I work with. This is the best way to find out what is going on around you and to get to know people. Bob Waterman, a friend and former boss of mine from my days working as a consultant for McKinsey, popularized this idea of "management by walking around" in a chapter of his best-selling book, *In Search of Excellence*, published in 1982. It's an amusing expression that I have become fond of, and which perfectly describes what has been, and continues to be, my practice.

I picked up this habit early, and I can date it to an experience I had as part of McKinsey's first office in Japan, in the late 1960s. My team of consultants and I were on a study for Japan Airlines and were working in temporary premises within an office complex that belonged to the client. We had no assigned desks or personal phones, no conference table, no individual office spaces, but paradoxically this allowed us to function very efficiently as a team and brought about an innovation in the way we worked. We shared two phones between the four of us, built up an awareness of each other's work patterns, shuttled back and forth from the team room where we were all based to interview managers in this or that building, and all the while we discussed our research and findings standing up or walking through the corridors with an energy that was unmistakable.

When we ultimately rented space for our own offices in the Marunouchi area of Tokyo, bought furniture, set up a conference room, and so on, we realized that this organized, formal atmosphere was not the same as our six-month mission in the temporary space working for Japan Airlines. No one was used to sitting for hours in a conference room, a reluctance to interrupt the person speaking established itself, and everyone began feeling stuck. By popular demand, we therefore changed the layout, restored the model we had previously developed, and began to hold our discussions in the open. We brought back movement, walking, and dynamic desk-hopping into our office culture, and all this physical momentum quickly lifted our team spirit back up to where it had been during our first assignment. I smile thinking about this today since we had no idea how good this was for our health.

THE EFFECTS OF SEDENTARISM

More and more of the activities we fill our lives with in this day and age involve little to no physical activity at all. One study carried out by the European Commission among EU member states in 2017 found that, on average, 39% of workers spent most of their days sitting down, whereas only 12% had to perform heavy physical effort. The rest of the workers spent most of their time either standing or performing moderate physical effort. In certain countries such as the Netherlands, Germany, Luxembourg, the number of sedentary employees was found to be above 50%.

But this trend does not stop at the workplace. Whether it is at school, in the car, on a train, on the living room couch, or in front of one of the many screens that surround us, our occupations are increasingly sedentary. If we are going to tackle this problem, it will require ingenuity, and if it is not tackled we will begin to see the health implications at an increasingly young age in coming generations. In fact, that is already the case. Teenagers have some of the highest sitting times of all age groups. In a 2019 study of schoolchildren worldwide, for example, the WHO discovered that a staggering 80% of adolescents do not meet recommended exercise guidelines, and there are warning signs for younger children as well.

The scientific research that has been done on the effects of sitting disease and sedentariness (or sedentarism, as it is sometimes called) is a patchwork of case studies that all point to excessive sitting as a contributing factor to a multitude of health problems that are increasingly plaguing our society. Have you ever felt the stiffness that sets in when emerging from a long drive, a long stretch at your desk, or getting up from a comfy couch after a film? Then you intuitively know what researchers are trying to explain. Some of the results are startling, but frankly, they do not come as a surprise. Excessively sedentary behavior can lead to cardiovascular trouble and heart disease, diabetes, various types of cancer, depression and anxiety, weight gain, muscle loss, and problems with your joints, hips, and back.

When our body stays in a sitting position for too long, our metabolic rate slows down. At the same time, the awkwardness of the posture puts steady strain on certain muscles and organs. Sitting for prolonged periods can lead to some of the following effects: muscle atrophy, back problems, digestive trouble, poor cardiovascular health, increased risk of heart disease, reduced capacity to break down fats, weight gain, particularly around the waist, slowing of brain function due to reduced air intake and a generalized under-oxygenation, increased levels of fat accumulated in the liver, as well as a decreased ability to break down sugars, and the list goes on. Pretty scary, right?

Studies have shown that despite the preventative benefits of physical activity, even regular bouts of exercise may not be enough to compensate for excessively long hours of sedentariness. Even though the recommended amount of daily exercise, according to the WHO, is only 30 minutes, everything that you do for the rest of the day matters too. In other words, going to the gym on a regular basis does not fully offset the metabolic effects of excessive sitting. This is bad news, given that we spend, on average, more time sitting than sleeping. Let's repeat this point, to be clear: if your lifestyle is predominantly sedentary, going to the gym is not enough to counteract the potentially devastating effects of the time you spend sitting down. You need to be moving throughout the day as well.

Even though certain countries, such as Australia—which commissioned a detailed report on sedentary work, published in 2016—and the UK, have begun taking notice of this problem and have released recommended limits for daily sitting as well as advice on how to avoid sitting for long periods, the topic remains sensitive, which is not to say taboo, for many reasons. Some of these are socio-economic, such as the overwhelmingly sedentary nature of so many professions, while others are cultural, like the degree to which we have become accustomed to and dependent on sitting, its functions, its joys, and its comforts. Just think of the primary role that entertainment holds in our lives, or how many activities require physical passivity. Compounding these problems are the methodological difficulties involved in understanding exactly what effects sitting has on our health. Because of the many factors involved in attributing causality with any accuracy, evaluating the negative impacts of sitting is a tricky topic, one which many of the leading authorities often shy away from.

The biggest barrier to the kind of shift we have yet to see in our sitting habits is very likely the status quo. Changing the way we think about sitting will have far-reaching effects on most aspects of our lives and will require us to change our ways across the board. If we recognize sitting as a kind of disease, and begin to take action to reverse its effects, it will transform the world of work—and, before that, the world of school—and reshape how we see and approach our private, professional, and social lives.

It is difficult to infer causality between rates of disease or mortality and rates of sedentariness. There are a large number of contributing factors associated with the occurrence of disease, as well as some degree of mystery. This makes it very difficult, and perhaps even futile, to try to pinpoint a single factor. One study following over 17,000 Canadians for an average of twelve years found a strong association between sitting time and mortality rates. Those who reported sitting all the time were 54% more likely to die of either "all causes" or cardiovascular disease. In another relevant metric for our times, television-viewing time in a group of close to 9,000 Australians was examined as a predictor of mortality rates. It was found that those who watched four or more hours of TV a day experienced a 42% increase of risk of mortality, all causes included, and were 80% more likely to die of cardiovascular illness.

While the average person today is leading an increasingly sedentary life, it is of course impossible to put all the blame on the individual alone. Just like the broader issue of lifestyle, rates of sedentarism are in large part due to the evolution of our society. We must recognize that there are powerful forces at play which shape our behaviors and habits. Whether it is the irresistible appeal of a rich and sophisticated entertainment industry, or a professional world that, by and large, still measures productivity by desk time, what we do with our time and our bodies is never entirely under our control. There are also public policy dimensions to these issues, which we will return to later. But at the end of the day, it all begins and ends with us, as men and women, fathers and mothers, living our lives according to the choices we make. Despite the forces that shape our waking hours, we are alone in having to deal with the curve balls that the world throws at us, and this includes the health consequences of our lifestyle.

WHAT WE CAN DO

In an ideal world, we all ought to be able to recognize our body's need for movement and exercise and act upon it. Instead, however, the treatment we inflict upon our bodies is driving down our health at an alarming rate, while simultaneously causing healthcare costs to rise dramatically. A lot needs to be done to reverse these trends, both on an individual and an institutional level. Not everyone can afford to quit their job because it requires sitting for nine hours a day, but most people could get up, stretch, and walk around the office once every hour. Why not leave the building for a brisk 15 minute walk during your lunch break? Employers, too, could actively encourage staff to move around more and build more flexibility into the way we work. Even when the options are limited, it's important to remember that small changes can go a long way.

There is an undeniable element of individual responsibility in improving one's fitness, and this responsibility should extend around us to our professional and social circles, as well as to future generations. Young people are heavily influenced by the behavior of their elders, and I would argue that it falls upon us to set a better example than we are currently doing. The health of our children, our grandchildren, and their children is at stake.

If you must sit for extended periods daily, here are just a few ideas of the things you can do to reduce the harm:

- Get regular light exercise as often as possible throughout the day. I'm not talking about working out, just get up and move around however you can.
- Stand up regularly (once every half an hour, for example, or every time the phone rings) and walk around, if possible, to stretch your legs and get the blood flowing. Walk or pace while taking calls, for instance.
- Install a stationary bicycle or a treadmill in your office. It is even possible to purchase small, portable pedaling-machines, or to install a treadmill under your desk and walk at a slow pace as you work on the computer. These solutions have a financial cost, but they will get you moving and if you can afford it, then why not give it a try?
- Use a standing desk. Studies show that alternating between sitting and standing position has a beneficial effect on your health. Also, standing burns more calories, in case that's a factor for you.
- Turn sitting events into mobile ones, when possible. Discuss a project with a colleague while walking in the park, do more hiking and less lunching with friends, have coffee on the go, be creative in the ways you meet with people.

From standing desks to walking meetings and remote "work from anywhere" models, from increases in the use of bicycles for commuting to the rise in the number and diversity of gyms available, some shifts are already happening, and there are positive signs of movement. Still, it remains largely up to us, individually, to make a difference in our lives and the lives of those around us. We can do this by leading more active lifestyles and spending less time sitting down. If the tingling in your legs at the end of the day is a familiar sensation to you, if you can feel the metabolic slowdown associated with inactivity, and if you consider your health to be a priority, then you should probably think about making some changes.

The bottom line is that sitting is far from harmless, it has the same effects as a disease. This may be the single most important factor in long-term health. Given the epic proportions of our sedentarism, you should avoid it whenever and wherever possible. The less you do of it, the better. Remember that even if you are someone who works out regularly in isolated sessions, you may be at risk of losing the benefits of this exercise if most of the rest of your time is spent sitting. Short stints of exercise will not be enough to offset the accumulated damage of otherwise overwhelming sedentariness. Keep moving by any means necessary. Keep your body moving *every* day, don't stop, don't let up. Exercise in all its mundane and mildest forms should be the rule, not the exception. Our bodies need to be in motion, and we need to find ways of staying active throughout the day, every day, all year round—the rest of our lives depend on it.

9
WEIGHT MATTERS

Bring balance into your life and your weight will follow. You don't necessarily need to lose weight to live an active lifestyle, but living an active lifestyle will certainly help you manage your weight. For most people, weight is also something that ought to quickly come under control as you begin to implement lasting changes in the way you live. If you pay closer attention to *what* you eat, *how much* you eat, get enough sleep and exercise on a daily basis, and keep your stress levels under control, your weight should naturally balance itself out over time, and your body will begin to function more efficiently, leading to better overall health and wellbeing. The trick is in finding the right balance of all these elements.

CIRCUMSTANCES ARE EVERYTHING

In the early 1990s, I organized a trip to Morocco for my cycling group. I got the idea from Jean-Claude Killy, the French ski champion, who had cycled there himself and spoke very highly of the experience. The trip was an adventure in every sense of the word, since Morocco at that time was something of an eccentric destination to go riding. The roads were not so great and there was a lack of services readily available to accommodate a group like ours. Nevertheless, through a local travel agent I was able to hire a driver and a sag wagon for all the materials, spare tires, and luggage. There were ten of us on that trip and we aimed, as per our habit, to cover about 900 kilometers over the course of eight days, so some level of logistics was essential.

Despite the rather rustic nature of most of our accommodations on the trip and the dubious condition of some sections of the roads, it was a fantastic experience. We began in Casablanca, with its great souks and old medinas, rode down along the coast to the charming cities of Essaouira and Agadir, then turned inland and up into the craggy Atlas Mountains, where small Bedouin villages subsist on hardscrabble farming and goat herding. We climbed through a few passes at about 3,000 meters and from there we rode down into the lush plains around Ourzazate and Marrakech, where we spent a night at the famous La Mamounia, a hotel Winston Churchill was particularly fond of. Built within the walls of a vast garden gifted by the 18th century Moroccan Sultan Mohammed III to one of his sons, it is the most grandiose place I've ever stayed in my life. From Marrakech we circled back up to Casablanca, and ended our tour there.

Apart from the bit of luxury at La Mamounia, the main difficulty was finding appropriate food supplies for the road. Each day, there were few places to stop along the way and little by way of facilities for tourists. We ate sandwiches for our lunches and had local dishes for dinner in the evening. These were, for the most part, soupy tagine-like dishes served with rice. While they were delicious, they were also a significant departure from our normal diets and the effect, we agreed later, was that we probably all ate less than we normally would. After a stop in Agadir, most of us developed a terrible stomach ache, and two of us got sick enough that we had to take a day off and ride along behind the group in the truck. We slept through most of that day among the gear under the flapping canvas that covered the back of the vehicle, both of us fighting high fevers. Because we always did all we could not to give in and miss out, this was a rare occasion on these trips. But something in the food or drink had gotten to us.

With two of us down and the rest of the group suffering from an upset stomach to one degree or another, we loaded up on bottles of Coca-Cola, which were widely available, and I bartered for an old icebox from the hotel we were staying in, which we filled with ice and stored in the truck. In addition to containing huge amounts of sugar which was welcome to fuel our efforts, the Cokes also had the effect of settling our upset stomachs. Because we were doing so many kilometers and putting in such a sustained effort, we were in the habit of regularly weighing ourselves on an old scale I took along. This allowed us to take stock of any changes and to make sure we never ran out of energy for our journey.

What we began to notice after just about a week of cycling was very surprising. It became clear that every single one of us had begun to lose weight! The amounts varied, but it was roughly between three to seven kilos. Despite the tagines and the large amounts of Coca-Cola we were drinking, the effort required to cycle over 100 kilometers a day in the scorching North African sun was forcing our bodies to begin converting fat reserves into energy. This had never really happened to us before on one of these trips, and here it was happening to all of us at once. We chalked it up to the change in diet, the climate, and the upset stomachs.

While my Moroccan experience is unusual for the intensity of the effort, and does not speak to the usual circumstances of daily life, it has stuck with me as an educational example of how the body regulates its own weight depending on its energy needs. This example illustrates what happens when the body runs out of energy, and shows how quickly it adapts to the situations we put it in. If we extrapolate, this story highlights both the need to eat enough if you are engaged in intense activity, as well as the importance of not overeating if you're trying to lose weight because, as we will see below, the body has its ways of dealing with excess nutrients and their calories.

WHAT SHOULD WE EAT?

It's hard to be prescriptive about what one should and shouldn't eat, because ultimately this is a highly individual question. The answer changes from person to person, and depends on the circumstances. Discussions around what constitutes a healthy diet can be confusing and are often fraught with contradictory advice, fads, and falsehoods. This is due in part to the complexity of the problem, its highly individual manifestations, as well as a wide-ranging set of beliefs and cultural practices related to diet and lifestyle. On top of that, there is no shortage of zeal and marketing hubris from the food and weight-loss industries. For not only does everyone have an opinion, there is often a vested interest behind what they say. That can sometimes be hard to navigate. As a general rule of thumb, however, you should try as much as possible to *eat real food*. Again, what this means depends on many factors. As a general rule, however, make sure your diet is built predominantly around fresh ingredients that you can prepare yourself, and try to avoid processed foods. This basically boils down to the idea that if it doesn't look like food, don't eat it.

Speaking for myself, I have never worried too much about what I eat. My biggest meal is often my breakfast, and it is usually composed of homemade Bircher muesli, made from grains, nuts, dried and fresh fruit. Lunch is a regular meal taken at home, if possible. Dinner is usually light––soup, salad, and some bread and cheese––and taken early, preferably around 7:00 p.m. I don't have too many rules when it comes to food. I will eat and drink pretty much everything, but I do pay attention to the quality of ingredients, and I stay away as much as possible from industrial processed foods and refined sugars. In terms of what I avoid, however, that is about it. Above all, I am very disciplined with regards to quantity, and do not give in to excess. If at any given time I am doing a lot of sport, I will eat a little more than I would in a period where I am less active. While I am not selling a particular diet here, a Mediterranean diet is a good go-to baseline for most people: lots of fruits, vegetables, and grains, beans, nuts, eggs, fish, and some dairy. I eat less meat now than I used to, but I have no qualms bringing white or red meat to the table, and I will enjoy a glass or two of wine on a daily basis.

It's up to each of us as individuals to determine what combination of foods, in what quantity, at what time of day, is best for us. We all have different bodies, patterns of behavior, and activity levels, and we live in different environments with a broad range of effects on our physiology. And even when we do live an active lifestyle, our fitness objectives are often different. I tend to believe that everyone should do, eat, and live as they please and as suits their needs, with the caveat that any excess will create problems, and the observation that many people's notion of what constitutes a normal diet, both in terms of quantity and quality, is often wildly misguided.

"Know thyself" is a good rule of thumb. By watching for kilos lost or gained and comparing them with my activity levels, I have become pretty good at judging my needs in terms of both nourishment and exercise. Believe it or not, my weight has remained relatively stable at seventy kilograms since my twenties, give or take one or two kilos. I regularly step on the scale to monitor the situation, and I do this mostly because I can feel the way too many kilos or too few affect my performance and energy levels. This is a very personalized process which helps me optimize my fitness. If I find that I am too heavy, I may reduce the quantities I eat, but I certainly will not deprive myself of food. If on the other hand, I am too thin, and my activity levels are the same, I may eat a little more to compensate. The truth is, I have come to trust my own internal signals before I even weigh myself. I will generally feel it if I've put on weight or if I'm on the light side, and the reason for these changes is most often related to my eating or exercising habits at that time. My ability to judge these differences, however, is inherently linked to the fact that I remain active. The exercise I get is my barometer.

DIET MATTERS

Although I won't be the one to disentangle the complex web of half-truths that surrounds the issue of food and nutrition, in the interest of helping you make informed decisions I would like to go over a few basic and uncontroversial metabolic processes that will shed some light on what happens to the food we eat and how it affects our health.

Most of the foods we eat are made up of three types of macronutrients, of which we need relatively large amounts on a regular basis to remain healthy: carbohydrates, proteins, and dietary fats, or lipids. Vitamins, minerals, dietary fiber, and water are also often included since they are also essential, but we won't go into them here. The amounts of these macronutrients that we need varies, but each fulfills very specific and essential functions. After a meal, our digestion breaks down the food in stages so that it can be absorbed and metabolized. It is during the metabolization of these nutrients that energy is released for the proper functioning of the body.

The term metabolization refers to the myriad chemical reactions that break down and reconstitute molecules according to our physical need. These transformations are the basic way our body builds itself up, creating, maintaining, and fixing itself over time with elements ingested from our environment. Without going into too much detail, it is useful to know that carbohydrates are broken down into glucose––sugar, basically––the proteins into amino acids, and the fats mostly into fatty acids. These nutrient-molecules are then used to power everything from cell growth to the building and maintenance of tissue, enabling proper functioning of all our body's systems.

You should know that the body takes efficiency very seriously and it will tend to use whatever is most readily available, even if the efficient choice is not the healthy one. This is where your decisions concerning diet come in. Our bodies are only able to work with what we give them, and therefore it is important to figure out how to make decisions that will benefit our health. All the body can do is send signals as to what works and what doesn't. Some of these signals are confusing; for example, we are hardwired to love sugar because it is literally what fuels us, but that doesn't mean we should be guzzling soft drinks all day.

Oversimplifying a little, we can say that most of our body's energy requirements are met by the sugars that make it into our blood. The question of how much sugar enters our system—and in what form—is therefore at the center of many debates about diet. These sugars come in different forms from different sources, so their quality matters. Because carbohydrates are basically chains of sugars, they are metabolized quickly and usually become the body's main source of energy, whereas dietary fats and proteins have to undergo several chemical transformations before they can be used as fuel, making them slower sources of energy.

How fast the body can metabolize sugar from a nutrient determines what is called its glycemic index (GI). So while carbohydrates are usually the main source of sugars, not all carbs are created equal. Fast is not necessarily a good thing—it all depends on one's energy needs. A football player in the middle of a game will burn the sugar from a chocolate bar in no time because of the explosive nature of his or her physical effort. Someone sitting on a couch watching TV will not. Our energy needs depend on how much our body is working, and this is why exercise matters, a lot. We need sugars for energy, but the form in which we get them matters. Sugars from a chocolate bar will enter the blood much faster than, say, the sugars from a plate of pasta. The pasta will thus have a lower GI score than the chocolate bar. And the sugar obtained from lentils, oatmeal, or beans will be even slower to enter the blood than those obtained from the pasta, giving them an even lower GI score.

When it comes to sugars, our body's efficiency tends to work against us. If we flood our bodies with fuel that it has no immediate use for, it puts it into storage for a rainy day in the form of fat—a slower source of energy, as we have seen. In times of need, the body can access this fat and burn it. This useful trait evolved over millennia to enable our human ancestors to survive periods of drought, cold, poor harvest and hunger. But in a time of abundance and industrial food production, it has led straight to the epidemic of obesity plaguing much of the world today.

As a general rule, slow sugars are better for your health than fast sugars, because they deliver energy at a slower rate over a longer period of time. This is good for several reasons. First, it takes time for the body to evacuate the sugar and turn it into energy, and the metabolic processes required to do so are themselves a source of health. Second, it is the very speed of fast sugars, which creates spikes in blood sugar, that the body struggles to manage. High blood sugar, also known as hyperglycemia, can cause serious problems such as damage to the blood vessels, which in turn can lead to other complications. Chronic hyperglycemia also puts strain on the endocrine system by requiring increased production of insulin, the hormone responsible for transporting sugar to cells, where they are converted into energy. Over time, if the body is unable to evacuate these sugars, blood glucose will stay elevated. This can often lead to the onset of type 2 diabetes, a condition in which the body is either unable to produce insulin or develops a resistance to it. In short, our body is healthiest when it works hard for its fuel.

One of the main advantages of slow sugars is that energy is released more steadily into the bloodstream, thus continuing to provide our cells with a more stable source of energy over a longer period of time. In the average diet, we usually end up metabolizing a variety of sugars from a variety of sources. All three macronutrients can be converted into glucose, but they do not take the same pathway, and the body will privilege carbohydrates over dietary fat, and dietary fat over protein. Thus, while carbohydrates are often considered to be the main source of energy, dietary fats also can be metabolized to provide glucose for the cells. Natural dietary fat is a good source when you want a slow release of energy. Think of the trail mix prized by hikers, which contains a variety of grains, dried fruits, and nuts. The fruit gives fast sugar, the grains give slow sugar, and the nuts are a source of dietary fat which can also be converted into sugar if necessary, making it even slower still. It's fuel in three phases, so to speak, which is perfect for long walks that require a slow but steady source of energy.

One last thing on the subject of dietary fats. Contrary to popular belief, which has demonized fat somewhat unfairly, you should definitely include some in your diet, for it is also essential to a number of metabolic processes, including the metabolization of certain vitamins. The only fats you really want to avoid are industrially manufactured trans fats. These are often listed in the ingredients of processed food as "partially hydrogenated vegetable oil." They have been shown to have a devastating effect on health in the long term when consumed in large quantities.

HOW MUCH SHOULD WE EAT?

If this is framed as a question, then the answer should be: as much as necessary. Evolutionarily speaking, our bodies are designed to plan for harsh winters by storing away our dietary surplus as body fat so we can survive prolonged periods with very little food. Nowadays, this is backfiring and making us sick because we never give our bodies the chance to burn off that body fat.

When it comes to monitoring our diets, we often talk of calories. This is a term that refers to the energy value present in food, which we can then match up against our daily needs, estimated based on a number of factors related mostly to exercise levels. The term "calories" sometimes gives rise to confusion, however. There are no "calories" in food: it is merely a unit used to measure the energy the food generates. A calorie with a small c, or "small calorie," is a unit of measurement that corresponds to the amount of heat needed to raise the temperature of one gram of water by one degree Celsius. When spelled with a capital C, a Calorie, or "large calorie," refers to kilocalorie, the equivalent of 1,000 calories. Somewhat confusingly, it is this large calorie that we use to measure energy produced by the food we eat, even though it is spelled with a lowercase c. Be that as it may, when you measure caloric intake or hear talk about calories turned into fat, just remember that the "calories" themselves are neither in the food nor in the body fat itself. Calories are not a "thing," they are just a unit of measurement.

From alcohol to nutmeg to the sugar in your coffee, chances are that too much of anything will have a negative effect on your health. Almost anything can be poisonous at the right dose. So the quantities of food you eat really matter. This is perhaps the biggest issue for me. Your body only needs so much of the various nutrients you ingest. Food can be a tremendous source of pleasure, addictively so, but do not forget its primary purpose is nutritional. Learning to understand your caloric needs is a crucial skill, and each person's needs depend on several factors, prominent among which is the amount of exercise he or she is getting.

How much energy you are consuming on a daily basis has a huge impact on how you should be regulating the amount of food you eat. The difference in caloric intake requirements between athletes and the average sedentary adult is enormous. Not only does overeating increase your fat reserves, but it also makes it harder for your body to break down these reserves, simply because there are nutrients already present in your blood and readily available to be turned into energy. This principle applies whether you are exercising or not. Monitor your diet, listen to the signals your body is sending you, and you should be able to figure out how much food is right for you. To summarize what you need to remember, there are two things which will mobilize your fat reserves to meet your body's energy needs: exercise and hunger. I'm certainly not suggesting anyone starve themselves, but eating less won't hurt, and exercising more is what I'm really rooting for.

WEIGHT MANAGEMENT IS A BALANCING ACT

When you eat a meal, your body takes what it needs to meet its immediate nutritional and functional requirements, then it stores what it cannot metabolize as glycogen in the liver, the first go-to when energy is required and nothing is immediately available, and, once these relatively modest reserves are full, the body stores the leftover excess nutrients as body fat. This is the body's natural, healthy, and rather ingenious way of keeping a little for later, and there is nothing wrong with it as such. Body fat is stored in what is called adipose tissue, which does three things: it keeps you warm, forms natural padding, and stores energy for the long term. So far, this is all pretty straightforward and nothing is wrong with the picture. Remember, you want all these things. The problems begin to arise when food is regularly ingested in such large quantities that the body, getting more sugars than it needs to convert into energy, tries to store as much of this as it can for later. Our fat cells are the body's larder, or pantry, and they have enabled mankind's survival for thousands of years. Fast-forward to today's chronic overeating and overwhelmingly sedentary, inactive lifestyles, and you have the perfect recipe for weight gain.

Once fat reserves are established, they are broken down when the body needs the energy. And here is where exercise comes in. Fat reserves are made available during exercise as an energy source, but the rate at which they are broken down will depend on the carbohydrates and fats you've recently consumed. This is because, as we have just seen, the body seeks the path of least resistance, and will privilege recently ingested nutrients and glycogen stored in the liver before it begins to break down any fat cells from the body's adipose tissue. What this means is you need to balance how much you eat with how much energy you need. If you're within the norm, this probably means eating less and working out more, but that's for you to figure out. It falls upon each of us individually to find and achieve the right balance.

I won't recall the statistics available everywhere, except to say this: if you are overweight, you are at an increased risk for a plethora of undesirable health conditions that may tragically shorten your life and dramatically reduce its quality. The fact is that an alarmingly high number of people are overweight or obese today, and this trend is on the rise. There are many reasons and circumstances that lead to being overweight, some of them are within our control, others are not. I certainly have no intention of making anyone feel guilty. That said, bringing one's weight under control can have a lot of benefits.

Losing weight will help take the strain off your joints, reducing discomfort, pain, and the potential for further complications. It also makes moving around a lot easier and more enjoyable, and has a profound influence on how you feel. Energy levels, mood, stress, and libido can all be negatively affected by excess body fat. Perhaps most importantly, losing weight will ease the pressure on your metabolism by lowering your blood pressure and improving your cholesterol levels, thus greatly reducing your chances of developing a non-communicable disease.

For some time, the main focus of the medical community has been on body mass index (BMI), but this is shifting because it seems increasingly likely that the place you carry your fat matters more than the amount. According to some voices in the scientific community, the fat that accumulates around your midsection–– the so-called abdominal, visceral, or deep belly fat––is the most nefarious kind, whereas subcutaneous fat actually has redeeming qualities. How much abdominal fat you have may be the best way of predicting your risk level for developing a non-communicable disease such as type 2 diabetes. That is because this abdominal fat secretes hormones that have an inflammatory effect on the body, and additionally seem to be linked with a decrease in insulin sensitivity.

Calibrating how much we eat with how much we move should be the goal. These are not the only factors, but they are the main ones. I do not mean to say that exercise alone will make you lose weight; depending upon your physical condition and type of workout, a number of things may happen. As you begin to exercise, you may find that you actually put on some weight, due to the increase in muscle mass. Or, even as you witness a slimming down of your waistline, you may find that your weight stays the same. This may be due to the fact that muscle is denser than fat, which takes up more space. Another short-term reason for weight gain can be levels of water retention in your muscles. Overall, however, you should keep in mind that this is just a transitory phase, a single step towards a more balanced metabolism. Exercise is an essential element in any effort to bring your weight under control, because exercise is an essential element in being alive, period.

WHEN SHOULD WE EAT?

As I have said, I eat my bigger meal in the morning after my exercise routine, then I eat again at lunch and have a light dinner in the evening. I try not to eat too late, because I know that I don't sleep as well on a full stomach. I sometimes break this rule if I am out for dinner, but I like to be regular because that is what agrees with me best. Since I monitor my weight on a regular basis, if I ever find that I am gaining a kilo or two, I will generally skip a meal and reduce my caloric intake. This happens on a semi-regular basis.

Research shows that this kind of intermittent fasting—refraining from eating during relatively short periods of time of less than twenty-four hours—can have a positive effect upon our metabolism. What happens, in a nutshell, is that your body goes into fighting mode to prepare against the possibility of not getting any food, and cell functioning is improved. Skipping meals from time to time can thus have very positive effects on the body. I learned about the research on this topic during the writing of this book, but it happens to be a practice I have followed for years. It's a way for me to keep my weight under control, and has always felt like the right thing to do. Alongside my regular regime of exercise, and despite a rather liberal diet, skipping a few meals here and there seems to be enough for me to maintain a stable weight. Remember, however, that this is not a miracle cure and it does not replace the need for a balanced diet.

If you are fasting for more lengthy periods of time, something I neither condemn nor condone, exercise continues to play an important role because by using your muscles your body will privilege fat reserves as an energy source. Know that you should definitely continue to exercise, even during a fast, for if you are inactive your body is likely to metabolize its muscles for energy first, rather than its fat reserves, which can lead to an undesirable reduction of muscle mass rather than fat loss. If you do plan to fast for a period of more than twenty-four hours you should discuss it with a doctor or do so in a supervised setting.

I will close this chapter by pointing out that while eating provides us with pleasure and sustenance, it also has a powerful social function. People come together and around the table. Meals are a convivial way of building relationships and exchanging news, jokes, stories, advice, and other pleasantries. In terms of information gathering, intellectual stimulation, humor, and your ability to express yourself, it changes your life and brings to it an incredible and irreplaceable wealth. Meals are also a time for people to talk about favorite recipes, foods they love, and what they eat to stay healthy. I think these occasions are not to be missed, and should be built into your life, whatever your fitness or dietary program may be.

Just like building better fitness and strength, improving one's diet requires a long-term commitment. There is no simple formula. It is a process that involves sustainably reordering your life around new principles and wellness objectives, and it means changing your behaviors and habits. In short, same as all the other lifestyle changes discussed in this book, it is part of a bigger picture that requires putting your body at the heart of your decision-making process. Creating and adopting a new lifestyle is not easy, but it will bring positive metabolic changes that will make the effort worthwhile.

10
YOUR BODY IS YOUR GUIDE

Developing a deeper connection to one's body is a crucial skill that anyone can learn. Everyone's body has different needs and thresholds, and while one person's workout may be another's warmup, what we have in common is that we all need some form of exercise, and we need it regularly. We would be better able to grasp this biological imperative if we were more attuned to ourselves, if we knew how to listen closely. Our bodies send us signals all the time, when we do too much or when we do too little, but we are often too busy or too distracted to pay close attention. This "listening" allows us to develop a better feeling for what type of activities we *need,* how best to perform them, how much of an activity is enough, and when we start to reach our limits. In short, we improve our ability to recognize what feels good, sustainably and durably so, and what doesn't.

RELEARNING TO WALK

Despite our best efforts, things go wrong anyway. Over the years, I have had a number of accidents requiring rehabilitative care, including relearning how to walk on my left foot again at age seventy-two after my operation for spinal stenosis. One side effect from the operation was losing the nerve sensations on the bottom of my left foot, which is now numb to touch. This completely changes the way you walk. A large part of my rehabilitation, therefore, was adjusting my walking style to what it was before the operation. In fact, it went further than that because I had to adjust to what it *should* have been before I started compensating for a bad back. This was probably the hardest part of the rehabilitation process for me. I had to learn to walk with my eyes on a target ahead of me, trying to keep my shoulders, hips, and legs aligned with the direction I was walking in. This was harder than it sounds. I replicated this exercise wherever I went, a constant process of trial and error. It is surprising how much we take for granted the basic nerve sensations on our feet. Walking seems easy enough until you have to do it without feeling exactly where your foot is. In any case, with a little work and a conscious effort to systematically raise the height of my step at the level of my left heel, I was able to restore something close to a normal gait and a balanced walking pattern.

This training process took me about three months, at which point my physiotherapists were finally satisfied that I had mastered the technique. Every morning since then, I have walked towards a target in full view of a mirror, diligently checking to make sure my shoulders and hips are aligned and my foot is falling as it should. As long as I keep good balance, straighten my back and shoulders, and properly align my left and right sides, everything seems to work fine, and it now feels pretty much as normal as can be. I do not particularly feel at a disadvantage for lacking the sensation on the bottom of my foot, mostly because of the new exercise habits I have acquired, but also because the muscles and joints still give me a good sense of what I'm doing. This means I continue to be able to walk and run, and I am relatively good at adapting to terrain. Thanks to the quality of the rehabilitation, this significant injury which could have led to a complete loss of mobility only remains as a minor handicap, which I have taken in stride, if you'll excuse the pun.

The correlation between what feels good and what truly is good for us is not exact by any measure, of course, but practicing a better connection with our bodies and developing better listening skills will significantly improve our ability to make accurate judgements. Unfortunately, too many people are out of touch with the material reality of their bodies. We are exceptionally versatile creatures, designed to move around and ideally equipped to walk, run, jump, squat, swim, climb, and so on. Doing all of these things is resolutely good for us because it is what we evolved to do.

The fight we have before us today, if we want to bring back a healthy way of being in the world, is a tricky one, because we are fighting an imaginary version of ourselves, one that has slowly materialized through the centuries, and come to a head in our age of unprecedented comfort. We are fighting an idea of the human being where exercise is relegated to the margins, as an appendix, and physical activity becomes merely a hobby rather than an essential part of what it means to be alive, to eat, to struggle to survive. I am neither a luddite nor an opponent of progress, but we cannot abandon the physical prerogatives we have inherited from evolution. When we talk of living an active lifestyle, it is not a fad or a fashion statement. This is not just a question of aesthetics; it is your quality of life, and possibly your very survival that is at stake.

Just because we have access to highly developed and efficient healthcare networks does not mean we ought to relegate all concern for our wellbeing to the experts who assess our health during appointments which are short and focused by design. Doctors cannot possibly integrate all the information required to gain a holistic understanding of our physical state with a few tests or office visits. In the end, we are sole custodians of our bodies. There are many ways of achieving a better mind-body connection. I suggest some avenues in this chapter, and while some of these may help, you should try to develop your own.

REFUSING TO LISTEN

It's very easy to lapse into a state where you are deaf to the signals your body sends you. After my shoulder injury due to a bike accident in 2019, with all the tendons ripped from the bone, I was unable to properly exercise, and it wasn't long before I began to feel increasingly useless and impatient. This was before I made the decision to go ahead with the operation and so, to avoid going stir crazy, I talked Claire-Lise into organizing a "short" bike tour in the Piedmont, in Italy. She was skeptical, but I stubbornly pushed through with this foolhardy plan. I was unable to lift my arm past my shoulder, and the pain was tremendous, but I ignored it and off we went.

This trip lasted one whole week and I did manage to ride— more or less. This was not one of my most glorious moments. By keeping my arm perfectly straight, I was able to hold on to the handlebar with my left hand, and although it was awkward, and every time I hit a bump in the road it sent shards of pain through my shoulder and up and down my spine, I somehow powered through it. All through the trip, my body was screaming at me that something was terribly wrong, and I chose not to listen. I ignored the signs. At the end of each day, I was unable to lift my bicycle and, for the first time in my life, I had to ask a porter to carry it into storage.

Ultimately, we did have some fun on this trip, despite the pain I was in, but it could have gone very wrong. On this occasion, it wasn't only my body that was sending me signals. The owner of the hotel where we stayed thought I was nuts, and many of the passersby thought I was handicapped. Whenever the topic came up, my wife just threw up her hands and sighed, although she was relieved that nothing went as wrong as it could have. There was no question in my mind as we drove back home that this had been a bad idea. I resolved to accept the obstacle that had been thrown at me and, immediately upon our return, made arrangements for the surgery.

RELEARNING TO LISTEN

Building a keener awareness of the signals your body sends you can go a long way toward getting you into shape, despite the difficulty in remaining open to them and the changes or actions they require. You may even find this helps correct some of the health issues you are experiencing. Staying in tune with your body can help you choose the right exercises and avoid injury, adapt your diet, decide upon and follow your routine, and in this way help you take significant steps toward achieving your workout goals.

Everything that goes on within us is based on complex signaling mechanisms that regulate the body's own internal systems, allowing it to react to the environment and elements that we expose ourselves to. Whether we are talking about the secretion of hormones, the functioning of the immune system, or the process of coagulation, most of the "signaling" is happening internally, at a level which is invisible to the naked eye. This is partly because it does not require our intervention and happens automatically, as a part of the body's routine, so to say, as long as we are sufficiently and sustainably active. It is mostly when things start going wrong that we begin to experience the signals our body generates. These are what we usually call symptoms. They are the body's call to action.

I am looking to draw attention to the way this listening can help you manage your return to physical exercise and an active lifestyle, but it's important to understand that it applies to the entirety of your experience of life. This is not a spiritual matter, it is not a question of belief, it is the observation that your body is an inherent part of who you are. We often think of our body as separate from our self, maybe we think of it as the vector or vessel for everything we experience in life. While this is not wrong, per se, it obscures somewhat the fact that our body cannot be just the means by which we have access to experience, for this is too reductionist. The experience of life would not be available without the body. The very notion of experience is dependent upon physical sensations and their interpretation. Whether we are referring to eating, laughing, playing, feeling, or even thinking, these are all physically embodied experiences.

It follows that we should pay closer attention to the signals our body sends. Everything from the foods we eat to the spaces we occupy, the clothes we wear, the sounds and smells we take in, and the people we spend time with will elicit bodily responses. When we recoil in disgust at a disagreeable smell, sneeze due to the presence of foreign particles in the air, or suffer from excessive gas after a particular meal, our body is telling us something is wrong. Passing gas after a meal is not the end of the world, but if your regular diet makes you do it all the time, you might want to look into the matter.

It can be overwhelming to feel these changes—and the many sensations produced by the body on a daily basis—as they occur. It can also be difficult to know how to respond. Once you tune into this awareness, however, and begin to listen to the signals your body sends, you will become better at connecting the symptom to the cause. We will go into some examples below, but this can be applied to a number of situations. Monitor how you feel during and after a given meal, during or after an exercise session. Pay attention on an ongoing basis and note the changes that occur over time. It takes some time to develop a good sense of our bodies. No one is in a better position than you to vigilantly monitor your body. This is just another way of being proactive about your health.

LEARNING ABOUT YOUR BODY

In addition to listening more closely to the body's signals, I highly recommend that you take an interest in your anatomy and physiology, if only superficially. Do some studying to try to better understand your physical makeup. This will unlock insights and help you achieve a deeper and more accurate connection to everything going on inside of you. There is a wealth of information available everywhere around us—the internet, libraries, bookstores, podcasts, and audiobooks are all great resources. We are lucky to live at a time where science is able to provide us with incredibly detailed information on how our bodies work. It is a fascinating subject, and one marvels at the complexity of how it all fits together.

Specialists everywhere make it their job to understand and relay the state of our knowledge, and so any questions you have can likely be answered, or at the very least partially illuminated, with the right questions, a few clicks, and a little research. Even if this only has the effect of firing up your imagination and building your understanding of what is happening under the hood, as it were, it will truly help you visualize the types of symptoms you may be feeling, and it may help you find the most appropriate treatment and prevention techniques.

The human imagination has a tendency to lump things together, a necessary skill so as to not get lost in details. But behind our need to simplify and make reductive generalizations for the sake of coherence, the complex and intricate details of reality remain. If you have never looked closely at a drawing of the human musculoskeletal system, for example, then I urge you to go online and type in anything from hip flexor to scapula (hip muscle or shoulder muscle) to see how complex these systems really are: dozens of muscles working together to ensure the most basic human movement such as walking, squatting, reaching out and picking up an object, and so on.

SOME THINGS TO LISTEN FOR

The idea is to make better use of the science and tools available today in order to live more holistically in a way that is more connected to the body. Listening to your symptoms and putting them in the context of your behavior and actions will go a long ways toward establishing causal relationships that can expose things you may be doing wrong, things you may be lacking, or things you may be getting too much of. Here are some very broad examples of some of the areas where you can bring your attention to bear to get in touch with your body's internal workings.

Your digestion. What you eat, how, when, with whom, how fast, and in what quantities—all these factors will influence the way your diet and eating habits impact your body. Everything from your weight to your mood, from your energy levels to the quality of your sleep are impacted. The relationship between what you eat and how you feel is crucial. Take the time to focus on any symptoms you may feel in relation to your digestion, whether it is a pleasant sensation or a negative one, such as feeling bloated, experiencing heartburn or acid reflux, or passing excessive gas. There is always the possibility that you have developed a medical condition, but you also may be making poor dietary choices. Changing your diet to eat more real food, cooked from scratch, and fewer processed food products is a good rule of thumb.

Your heart. When you work out, your heart starts beating faster than normal. This is good if you do it in a controlled fashion on a regular basis. You will see improvements in your cardiorespiratory capacity, including a lower resting heart rate, better heart pumping capacity, and an increase in comfort during physical effort overall. Be on the lookout, however, for any signs such as chest pains, pressure, unexplainable fatigue or shortness of breath, or erratic pulse—these could be signs that you are experiencing heart trouble. Don't hesitate to seek medical help.

Your skin. Your skin is the first and foremost barrier between you and the world. It keeps you in, and most of everything else out. But more than just a physical barrier, the skin is your body's largest organ and it contains a whole world of activity. From the substances, materials, and organisms that you come into contact with, your body's reaction and relation to your immediate environment emits a number of signals that help you manage your health. Unsurprisingly, itching, swelling, redness, and dryness call attention to something going on inside your body that requires your attention.

Your memory. It is normal for us to have a selective memory, and we all get somewhat forgetful in one way or another throughout our lives. But while memory loss can be a symptom of dementia or a progressive condition largely out of your control such as Alzheimer's disease, it may also be directly related to your lifestyle, and there are things you can do to improve your chances of staying sharp. Staying interested and curious, engaging in life-long learning, staying involved in the world, in one's social life, and keeping on top of a diversity of activities and interests are all important. I don't know that there is a perfect recipe, but I do know that it all adds up.

Your mood. While none of our body's systems function in a vacuum, the interrelated nature of all our sensations are particularly evident when it comes to mental health, precisely because it is at once so intangible and undeniably influential at all times. Look out for any changes in the way you feel about yourself and your life. Be conscious of any negative thoughts, sadness, or persistent sleep loss, lack of energy, or general listlessness. Small changes to your lifestyle can have big impacts on the way you feel. Exercise is only one of many factors having an influence here: your diet, sleep, general activity levels, stress and anxiety, social life, emotional state—all of these will have an effect on your mood and mental health. No need to suffer through your troubles alone, there are people you can talk to and concrete steps you can take.

Your muscles. How our muscles feel prior to, during, and after exercise, is a very valuable source of information as you learn to find the right exercise patterns. Tightness, numbness, fatigue, various types of pain and soreness, all of these are messages that your body sends you to report on the physical activities you engage in. These may be especially noticeable when you are working out and exercising again after a period of inactivity. Some degree of discomfort here is unavoidable, but with time you should become more adept at distinguishing the nature of these sensations. Start jogging again, for example, and you may feel pain in your knees, calf muscles, thigh muscles, shins, and buttocks. Do not overdo it in the early stages, and respect the way you feel. After the initial complaint due to long-term inactivity, however, these muscles should gradually start to buzz and hum with the energy you move through them. As you bring physical activity back into your life, your muscles begin to regenerate, to grow in size and capacity, and to assert their presence and inherent function in your body again. Depending on where you are coming from, regarding activity levels, this can involve very serious changes in the way you feel—for the better.

Pain. From the throbbing under your big toe that allows you to find a splinter, to the headache that reminds you to stay hydrated or signals that it's time to get out of the sun, our body is very adept at sending messages through pain. These signals can mean any number of things, but over time we learn inherently how to manage our responses to them. As we will see below, when we think of exercise, it is possible to make a clear distinction between "good" and "bad" pain. In addition, it will also be useful to think of one more distinction: the difference between *acute* and *chronic* pain. If you prick your finger or burn your hand, you know it immediately and are able to react. These examples are cases of *acute* pain. Instances of *chronic* pain stretch out over time, but just like the sharp feeling of pain when you prick your finger, there are also specific causes behind the slow burn of chronic pain that may require our attention.

LISTENING IS THE BEST WAY
TO MONITOR FITNESS

It is important to underscore that, when it comes to getting physical, there is no reason to experience excruciating pain. The first thing you need to distinguish before, during, and after exercise is the "good" pain from the "bad" pain. While it can be hard to put precisely into words, there is a concrete difference in the way it feels. It's one of those cases where you need to trust your instinct, an *I know it when I feel it* kind of situation. If you are truly in pain, which is to say pain that is not soreness or stiffness due to proper exercise, then you probably have done something wrong and should change your activity, or your way of doing it. It's important to push yourself, for this is the only way you will progress and make headway on your fitness objectives; however, you should always do this responsibly, paying very close attention not to overdo it.

Slow, steady, consistent and, yes, pushing—but *not destroying*—your limits, this is the way to go. If you are careful in the way you exercise, there is no reason for you to experience soreness or even "good" pain. In fact, you want to shoot for consistency and duration when working out, and should always physically feel like you are able to start again the next day. If you wake up the next morning completely exhausted, cramped, unable to walk or use whatever muscles you were training, then you are overdoing it. If you need three or four days to recuperate after physical activity, then you are overdoing it. You want to be mobile and fit for your everyday, so don't run yourself into the ground every time you exercise. Make sure that you do enough physical activity to get the benefits, but not so much as to injure yourself or wear out your body.

The relatively harmless aches and pains that come with an increase in physical activity are a small price to pay for the benefits you will achieve in the medium and long term. The kinds of chronic problems that we find ourselves suffering from when we abandon exercise and relegate our body to the ravages of time, entropy, and disuse are far worse than the discomfort you may sometimes experience during or after a workout. Without going again into the issue of non-communicable diseases such as diabetes or cardio-vascular conditions, a deteriorating physique is likely to bring with it a whole range of muscular problems. You become more likely to develop generalized weakness, sarcopenia, and chronic back pain, among other conditions, and you become increasingly vulnerable to falls. In the same way that a bed-ridden patient gets bed sores, our bodies begin to fall apart when they are consistently asked to underperform.

If you do have chronic pain, however, this is something you need to address. An inactive lifestyle is the perfect breeding ground for such problems, but they can be remedied with the right regime of corrective exercise. By underperforming certain movements in your daily life, you are depriving your muscles of the chance to build themselves up, and therefore you develop weaknesses, some of which you may not notice. Over time, you run the risk of developing pains related to these weaknesses which, as you shift your weight and overcompensate, lead to further pains that can easily spread throughout your body.

Pain associated with a deteriorating physique often leads to an amalgamation of many problems, and this can sometimes make it hard to identify the source of the problem. The pain, in other words, rarely has a single cause and often involves a variety of different ailments that all flare up at once, or in turn. It is often very easy to mistake the symptoms for the cause, and strangely enough, this seems to be something that doctors sometimes do too, for lack of time or attention perhaps, or simply because the patient is not able to effectively communicate the nature of the pain. Be this as it may, recourse to drugs to address the symptoms are very common in instances where the underlying cause would be better addressed through curative and preventative exercise, osteopathy, or physical therapy.

Chronic back pain is a prominent example of this. A huge proportion of people suffer from back pain, which is overwhelmingly linked to occupational habits such as excessive sitting. Some figures suggest as many as 80% of older people suffer from what is colloquially known as "a bad back." Although a sedentary lifestyle will create the conditions for the pain, it can also be triggered by a specific injury, the threshold for which, as fitness declines, gets lower and lower. Chronic back pain is thus very likely to be linked to lifestyle and often involves one or more local muscular injuries. It is also very likely to manifest as a result of muscular imbalance.

Muscular imbalance caused by excessive sitting—and the resulting changes in musculature—can be relatively easily addressed through targeted exercises. As such, you may have a good chance of limiting your back pain by simply strengthening your abs (stomach muscles), gluteals (buttocks), and spinal erector muscles (lower back), as well as simply stretching out and relaxing your quads (thigh muscles). While our quads tend to be among the muscles we continue to activate frequently––to stand and to walk, for example––our abdominals, gluteals, and spinal erectors, on the other hand, tend to fall into disuse.

To counteract this, you can adopt a training program that includes exercises designed to address this muscular imbalance. If followed properly over a period of time, this will likely alleviate some of the pain you feel and allow you to begin disentangling or isolating any other pains that might be involved. Additionally, a good strategy to prevent back pain is to find and engage in some form of core training, such as Pilates or yoga, in order to strengthen all the muscles around your trunk, including your spine, your pelvis, your hips, and your torso.

Whether you are recovering from an accident, emerging from a long period of inactivity, or simply struggling to be regular in the way you exercise, you will benefit from cultivating a sense of awareness of your own body. Once you learn to focus your attention on the way your body moves, you begin to notice things like your strengths and weaknesses, and this allows you to adapt your efforts and activities to be more effective. A concrete example of this would be learning to feel with some certainty when you need to take a break, or, inversely, when you can push yourself more.

The sensations you begin to connect with will no doubt surprise you. When we are inactive, these sensations fall out of the realm of those accessible to us. Whether it is touching your toes, being able to lift your own body weight with your arms, or walking up a flight of steps without losing your breath, you will begin to feel muscles you had forgotten you had, or thought would never return, and you will begin to take enjoyment from being able to perform even simple movements that had once been difficult. A simple pleasure, for sure, but essential to the kind of awareness we are aiming for here. Your muscles extend to their maximum reach as you go for that jar on the top shelf, or you feel your legs and core contract and stretch as you squat to pull out the pan from under the counter. This may sound strange to some readers, but trust me when I say there is true joy in simply being able to perform basic movements with more ease, confidence, and strength. This is especially true as we get older.

It is a fact of life that despite our best efforts, accidents occur, and our bodies do change. Things happen that raise roadblocks and make it harder for us to meet our fitness goals. We get tired and suffer from stress, we overdo it and pull a muscle, or we let ourselves slip into unhealthy habits, even as we are making progress and living more actively. The best you can do is take preventative action, try to maintain yourself in as good a condition as possible. Learning to listen to your body is a great first step.

You must listen for, recognize, and accept these changes as they occur. Opt for a brisk walk if your ankle hit the ground a bit funny last time you went jogging. Leave that shoulder alone for a couple days after that uncomfortable pinch you felt. Whether we are talking about your body and fitness, or life in general, it pays to be receptive and ready to adapt to new circumstances, whatever these may be. If and when an injury or setback keeps you down, there are ways of steadily working your way back into action, one day at a time. It is a fact that we can get our energy and physical prowess back to a large degree, even at an old age.

Much of what I want to convey in this book boils down to the notion that you are your body, that your body is adaptable and capable of more than you might expect, and that it is possible to get fit if you put both your mind and back into it. But in addition to this, I want you to come away believing that you are better equipped to manage your own health than you think. Pay attention to your body's natural intelligence, listen to your body's signals, and treat it with the care and respect it deserves; use it as your barometer and guide as you embark on your journey to increase your levels of exercise, develop your physical abilities, and lead an overall active lifestyle. Stay with it. Stay steady. Stay strong-willed. Be ready to adapt. And be ready to try new things in order to integrate the wisdom your body is trying to communicate to you.

11

ROUTINE IS YOUR FRIEND

A successful routine is the solution to a problem you never knew was there in the first place. In order to bring physical activity back to the center of our lives, we need to reconsider our day-to-day activities and plan to make exercise a regular fixture. There are no shortcuts. You cannot get healthy, or fit, on a weekend-only basis. And while you don't need to turn yourself into a high-level athlete to see results, the necessary lifestyle changes are full time. Learn to wield the powers of routine, and it will become a formidable ally.

IT'S JUST AS EASY, AND JUST AS HARD, AS A MORNING RUN

Throughout my life I have often been involved in business abroad, requiring that I travel both frequently and extensively. One of the downsides of this constant traveling for business was that it upset my usual workout schedule. I accepted this, reluctantly, trying to find what opportunities I could to exercise while I was away. But these business trips were always packed with meetings, lunches, dinners, commutes, time changes, and hotel stays, which left little time for anything else. Tight schedules in foreign environments where one cannot eat, sleep, and exercise as usual easily lead to exhaustion and can be a real health hazard.

After struggling with this problem for a few years, I stumbled on a solution that would truly anchor my reliance upon routine as a recipe not only for getting my regular workout in, but to ensure success in my professional life. The breakthrough came early one morning while I was on a business trip in Frankfurt. This was in the days before the internet and I was getting increasingly frustrated while studying a map of the city to try to figure out what the best neighborhood for dinner would be. I couldn't make heads or tails of the thing and realized I had no idea how to get oriented or how to make a good decision about the location for meeting with my clients. Being inclined toward decisive action, it struck me that all this time I was wasting trying to organize myself would be much better spent scouting out the terrain in person. I decided then and there to put on my running shoes and set off to discover the city on foot. I committed to this regimen with dedication and, each morning that week, woke up at 6:00 a.m. to run through the city for an hour. I brought the map with me, explored different neighborhoods, and marked the interesting spots I found along the way. I located not only the restaurants, but the cathedrals and museums too. It worked like a charm.

I went running regularly at home, but until that trip I hadn't thought to take this habit with me abroad. From then on, I kept up this ritual during all subsequent business trips and it became a fixture of my travel routine. In this manner I discovered a number of cities, the most prominent of which was London, which I visited very frequently. I ran through St. James Park, Kensington Gardens, down Oxford Street, across Waterloo Bridge, and up and down the Thames on both sides, slowly inching my way through the capital's streets in the early morning, often in the dark, equipped with a headlamp and reflector jacket, before my workday began. In this same manner, I also ran along the Seine, in Paris, and explored not only Milan, Turin, Barcelona and Madrid, but also Tokyo, Osaka, Singapore, Taipei, Manila, and Hong Kong, to name just a few. I even ran a few times in Saudi Arabia, where one morning I was chased by a pack of wild dogs and had to scramble up a wall for refuge until a man, woken by the commotion, chased them off with gunshots. By the time I walked into a meeting room on those days, I was wide awake, my body was primed, my mind sharp, and my confidence boosted by my morning adventure.

ROUTINE IS A TOOL TO MAKE THINGS HAPPEN

Establishing routines is a way of selecting what you want to prioritize in your life. It is the best way to schedule your exercise, but it can also be applied to most of the things you fill your day with. If you want or have to do something every day, you should consider building it into a structured routine and sticking to this schedule. Following a routine will help simplify your life, because you don't have to think long and hard about the how, what, why, and where of every little action or activity you fill your time with. The consistency and the persistence required to make happen the thing you want to do will build a solid foundation of habit, enabling a smooth process, as well as unlocking progress and results over time.

Whatever you dream of or strive for, it will only come about as a result of your habits and daily routines. We've been talking mostly about fitness, but the same applies for the arts, music, and any form of business. Practice makes perfect, and you have to put in the groundwork to build up your level of performance and hone your craft, whatever it may be. Same as with the athlete, when we witness a craftsman, an actor, or a musician, for example, what we see is the performance, the relatively short lapse of time during which everything is set into motion and the magic happens: we hold our breath for the duration of a sprint, are fascinated by the deft and practiced movements of a potter's hands, we are drawn into the plot of a good film, and we forget ourselves in the harmonies of a symphony. But what makes these performances possible is hours and years of regular, daily training, preparation and practice, the mental and physical conditioning around which lives and livelihoods are built.

Once you begin to examine your activities and responsibilities, it becomes a question of setting priorities. This process of introspection, of organizing everything that you need, want, and have to do by order of importance will help you efficiently schedule your time. The function of a routine, one that really works, is to allow you to do everything you need to do within the limited amount of time you have each day or each week. Routine helps you to organize your life in order to maximize your own wellbeing and efficiency. It maps the path that you will follow to achieve your goals, and sets the true north by which you will take your bearings each day.

To get enough physical activity on a regular basis, you have to insist that it consistently get done on the days and times that have been selected—*no matter what*. This holds, even in the event of disruptions, problems, and setbacks. A dodgy knee, a long phone call, a late night, a big work deadline—the reasons to put off exercise are many and frequent.

Work is often the biggest obstacle on the list for most people. For those who are still working, professional obligations take up a lot of time. In my life as a businessman, I have learned that everything from managing a company's operations to the negotiation of new contracts is a very time-consuming process that can represent an infinite drain of one's resources if you do not put limits on it. Household chores place demands on our time, from doing our taxes, to food shopping, housework and caring for children or older relatives. Equally important is family and social life, reading books, keeping abreast of the news, lunch meetings, haircuts, dental appointments—the list goes on and on.

The latter examples are usually the easiest to plan because they rely on someone else's schedule. We stick to these appointments because we need the service and because we respect the other party's time. Why not extend ourselves the same courtesy, I would ask? The strange thing to realize is that we rarely think of the mundane things that actually fill our days, and therefore we tend not to plan as rigorously as we could. If we were as respectful with our own time as we are with that of others, how much more efficient we could be!

Think of it, if you will, as making appointments with yourself, and religiously honoring those engagements. When we are not careful with our time, daily activities and chores tend to be precisely the kind of obligations that take up the most space. This may be because we take these activities for granted or because we try to avoid doing them all at once, which can be overwhelming and cause us to shy away. But ignoring the reality of all the things we have to do will never make them go away. Bringing the discipline of rigorous routine into your life is a great way to address tasks that need to be completed in order to make room for more important priorities.

WHAT A ROUTINE CAN DO FOR YOU

Whether they apply to your physical activities, daily chores, business endeavors, hobbies, or civic responsibilities, the routines that you cultivate are an essential part of making you who you are. Routine comes with very significant benefits. It is an incredibly powerful tool that can help improve not only your fitness, but your health, your wellbeing, your productivity, your social life, and more. We can boil it down to the following principles:

Better focus and productivity

A routine eliminates the constant recurrence of choice and the need to make decisions, which is a huge drain on your mental and physical resources. Setting a routine, enables you to make decisions in advance, and then stick to the plan. This paves the way for greater energy and an enhanced capability for focus. Unless we are disciplined, our brain expends significant amounts of energy on dealing with choices that are often insignificant or purely logistical, but nevertheless end up clogging the works. I call this brain fog. When you follow a pre-established routine, you spend far less time and energy making these small decisions: you just get on with doing what needs to get done. All the brain power that would otherwise go to waste is put to better use. You will find you are fresher, more alert, and more intellectually agile when you get down to the tasks you have set for yourself.

More free time

It's somewhat paradoxical, but by prioritizing your activities and obligations, carving out the time to do them, and sticking to a schedule, not only will you maximize the potential value you can get out of every day, you will also greatly increase your free time. The constraints you place on your routine activities will eliminate or at least greatly reduce procrastination and wasted time. This holds true whether it is going for your daily run, paying your taxes, or spending time with your kids or grandkids. A routine does not have to mean squeezing every minute out of every twenty-four hours, but it does mean getting those things you have to do out of the way, and thus bringing value to the time that is suddenly freed up.

Enhanced wellbeing and peace of mind

When you adopt and stick to a routine, the predictability of your activities brings with it significant wellbeing and peace of mind. We are creatures of habit, and both our body and mind are positively impacted when we regularize what we do and complete the tasks we set ourselves. Whether they are things you enjoy doing, or things you simply have to get done, you will derive a sense of achievement and pride from your routine. From the clearing away of anxiety that comes with a simplified schedule to the comforting feeling of performing tasks in a repetitive and automatic fashion, from the satisfaction of expediting troubling paperwork as soon as it lands on your desk to the digestive calm that sets in when you eat your meals at the same time every day, there are examples across the board that point to the deep effects of routine upon our quality of life.

THE DEVIL IS IN THE DETAILS

The idea of a routine sounds pretty simple, right? It is, and that's the beauty of it. The challenge, however, lies in the nitty gritty details of implementation. I keep a calendar and access it through my phone, but mainly as a reminder, because, having kept at it for over half a century now, the main elements of my routine are pretty much ingrained in my DNA. Nevertheless, my routines are split into daily and weekly tasks which I know I have to complete. At the beginning of the week, I fill in the details of my office hours, appointments, meetings, and tasks for the week, and depending on where I am with my morning workout, I pencil in times for up to three aerobic and three strength training sessions on top of that. I put these in where there are holes in my schedule, and will do them as long as my health permits.

You need to constantly adapt to the situations that the world throws at you. This can be problematic. Here are a few tips for implementing a routine, and getting your system to work smoothly:

Put out fires when you have to. No routine is bulletproof or impervious to unforeseen events. If something has to go, that's OK. We have to be ready to deal with the unexpected, but when doing so, we also need to be aware of how it stacks up in our order of priorities. If an urgent matter arises, I will give it priority and delay or cancel less important tasks. Typically, with regards to physical activity, very little stops me from getting my daily morning workout, but on the other hand I may more readily shift around my aerobic or weight training sessions. If and when necessary, I will also cancel non-essential meetings to deal with emergencies.

Can someone else take care of it? This may seem obvious, and ought not to be an excuse for laziness, but you should realize you may not always be the best person for every single task. Your time and attention are valuable, and if you have to spend too much of them doing things which could be better done by someone else, it's probably worth considering stepping aside and finding another person to take care of the matter. Throughout my career, I have surrounded myself with people who were good at their jobs and allowed me to be better at mine. Understanding this is a very powerful productivity tool. One's private life is a little different, but some form of task distribution can make everyone happy and allow everyone to contribute according to their skills and interests.

Temporary solutions are better than no solutions. When you are dealing with a difficult or evolving problem which you can't resolve immediately, I recommend finding a temporary solution so that you can move on to other things. It's important to know how not to become overwhelmed by recurrent problems that would eat up all your time if given free rein. A temporary fix will allow you to put the issue on the back burner until a permanent solution can be found.

Start with the least attractive tasks. When it comes to routine tasks, you want to be as efficient as possible. Don't let things like paperwork, correspondence, and email gobble up your day. These are important tasks, but they can be a time sink. On my work desk, I have "in" and "out" boxes. I separate my inbox into two piles, one with what I want to do, and the other with what I don't want to do. I then give myself a limited amount of time and simply work through both piles, but *always* starting with the "don't want to do" pile. Getting the difficult stuff out of the way first is a great way to keep productivity up, it accelerates the process and ensures that everything gets done.

Do one thing at a time. Focus is a finite resource. Don't squander it by spreading yourself too thin. Sometimes, multitasking is a good idea, but only *sometimes*. As a general rule, you should focus on one thing at a time and allow yourself to deal with the problems on your to-do list one by one in a concentrated manner. This keeps you on track, doesn't split your attention, and pays off in the end. We're only human after all.

Finish what you start. This one follows from doing one thing at a time, and it is harder than it seems. It means making decisions and accepting the consequences. It means putting in the effort when you say you will, sticking to your word, and keeping the promises you make to yourself and to others. It means being brave enough to be imperfect, but sealing the deal. It also means you will make mistakes, but that's OK. Most importantly, it means moving forward and moving on.

Create rituals for yourself. In a way, many of the tasks and activities you choose to include in your routine will become somewhat sacred, in the sense that they will become fixtures that anchor your days and bring a sense of rhythm to your life. I don't mean this in a spiritual way, but ritualizing even the simplest actions in your life can have an impact on your wellbeing. It can be the smallest of things, such as putting your shoes away in the same spot as soon as you get home or a cup of coffee with the morning paper. Some of my main rituals, apart from my morning workout, which I've already discussed, include starting work at the same time every morning, trying to arrive home at the same time every evening, and keeping regular mealtimes. Another important ritual for me is my daily walk, usually taken just before or after lunch. And while it's great to get my blood flowing and give my legs a stretch, I also take advantage of this time for any phone calls I need to make, or to go over my mental to-do list to get a head start on the afternoon's problem-solving.

Learn how to say *no*. Whether it is to people, activities, or temptations, it is hard to understate the importance of knowing how to put your foot down and simply say *no*. Spending time with others is fun and generosity is an admirable and valuable trait. To be able to help others without feeling overwhelmed, however, we need to take care of ourselves first. Saying no to other people's demands on your time will empower you to gain better control over your schedule. Be firm in your refusal and don't feel like you have to find excuses. Be polite and courteous, but stay focused. Also, bear in mind that telling the truth is often the best way forward. Saying *no* is an important source of self-discipline and a reliable time-saver.

Make time. A big part of doing anything in life—getting and staying fit included—is finding and taking the time. Perhaps you have loads of time, and if so, that's *great,* but even if you do not, you need to shuffle your schedule around and *make* time. Structuring your time around certain activities that you perform on a regular basis will help you focus on what is essential. Ask yourself what activities you can better plan and optimize for them to take up less time. And, conversely, what activities would you like to make more time for?

Invest time. Another way to think of this issue of time is in terms of investment. Whereas the notion of *spending* time has a finality to it, reminiscent of an all-or-nothing transaction, the idea of time investment highlights the potential for long-term returns and meaningful gains. It broadens the concept of time usage to include a concern for the future. This should shift your thinking about time in so far as the activities, practices, or habits you *invest* in should be those that result in the most desirable long-term outcomes.

OUR ROUTINES EVOLVE

My need to develop and follow a routine really began during my university days, because I had a full schedule of activities to juggle both in and outside of class. Alongside my studies, I worked for a private military academy in Palo Alto, first as a swim teacher, and then as a bus driver. I would be up every morning at 6:00 a.m., pick up the bus a half hour later, and go straight into making the rounds to pick up the kids. I was paid for two and a half hours' work and was just in time to be late for my 9:00 a.m. class at Stanford University. My sophomore and senior years, I also worked as a waiter in a restaurant from 6:30 p.m. to midnight on weekdays. These jobs allowed me to pay my way through university. But between the studying, the jobs, and the sports, I had to learn to run a pretty tight ship because socializing and having fun was also, I have to admit, high among my priorities. Needless to say I maximized what time was available on the weekends.

Today, I find myself at the other end of a long professional career and my student days are but a fond memory, yet I continue to draw on the power of routine even as I ease into a lifestyle that is more adapted to my age. Although it has evolved over time, my routine remains at the center of my ability to stay organized and, more importantly as I grow old, my ability to stay mobile and active. Although I continue to work on several projects, including the Fit For Life Foundation, I have reduced my obligations, given much more priority to my family, and singled out the goals I want to meet in the near future.

The key idea behind the power of routine is that it can help you bring about substantial improvements to your productivity, health, and wellbeing. If you want to live an active lifestyle at an advanced age, this requires you to reevaluate your habits and establish a routine that can raise you up to where you want to be. So much of life is out of one's control: accidents happen, illness strikes, other people take actions that affect us. The power of routine enables you to introduce some sense of order by controlling the elements in your own life that you can control and ceasing to worry about what you cannot.

Alongside its other benefits, a routine will go a long way to help you fit in some exercise on a daily basis. Stop thinking of exercise as a burden, a one-off event, something to get out of the way so more important things in life can take place. Think of it as one of the core pursuits that you build your days around and one of the wisest investments you can make of your time.

No matter where you get your physical activity—whether it's in the form of a morning workout, like mine, by walking the dog or swimming laps in the pool—it should be near the top of your list every day and have the place it deserves in your schedule. In time, you may just find that you cannot live without it. Make exercise an enjoyable daily ritual and you're well on your way to developing a routine that will support your health and mobility for years or decades to come.

12

FEAR MAY BE HOLDING YOU BACK

Fear can be a motivating factor, but more often it is a hindrance. They say that there is nothing to fear but fear itself, and this does suggest an important insight into the psychology of fear. When we are afraid of something and do not take measures to deal with it, the chances are that it will end up having an undesirable influence on our lives. Left unchecked, fear can be disruptive—it may keep you from activities you would otherwise benefit from and take pleasure in, steer you away from places you could discover, or prevent you from meeting people you could become friends with. In light of this, you might want to ask yourself whether your fears are holding you back.

Our fears vary in intensity, from mild aversion to full-blown terror. But we all have fears, to a greater or lesser degree, whether we are conscious of them or not. They originate in any number of causal factors including, among others, past experiences, ranging from the unpleasant to the traumatic, an overactive imagination, or an anxious temperament. Some fears work for us, by keeping us safe from danger, for example. Others work against us, holding us back, keeping us locked within a self-made prison. You may be afraid of dogs because you were bitten as a small child. Perhaps a particularly bumpy flight has made you anxious about taking the airplane. If these fears mean you miss out on doing things you enjoy, like walking in the forest where dogs might be off the leash, or visiting family abroad, they are holding you back.

In this chapter we will focus on a set of fears that many of us experience and that are particularly relevant to exercise: fear of judgement or ridicule, fear of discomfort or pain, fear of injury, fear of failure, and fear of getting started. The good news is that these are all aspects of our psychology that we can work on overcoming and change for the better.

While not all fear acts as an obstacle—one can easily imagine how, for example, a fear of failure might be an incentive for performance—there are ways of mitigating or even reversing those that are holding you back. It all begins with taking stock of the situation and realizing that some kind of fear is there in the first place. Only when you accept something is a problem can you begin to take steps to address it. If you are allergic to bee stings, for example, then your fear of bees is justifiable, but it does not mean you cannot leave the house from April through October. There are precautions you can take to protect yourself. When it comes to physical activity and getting back into exercise, it is especially important to face and tame our fears, rather than be ruled by them. The stakes are too high to let any hang-ups hold us back. Exercise-related fears are our focus here, but the lesson is one that can be applied to all aspects of life. Facing and dealing with your fears can make your life a whole lot easier.

TWO SIDES OF THE SAME COIN

In the early 1990s, I went on a trip with my family to Lizard Island off the coast of Australia. After some wonderful snorkeling around the island, we went down for a diving expedition to the Great Barrier Reef, only about a fifteen-minute boat ride away. There were about twelve of us diving under the guidance of two dive masters, and we made regular stops to see reefs and various colonies of fish. These ecosystems were astounding and teeming with life. Fish of all colors and sizes swam about the corals, shoaling and intermingling in dazzling swirls. We saw rays and sharks and impressive specimens of fish like Napoleon wrasses and groupers, enormous fish that in some cases are known to weigh up to 180 and 390 kilograms, respectively. It was a relaxed atmosphere, and everyone was happy to be out getting a few precious glimpses of what was going on under the waves.

We dove down to depths of about twelve to fifteen meters in groups of two according to a buddy system, for safety. My partner was a man in his seventies who I had not met before. Everything had been going as planned, but on the second dive, something happened. As we were going down, I began to see blood coming out of my diving partner's nose. It was seeping out from under his mask and clouding around his face in the water. I immediately felt a pang of alarm and my heart began to race. I had trained as a diver during my time in the military, and one of the things you learn is how to react in these situations. Whatever the solution is, and even when swift action is required, you must remain calm, and make sure that all actions you take are coherent, measured, and rational. You cannot let fear govern your decision-making.

We were lucky to be only about twelve meters down at this point. Even at that depth, however, you cannot simply speed back up, for this can cause decompression sickness and embolisms. I signaled to one of the dive masters, who swam over. The man's eyes were a blank stare. It was clear we both had the same thought—he might already be dead. But a few bubbles continued to trickle from his mask and the only thing to do was to act as if he still had a chance. We slowly made our way up, going just a few meters at a time, until, finally, we surfaced, only to find the boat had drifted off with the current. We waved frantically, but couldn't get their attention. We both had an inflatable vest which we used to buoy the unconscious man who, luckily, was still wearing his compressed air tank and mouthpiece. Once he was secured, I swam over in full gear toward the boat which was at some distance by now. I made it back onboard and we swung back around. We hoisted the man back on deck and found, to our relief, that his heart was still beating. One of the guides performed CPR on him until they were sure he was breathing on his own. About ten minutes later he opened his eyes and the first thing he said was: "What the hell happened?" There was a general sigh of relief when we realized he was out of immediate danger.

Several years later, and well into my climbing career, I was in a group that was planning on summiting the Aiguille d'Argentière, a mountain peak not too far from Chamonix in the French Alps. While the peak itself is not a very technical or difficult climb, to reach it you first have to cross a glacier that is full of deep, often hidden crevasses, so moving with caution is absolutely essential. We had two guides with us for a group of six climbers. It was projected to be at least an eight-hour climb, and we were making our way carefully through the glacier, all roped together, when we were overtaken by two middle-aged guys, unroped, going full speed ahead like bats out of hell. Our guides tried to talk some sense into them but they shrugged it off with a laugh and called back over their shoulder that they were late, that they would be fine, and so on.

About an hour later, one of them came running back in a panic. His friend had fallen into a crevasse. Our two guides took charge and we set out to look for the fallen climber. He was alive, we were told, but there was no saying whether it would even be possible to rescue him. By lowering a rope, we were able to ascertain that he was about twenty meters down a deep shaft in the glacier. Luckily he was conscious, talking, and able to tie the rope around his waist, despite having a broken arm and several other painful injuries. It took the six of us about two hours to pull him out, without his partner's help, for he had completely lost his nerve and spiraled into a counter-productive panic. When we finally got the fallen climber out, we had to carry him back across the glacier on a stretcher made from ski poles and ropes. This took another four hours. A helicopter met us at the refuge and took him to the hospital. In addition to his broken arm, he had a mild concussion, a dislocated shoulder, and a fractured tibia, but he was alive.

Whether you are diving or climbing, there is always the possibility that the unexpected may arise, and you will immediately be faced with the question: do I, or do we, have the resourcefulness to come up with solutions? You prepare as best you can, rehearse the logistical details and carefully plan out the expedition, or dive. Once you begin, you follow through with determination but not without caution. When you're in the moment, all you have is your preparation, your training, and your ability to react. Being physically ready for the challenge is one thing, being mentally ready is another, and this means there is little room for fear.

These two anecdotes are relatively extraordinary, and both involve extreme situations in inhospitable environments that are highly precarious. They are useful to consider and draw instruction from, however. I believe that a similar principle holds for life's extremes as well as for the quotidian situations we find ourselves in. Fear will hold you back when it goes unchecked, and it is very likely to do more damage than good. Now, this does not mean that you have to be fearless, it just means that you absolutely should not let yourself be governed by fear. Think of the foolish climbers who went recklessly stomping through the crevasse-riddled glacier. Their confidence was naïve and dangerous, and they were lucky not to have paid a steeper price than they did. Such fearlessness can just as easily lead to ruin as cowardice. But, to look at the other side of the coin, if I had panicked when I saw the blood coming from my diving buddy's nose, he may not have made it out alive. While it is crucial to evaluate the risks and identify the source of your fears, if and when you decide to go ahead with whatever project or action you are contemplating, you will have to find a way to mitigate and manage fear, lest it dictate the outcome.

SOME USUAL SUSPECTS

Fear of judgement or ridicule

We all need and desire the recognition of others to some degree, and it can be particularly painful when we feel negatively judged by those we care about or admire. But when it comes to exercise, you have to stop worrying about what others might think. Turn it into a source of motivation to work harder. You're doing it for yourself, not for them, so why should their opinion matter? You set your own objectives and advance at your own pace, and you need to keep this in mind at all times. Good fitness can only be achieved over time, and there are no shortcuts. There is no point comparing yourself negatively with someone who is further along in his or her journey into physical activity. They are at a different stage; you will get there too, but in your own time.

Afraid that you are going to look bad while you exercise? Forget it, it's irrelevant. Don't let it become a barrier. This fear should be the easiest to get rid of. So what if you look ridiculous? We are who we are. We have to come to terms with this, and own it. Whatever it is that's bothering you, whether it is the way you do the exercises, the clothes you are wearing, your weight, or your haircut, the overwhelming likelihood is that you are the only person passing judgement. Anyone who might be laughing at you is not worth the bother. And if you have persistent trouble shaking off this kind of anxiety, then take steps to mitigate it. If you are embarrassed about your clothes, buy new ones. Do what you can to eliminate the problem at its source, but manage the effects if you have to. It starts in your mind, but any tricks to rise above it are worth a try. Don't let people's prejudice or ignorance get you down. There's no use losing any sleep over it.

Sometimes we keep our mouths shut and don't say anything out of fear, but this is rarely a good tactic. There is always a solution, but without reaching out or voicing our concerns, we rarely get very far. I remember one year going on a bike trip to Norway, and being confronted with a situation like this. After several hours of riding, I broke one of the toe clips on my bicycle shoes. In the flurry of preparation for the trip, I had forgotten to bring an extra pair, and so I was stuck with a pair of replacement clips that—unlike the ones I had broken—were rigid and caused significant discomfort in my knee. I did not share this fact with the others in the group, probably because I knew how much it would slow our progress if we had to go out of our way to find a new pair for me. I just gritted my teeth and powered through. I cycled like this for the rest of the day and the pain kept growing until, finally, unable to take it anymore, I shared my situation with the others. I was resigned to throwing in the towel, and talked about finding transport back to Oslo. To my surprise, and subsequent embarrassment, one of the other riders had a spare pair of clips like my old ones that he was happy to lend me. After fitting them to my shoes by way of a screw designed for that purpose, we were off again, and the pain slowly began to subside. I should have spoken earlier.

Fear of discomfort or pain

Leaving one's comfort zone can be terrifying. Walking from what we know into what we don't requires a lot of courage. That dull dread we feel when we know we are doing the right thing, but also leaving behind what we are used to, is very uncomfortable. Nevertheless, it's very likely the best thing we can do. When it comes to exercise, this discomfort may significantly enhance and lengthen your life.

Not wanting to step out of your own comfort zone is perhaps one of the most common roadblocks to success. Anyone trying to make any kind of change in their life is likely to be held back by the simple pull of habit and comfort. But once you decide to move ahead, you should take no prisoners. You must be ruthless and leave your sedentary, unhealthy ways behind.

I can't resist the following declaration. We've all heard it: no pain, no gain. The key here is to know your body and do your best to understand the sources of your pain when you experience it. With regards to exercise, it shouldn't have to hurt. Or, to be more precise, it should never have to keep hurting. You should listen to the message that your body is sending you through the medium of pain, and take measures to manage it and make it go away, as we discussed in chapter ten, "Your Body Is Your Guide." This means you cannot let it take over and call the shots.

Just recently, after seven years of abstinence from running, on the orders of my neurosurgeon, I was feeling that this restraint was perhaps unnecessary. I had done a lot of walking during this time, a few long-distance, multi-day treks, and was confident enough that my body could manage running again. Running and cycling have always been the ideal combination of exercise for me. Their strength and aerobic benefits are perfectly complementary. Since quitting running, I had felt the fitness loss, and gradually became convinced that it was time to rectify this. I asked my sports doctor, expecting resistance, and his only response was: don't hurt yourself; if you feel you can do it, then go ahead.

The most difficult thing was overcoming the compounding effect of a seven-year hiatus. Jogging involves leg movements and muscle groups that are unlike any other activity that I do. As a result of the disuse, the hamstring and muscles going up the back of the leg tend to shorten and become more tense. As I began to run again, the main challenge was that my muscles would regularly freeze up and cramp. This was painful and debilitating, but I took the time to accompany this return to the sport with ample amounts of stretching—never overdoing it, but pushing forward, one step at a time.

If you too are experiencing debilitating pain, the first thing to do is to try to get the inflammation down or get the cramp to subside. The pain can go away fast if you take action, but it could also linger for a long time if you ignore it. Don't be afraid of it; do try to alleviate it. You can target individual muscles with stretches, try applying heat to sooth the muscles, or cold to lower inflammation, and rest up as appropriate. Try to teach your muscle to work again, and don't let these temporary setbacks take away your ability to use your muscles.

Learn to love the feeling of muscles that buzz after a solid workout. But learn also not to overdo it, not to injure yourself. This means learning to distinguish "good" from "bad" pain; and avoiding the "bad" pain that comes from having worked too hard. Navigating a balance between these two extremes is not only doable, it's easier than you think. Distinguishing "good" from "bad" pain will also allow you to be more efficient when seeking help, in the eventuality that you should continue to experience "bad" pain.

The fear of pain is understandable, but it should not prevent you from facing whatever is at the root cause of this pain. If you're feeling "bad" pain, you have to do something about it. Ignoring pain altogether can sometimes lead to further complications and is not a sustainable solution. If you experience an injury, for example, you may need to take steps to strengthen the muscles and avoid repeating the injury in the future. Know your weaknesses and take measures to prevent them from becoming a permanent vulnerability. If your problems persist over time, ask a physiotherapist or osteopath for further guidance.

Fear of injury

Fear of injury may manifest itself largely in the same way as fear of pain, and can lead to an avoidance of physical activity. Here we have another self-fulfilling prophecy: the more inactive you are, the higher the chances that you will injure yourself, or suffer an accident, when you do engage in any exercise more strenuous than you are used to. That is because when the body is inactive it becomes frailer and more brittle, and when your muscles aren't put to use, they won't be strong enough to protect you when you fall. When we work out on a regular basis and maintain our level of activity, our body is much less likely to suffer from serious injuries due to minor accidents and falls. An active lifestyle helps increase balance, dexterity, and flexibility, as well as strength, making us more adept at avoiding falls, more agile, and better able to watch our step and catch ourselves to avoid tumbling in the first place.

A trickier situation in this category is fear that stems from *previous* injury. People who have suffered serious injury and are returning to physical exercise after a "rest" period often experience fear and avoid using the part of their body that was injured. My philosophy has always been that when you fall off the horse, the best thing to do is get right back on it. But some caveats are in order here. You need to make sure you are taking appropriate measures to rehabilitate and prepare yourself physically for the strain that you will experience as you return to physical activity.

If you were treated medically after an accident, then chances are you went through a proper rehabilitation program. If you suffer from chronic pain, such as back pain, this may not be the case. It is likely that fear related to that pain is what is holding you back. I realize pain can be a true handicap, and the best advice I can give you is to consult a sports doctor with experience in these matters who will be able to help you get to the bottom of your pain. What you likely need to do is find out which muscles are weak, and how to strengthen them. The main difficulty here is that this is not always straightforward. Especially for those who have been inactive for long periods of time, there may be severe muscular imbalances which take time—and perhaps also the help of a trained professional—to address. Nevertheless, this does not change the fact that exercise is likely to help.

Getting yourself into shape is the best way to avoid injury as you age. It will also help you overcome your fear because you will gain confidence in your own abilities. As discussed in chapter six, "A Workout Will Make Your Day," getting in shape means improving your strength, your endurance, your flexibility, and your balance. If you can find a way to do this, you're already protected to a large extent against injury and pain.

Fear of failure

I have always tried not to get hung up on the possibility of failure, but I do realize that it is a very serious barrier. It is a barrier that can, in effect, be paralyzing and stop you from even trying. The way I look at it, however, is in terms of risk management. There will always be the possibility of failure, and I just need to be clear eyed about what's at stake. Ultimately, the more rational you can be about the nature of the risks, the less your emotions take over and call the shots.

Failure is a part of life. Ask anyone who has ever been successful at anything and you will overwhelmingly find that their journey is paved with failures. Learning to overcome the disappointments and setbacks of not achieving what we set out to achieve is a crucial part of what makes us good at what we do in the long run. It builds our resilience and gives credence to the idea that what doesn't kill you makes you stronger.

Clichés aside, if you allow yourself to get stuck on the starting block because of all the things that *could* happen or *could* go wrong, you are actively creating a scenario in which nothing happens and nothing gets done. Your capacity to react, adapt, and overcome is real—but only by trying and by getting started will you ever know what you are truly capable of achieving.

Fear of getting started

The first steps are the hardest. And yet, sometimes, you just need to stop thinking and throw yourself into it. That seems to me a perfect image of how one does it: jumping with both feet, into the deep end.

One of the most unnerving experiences in my life was my first private parachute jump. I had jumped once before during my time in the military, and had always wanted to do it again, with the liberty of deciding my own trajectory and appreciating the ride. I was working in New York when the opportunity came up through a parachuting school that flew out of Red Bank, New Jersey, just a short ride out of the city. On a whim, I called them up and reserved a date. As I hung up the phone, I immediately began to regret my decision and was consumed by anxiety for the next few days leading up to the jump. Did I really want to do this? What was the point? Would I be able to land in the right place? They had told me there was an instruction session in the morning, followed by a first jump right after lunch. Surely, I need more training than that, I thought.

Somehow, my curiosity prevailed, and I showed up on the appointed day at the airfield. We were brought into a room where they briefed us for an hour or so, and we were then instructed to fold our own parachutes into their bags. My heart started beating out of my chest. *I have to pack my own chute?* The one time I had jumped in the military, we were handed a chute, pushed out of a plane, and the whole focus was on the dangers of landing in water and managing not to drown. What if I make a mistake, miss a fold, or screw something up? The instructor was nonchalant, and showed me how it was done. I did my best to follow the instructions. I took notes, trying desperately to remember all the information I was presented with. My heart was in my throat. They showed us a film of first timers jumping in rapid succession out of an open door of an aircraft, just like the military does it. Everything from then on was a blur and, the next thing I knew, I was on the tarmac boarding a giant Swedish plane originally designed to carry cattle and reindeer to new pastures. The engines were revving up and the pilot, waving to us, flipped switches in the cockpit as we climbed up the stairs into the airplane.

And then, the door opened about half a kilometer over the ground. This was the moment of truth. People immediately began jumping out. The rest of us stood there, suited up, knees knocking. It was now or never. All of a sudden, I had a realization that all these people around me were just as terrified as I was. We were all "normal people," as it were, and this reassured me. It got rid of the notion that this was a competition, and unless these instructors were maniacs sending a bunch of innocent people to their doom, this was something that was within reach of any one of us. Maybe this thought simply coincided with the adrenaline rush kicking in, but it gave me the courage I needed. I was number six in line. Numbers one through four just jumped right out, but number five froze at the door. The instructor took his arm, said a few words to him, and out he went. As I advanced to the door, the instructor shouted in my ear not to land near the oil refinery, but he didn't go into details. I didn't want to look like a coward, so I jumped.

As I leapt from the plane, I felt the flooding sensation of adventure, discovery, elation, and adrenaline—a wild concoction of everything I loved. The experience of piloting my way down in a chute—which had levers for steering left and right—seeing the landscape from above as I flew through the sky, scoping out a good landing spot, and trying not to break my legs as I landed, all of it washed out any trace of the fear I had felt. That moment when you manage to face and overcome a fear is invaluable. I felt greatly empowered. I returned several times during my stay in New York, and also did a few jumps over Boston. Eventually, I gave it up because it made my wife, Claire-Lise, uneasy, but that was fine by me, for I had learned my lesson and gotten my thrills.

It's important to understand that a little dose of trepidation can go a long way. It can become a call to action, a source of motivation, or a way of staying on your toes. We should all find encouragement in our fears and allow them to motivate us to work on our outlook on exercise and on life. Everything goes, as long as fear doesn't take over and start calling the shots. When it does, I have found that the best form of defense is offense. Get out ahead of your fears. You don't have to jump out of a plane, but you can always find a way to leave your comfort zone, or take calculated risks. You might find it makes you stronger. And who knows, you might even come to love the activity you were so afraid to try.

13
REST IS OVERRATED

We all need our rest, but probably not as much of it as we think we do. Very often, for those of us leading relatively sedentary lifestyles, real exercise would do a lot more good than a lie down. Rest is a relative concept that occupies too great a space in our collective imagination, and we need to bring back some sense of just proportion. Everybody needs to rest after exertion, of course, when you're feeling what we've already referred to as "good" tired. But this feeling is very different from the exhaustion that comes from the slow grind associated with sedentariness, inactivity, or stress—the "bad" tired feeling. In these cases, your body is very likely to benefit from—and be reinvigorated by— more, rather than less, physical activity.

GOOD REST, BAD REST, AND CHRONIC FATIGUE

Since there is room for misunderstanding on this topic, I want to make sure the definition of rest as I intend it here is clear. I am taking issue with two things that I believe are problematic. First, with the notion that the dangers of physical activity outweigh its benefits. And second, with the notion of excessive caution and overreliance on the therapeutic value of rest. It seems to me that there ensues from these notions an aversion to exercise that has largely detrimental effects on our overall health. In a nutshell, the idea that exercise should be avoided whenever we feel discomfort, that exercise should only be undertaken when we are in full form, is mistaken. With today's better understanding of medicine and physiology, doctors and fitness experts are tending to prescribe more activity rather than less, the caveat being that it is always important to know, understand, and respect your limits and your weaknesses.

We tend to assume that rest is the solution to poor health, but we should probably be thinking of it more as just one part of the support structure that bolsters good health. Just as there is "good" and "bad" tiredness, there is also "good" and "bad" rest. We can say that good rest is what you do to recuperate from intervals of physical activity. No matter what your level of physical fitness is, you will benefit from rest after you've pushed yourself physically. For this reason, rest is an important element in the transition, or return, to an active lifestyle. It helps you manage the effects of physical activity by allowing for recuperation, and it is a powerful complement to exercise. Learning to know—and push—your limits will mean alternating between effort and rest, and developing a better ability to sense what your body needs.

Bad rest, on the other hand, is little more than a continuation of inactivity. This may appear counterintuitive at first, but I think that it's an important point to make: collapsing on the couch after a day at the office may seem like an attractive way of relaxing and getting some rest, but metabolically speaking it's just more of the same, and you are merely accumulating further hours of sedentary behavior. In the long term, excessive amounts of bad rest are likely to contribute to chronic fatigue and lead to the same types of problems that we associate with excess sedentarism, as discussed in chapter seven.

Chronic fatigue can sometimes be a symptom of illness requiring medical intervention, and you should consult a doctor if you are worried. That said, if fatigue is a regular problem in your life, you may find that lifestyle changes go a long way to helping you achieve wellbeing and balance. In a study from 2008, the University of Georgia found that regular exercise reduced chronic fatigue, particularly for people leading sedentary lifestyles. The study compared groups engaging in moderate- and low-intensity exercise with a control group that did nothing. The findings showed that low-intensity exercise was most effective at reducing chronic fatigue. After six weeks of engaging in twenty minutes of low-intensity exercise three times a week—in this case, the exercise was carried out on a stationary bicycle—test subjects saw a 20% increase in their energy levels and a 65% decrease in fatigue.

Apart from the benefits of regular exercise, here are some key factors you can work with in order to address fatigue that is not disease related:

- Make sure you get enough quality, restorative sleep. As we will see in the next chapter, this is absolutely essential to good health, and it is also the best kind of rest you can get.
- Try to lower your stress levels. Too much anxiety on a regular basis weighs down on your metabolism and can lead to exhaustion.
- If you are still working, make sure you are not overdoing it. Try to keep your work and your private spheres separate. This is, in itself, a form of rest.
- Pay attention to your diet. What you eat can influence your energy levels. Whether it is an intolerance to certain foods, or the nature of your eating patterns—for example, the insulin crash following the digestion of a meal—the effects of diet on energy levels and fatigue can be very pronounced.

KEEP MOVING

There is a specific event in my life that has always stuck with me as an important milestone regarding my own determination to stay active by all means. When I was fourteen, the family doctor diagnosed me with Osgood-Schlatter's disease, a growth-related condition that is common in adolescents and involves inflammation where the tendon attaches to the tibia underneath the knee. The danger, it was thought, was that a piece of bone might break loose entirely and lodge itself in the knee. As a preemptive measure, doctors were in the habit of prescribing extensive rest periods to their patients, instructing them to avoid any strenuous exercise. My sentence was firm: no sports for eighteen months. I was miserable, and in a matter of days I rose up in rebellion. There was no way I was going to spend a year and a half sitting around doing nothing, floating bone or no floating bone. And so, although I systematically favored my right leg and knee over my left, I went for anything that my body could take. American football, basketball, tennis, track and field, I did them all, and nothing ever happened. The only adverse effect I ever suffered from this was a muscular imbalance from favoring one leg—which remains smaller to this day—over the other, albeit with no great detriment to my performance.

Rest continues to be one of the main prescriptions for Osgood-Schlatter's disease today even though we are much more aware of the negative effects of inactivity. During an acute flare-up of the condition, leaving the injury alone and not aggravating it will promote proper healing. We need to take into account all the other health impacts of a period of enforced inactivity, however. The difference between a few days off—as many as it takes, even—and eighteen months is enormous. In a nutshell, it comes down to balancing the amount of rest needed for an injury to heal with our broader health needs, and the costs to other parts of our body from extended inactivity. It is not an either/or situation.

There are a few interesting examples from medical history that illustrate this strange deference we have for "rest." One of these is tuberculosis (TB). For a long time, TB was among the deadliest infectious diseases, and impossible to cure. Despite progress in antibacterial treatments, it is still among the top ten deadliest infectious diseases today, continuing to defy eradication efforts. For years, until the development of a vaccine, TB was treated with bed rest and fresh air. Apart from the compelling but misguided intuition that "broken" lungs needed peace, quiet, and rest to properly mend, there was, in fact, some scientifically-sound reasoning for the prescription of bed rest. The idea—later confirmed by studies of TB infection patterns in four-legged animals and bats—was that the disease consistently settled in the areas of the lungs that received less blood flow, due, simply, to gravity. Bed rest was considered a way of encouraging blood flow to the affected areas, and it was strictly enforced, often in sanatoriums. It was only in the late 1950s, with the development of more effective medicine, and after about a century of prescribing bed rest for the disease, that certain physicians began studying whether it was not, in fact, making things worse. It was concluded that there was nothing to be gained from strict bed rest, and that inactivity was likely to be further contributing to the ravages of the disease itself. More recent studies show that appropriate levels of exercise significantly improve healing and wellbeing, even during illness, which is consistent with what we know about the general benefits of physical activity.

These insights about the virtues of exercise over bed rest were confirmed by a landmark study which has become known as the 1966 Dallas Bed Rest and Training Study. Researchers from the University of Texas Southwestern Medical School wanted to test the limits of the cardiovascular system by studying the effects of three weeks of bed rest and eight weeks of intensive endurance training on five healthy twenty-year-old men. After the three weeks of bed rest, their maximal oxygen intake had plummeted (VO2max) and they found that the men's health had significantly deteriorated: they had increased heart rates, elevated blood pressure, decreased maximum heart capacity, a rise in body fat, and diminished body strength. Luckily for these men, and anyone leading a sedentary lifestyle, the eight weeks of training reversed these declines and in some cases, the test subjects were able to achieve a level of fitness superior to that with which they began the experiment. Thirty years later, the same men were invited back for a follow-up of the study. They were not asked to repeat the bed rest experiment, but their fitness levels were examined. The results were astounding. While their overall fitness levels had declined between the ages of twenty and fifty—their cardiorespiratory capacity decreased, they gained over twenty-two kilograms on average, and their percentage of body fat doubled, from 14% to 28%—this decline did not match the devastating drop in health that they had experienced during the initial three week bed rest period. To put it more clearly, three weeks of enforced inactivity aged these men more than thirty years of life did.

This damning evidence against the prescription of inactivity has implications for the medical world, and recuperation from heart surgery is another interesting example of the shift away from bed rest and toward responsible activity. As our understanding of recovery has advanced alongside medical technologies and techniques, it has become clear that our bodies need to move as much as possible. So, whereas it used to be that a patient recovering from heart surgery was advised to stay in bed for several weeks after the operation, today he or she is advised to start walking as little as one to two days after the operation. The prescription of light but regular exercise has become the norm. While caution is necessary for healing, and any heavy pushing, pulling, or lifting should be avoided, there is no debate about the importance of moving around to build strength during recovery. The main variable now is finding where one's limits lie, and learning how to gradually them without overdoing it. And this is not restricted to heart surgery patients: even patients who undergo hip replacements are up and moving within a few days of the operation.

PUSHING IT

It's important to understand and respect one's limits, and yet there are times when pushing these limits is worth it. I've always been attracted to, and motivated by, extreme circumstances. Whether it is mountain climbing or scuba diving, I love facing challenges that put me to the test. Apart from the appeal of adventure in general, these situations are great at teaching you ways of coping and making do with what you've got. They also show you who you are. Afterwards, you come away feeling like the everyday challenges of life are much smaller by comparison.

I should offer a disclaimer at this point to say that I am aware of the rather extraordinary nature of my stories, many of which take place outside of day-to-day experience, during high levels of sustained, intensive physical effort. Events that take place under such circumstances warrant different reactions from those you might encounter during more mundane situations. Nevertheless, they do give a good sense of what we are capable of when we need to perform under pressure or hardship. This applies to the following anecdote, which I can't resist telling here.

One year in the late 1990s, my cycling group and I were riding from Vézelay in central France down through Limoges and across the Hérault region to Bordeaux on the coast, which amounted to a journey of about 850 kilometers. Several of the riders wanted to see more of the coastline than we had originally planned, and so we decided to add a stretch of coastal roads to our itinerary. One of these was a very steep, winding, gravel road that dropped down from 450 meters to about 150 meters above sea level over the space of just a few kilometers. Everyone took this in good spirits in spite of the danger, for we were all on road bikes which aren't designed for such slippery terrain. A few members of the group threw caution to the wind and decided that, gravel or no gravel, they were going to take it at full speed. One of these people was my good friend John Beaupré, who was known for being one of the world's best ice climbers at the time. He took off like a flash and we lost sight of him until, some minutes later, we turned a corner and found him lying on the pavement—he had fallen hard and broken his arm. He was up again after a few minutes and, despite his injury, expressed the desire to keep riding.

It took a great deal of convincing, but we finally got him to a local emergency room, where we were met by the interns who had been left in charge while the doctors were out to lunch. They looked at him and decided he needed a full cast going from the shoulder all the way down to his fingers in order to fully immobilize the arm. John was aghast—he categorically refused the treatment and stormed out. Despite his injury, he insisted he was able to leave the hospital on his bike and finish the trip with us. There was some back and forth negotiation until a compromise solution was found. It so happened that one person in our group, Christopher Lambert, was a doctor. In his professional life, he was in charge of three separate emergency clinics in Santa Barbara, California, and was accustomed, therefore, to seeing bad breaks and all manner of sports injuries. He came up with a scheme that got John onboard, and it involved only a slight bending of the truth. His opinion was clearly that the break needed a cast, but that, if the pain was manageable, a smaller cast could do as a stopgap; and, in any case, a few more days probably wouldn't do much more damage. Back inside, he explained his credentials to the interns and convinced them to fit what he called a sports cast onto John's arm. They were intrigued and accepted to let him demonstrate this technique, so Chris got to work, showing them how it was done, lecturing all the while. He made a short plaster cast that went about halfway up to John's elbow, and theatrically answered all their questions. Every so often, as the interns scribbled notes, he would turn to us and wink.

On went the cast, I paid for the X-rays, and we left quickly before the clinicians in charge showed up after their lunch. As we rode out of the hospital parking lot, one of the riders asked Chris how many sports casts he had done in his life. "There's no such thing as a sports cast," he answered with a grin, and all of us burst out laughing. John, meanwhile, led the pack for most of the day, happier than I had ever seen him. He finished the latter half of the trip with us as planned, and I don't think he ever got a different cast. Not too long after that, he was back in the mountains, climbing ice falls as he had before. Needless to say, this story has gotten a lot of mileage since then.

DON'T GET TOO COMFORTABLE

There is a reason why we tend to gravitate to the familiar, the predictable, and the comfortable: it enables us to reduce anxiety related to the unknown, and this is not a bad thing. As we saw in chapter eleven, a routine can be a very powerful tool to help you optimize your schedule, activities, and productivity. A good routine can create a lot of freedom. Nevertheless, it's all about balance, and the predictability of a routine needs the counterbalance of the unexpected and the uncontrolled. Too much comfort is not a good thing.

Too often, we hold unjustifiably conservative and protective views of what we are capable of. This conservative approach as to what our body can handle has a number of detrimental effects. First and foremost, it trains us to avoid exercise rather than to embrace it. Small decisions—like choosing the elevator over the stairs, or taking the bus rather than walking for short distances—accumulate over time and create an unfortunate bias against physical exertion. We gear our actions and behavior toward comfort, and avoid all forms of discomfort wherever possible. These decisions are habit forming and, ultimately, become foundational for our lifestyle. This aversion to effort, discomfort, and unpredictability has skewed our sense of what is good for us and what is bad. Unfortunately, it seems we have become addicted to comfort.

Too much comfort will make your body suffer. In a sense, you can think of comfort as a form of entropy that will hold you back and drag you down, it will immobilize you and reduce you to a standstill. The physical effects of this are on par with, and closely linked to, the problem of inactivity and sedentariness, which we have already discussed—basically, grinding your body down and raising your risk profile for developing a non-communicable disease. Letting yourself fall into entirely predictable patterns that never change and never challenge you will also have a dulling effect on your cognitive functions. A recent primate study from Yale University, for example, demonstrated that too much predictability impairs the brain's ability to learn new information. The study concluded that uncertainty is a powerful stimulant of our cognition and learning faculties. Once our habits become entrenched and we become sure of ourselves and our surroundings, the brain has no immediate need to adapt in the way it would if solicited to react to novelty and change.

We live in a society which places too much emphasis on comfort, to the detriment of our health. The pursuit of comfort is right up there with, if not above, the pursuit of happiness. Unfortunately, however, these two pursuits do not tend to overlap for very long. It's a well-worn trope, almost a cliché, to say that leaving your comfort zone will bring positive effects, but it's the truth. You should never get too comfortable. Pushing outside of your comfort zone leads to new adventures and helps you stay sharp, ready to react as needed to whatever opportunities arise. When it comes to health and fitness, it means that your body is constantly having to adapt to the new situations it finds itself in, something that it is ideally designed to do.

I don't advocate putting yourself in harm's way on a daily basis, or taking too many unnecessary risks, but the human body is capable of so much more than we think, and we all have a great capacity for resilience, though we may not know it. You may be surprised at what you discover within yourself once you get going. My argument is that this resilience can, and *should*, be trained. As we have already seen, one of the biggest barriers to getting active again is figuring out what to do, and then sticking with it. In this fragile phase, before it becomes second nature, anything can be a deterrent—even if it is completely unjustified. Excessive caution regarding which activities we put our bodies through is among these very common barriers, followed by the exaggerated notion we have of the value of rest. What I've learned, and adopted as my motto, is this: if it doesn't hurt, keep moving.

14
SLEEP IS SACRED

A good night's sleep is our one-stop shop for physiological repair and recuperation. While rest tends to be overrated, very little is as beneficial for the human body as sleep, and an active lifestyle would not be complete without it. If you consider that we spend—or should spend—about one-third of our life asleep, which is to say eight hours a night on average, it seems fairly obvious that we should try to give this activity the attention and care it deserves. Sleep has always been a source of both fascination and endless speculation, and human beings have long sought to probe the mystery of what happens to us when we drift into unconsciousness. As the biological truth begins to emerge, the science is unequivocal: underlying every physical process and ability, every bodily function, is the need for regular, restorative sleep.

A POWERFUL RESTORATIVE

Most health authorities recommend that you get between seven to nine hours of sleep every night. Whether in the comfort of your own home or the discomfort of an unfamiliar setting, you simply cannot afford not to sleep. In 2000, during my mountain climbing days, I climbed a series of high-altitude peaks in the Andes with a group of friends. Among these peaks was the imposing Chimborazo, in Ecuador. Culminating at 6,263 meters above sea level, the peak is not challenging from a technical perspective, so much as it is physically demanding. To reach the summit, you must cover great distances in crampons at high altitude, and in the final stages of the climb the slope increases dramatically, which makes the going very tough. Given the very low temperatures at the summit, you have to get up and back down again within a relatively short period of time, and it isn't wise to linger too long in celebration.

There is an old saying among mountain climbers that the body has a memory of the altitudes to which it is capable of climbing. To undertake such feats, you need to have done enough climbing at high altitude to have acclimatized to an oxygen-poor environment, and you need to understand the effects this has on various metabolic processes, as well as the risks that are involved. This will help you avoid altitude sickness or embolisms, which can cause a lot of problems and, in the latter case, even be fatal.

Chimborazo was the fourth peak we climbed in Ecuador. It followed on the heels of three other peaks at 3,200 meters, 3,900 meters, and 4,600 meters, all within a period of seven days. Chimborazo, although incredibly beautiful, is also extremely physically demanding to climb. As soon as you begin to ascend, you feel the strain. Less than half of the climbers that undertake the challenge actually make it to the summit. The physical toll is such that it requires a great deal of endurance. But even though I was tired, I was determined. At these heights, your breathing rate is much higher than it is at sea level, and everything takes more effort. You can sometimes feel slightly light-headed while the rest of your body seems to be sluggish and weigh more than it normally does. It wouldn't take much—your crampons catching on your pant leg, for example—to trip you up and cause a fall.

Even though I had acclimatized, the 1,800 meters we descended that day from the summit of Chimborazo sapped my strength, and by the time we made it back to the cabin where we would spend the night, my legs were shot and I could barely stand. The final stretch of the descent—less than half a kilometer—took every ounce of strength I had left. I didn't even have the energy to eat. As I made it to my cot, I remember wondering what would happen to me. Although we had two more peaks left—both between 5,000 and 6,000 meters—I felt sure that my legs couldn't take anymore, that I would have to throw in the towel. All I could do was abandon myself to sleep. I fell into my sleeping bag and slept for over ten hours.

When I woke up the next morning, however, I had a feeling of great euphoria. My legs were stiff, but I felt great, and my body was buzzing pleasantly from the exertion, the altitude, and the necessary recuperation time after having pushed my body to its utmost limits. Sleep is what I needed, and I felt reborn. I devoured a breakfast so enormous that the rest of the team were dumbfounded. We made it off the mountain that day and went on to climb the remaining peaks without incident. This experience and the intensity of how I felt that morning remains with me to this day. It filled me with awe at the incredible resilience our bodies can develop when they are treated right.

SLEEP IS UNDERRATED

When I was at Stanford University there was a professor there by the name of William C. Dement. He had a reputation for being an anomaly because he studied something that most people thought was neither important nor scientific: sleep. In fact, he did more than just study sleep; he was among the earliest pioneers that turned it into a discipline deserving of study. His experiments seemed strange at the time, but they were extremely popular, and a number of my friends participated as test subjects. He would wire up the sleepers and track their brain waves throughout the night. A couple of nights in the University hospital—instead of a dorm—with good meals, no noise, and you got paid for it! If it weren't for my jobs at the time, I would have gone for it too.

If you read through the various definitions of sleep available in the dictionaries, it is remarkable how many of them, even in 2020, still contain little beyond the observation that sleep is a resting state accompanied by the absence of consciousness. This suggests that sleep is still considered by many as basically the fact of not being awake. The Collins dictionary, for example, simply states that sleep "is the natural state of rest in which your eyes are closed, your body is inactive, and your mind does not think." The Merriam-Webster is an outlier and exception in this regard, for it rightfully includes dreams, as well as "changes in brain activity and physiological functioning" into this definition, adding also that sleep is "made up of cycles of non-REM sleep and REM sleep [which is] usually considered essential to the restoration and recovery of vital bodily and mental functions." The importance of these final statements cannot be overstated.

In 1957, a team of researchers that included W.C. Dement published the first detailed study of the human sleep cycle. There are four distinct phases of sleep which we cycle through repeatedly during the night. All of them play an important role, especially the third and fourth deep sleep phases. This fourth stage of sleep is called REM sleep, short for rapid eye movement, and this is where most of our dreaming takes place. Many of the most beneficial physiological processes of sleep occur during this stage, which is also known as "paradoxical sleep" because the rate of breathing and brain activity increases while our body's muscles are kept in a state of deep relaxation to prevent us from physically acting out our dreams.

Changes in these cycles occur throughout our lifetime. It's not so much that we need less sleep as we age, but rather that the pattern of our sleep tends to change. Many people report difficulty falling asleep, a lighter and more fragmented sleep, wake up more frequently, or spend less time asleep overall. Under scrutiny, it seems that the sleep cycles of older adults tend to be more fragile, more easily interrupted, which means, unfortunately, less restorative deep sleep and REM sleep. Other identifiable factors potentially weighing into this decrease in sleep quality are the side effects of medication, changing hormonal levels—particularly for women around menopause—as well as a number of lifestyle factors such as our daily occupations, exercise levels, social life, and stress levels. While it is not clear that this deterioration in the quality of sleep is inevitable, one major finding has been established beyond doubt: when it continues over time, it is strongly associated with a deterioration of memory and performance. It also is a very serious influencing factor for depression, as well as the onset of dementia, and Alzheimer's disease.

Old definitions of sleep as merely the absence of consciousness at best miss the point, and, at worst, are utterly false. There is nothing passive about sleep: it is a time of intense activity within the human body. Much like the endless list of benefits that can be observed as a result of exercise, it is now widely acknowledged that sleep has a profound healing effect on our bodies and their internal processes. Sleep plays a key role in enhancing and maintaining our cognitive abilities, capacity to create and consolidate memory, reaction times, alertness, cellular health, tissue growth, muscle repair, immune system, cardiovascular health, and a whole range of other metabolic processes. In fact, levels of sleep have a direct correlation to our overall health, as neuroscientist and sleep expert Matthew Walker, whose book *Why We Sleep* has been bringing these issues to light in recent years, stated bluntly in an interview for *Business Insider*: "the shorter your sleep, the shorter your life."

The effects of losing out on sleep are devastating, and while most of us inherently feel that we're a little off when our sleep is disturbed, the true extent of the physiological damage that occurs is hard to grasp. Studies show that a single night of sleep deprivation is enough to seriously reduce our ability to react, reason, focus, and process emotion, with a number of brain and metabolic functions showing signs of impairment. This effect gets worse and accumulates over time. It only takes a few days of even partial sleep deprivation for all these markers of brain function to deteriorate.

Chronic partial sleep deprivation is a major health risk. Not only does it significantly increase the risk profile for obesity, diabetes, and cardiovascular disease, among others; it also has a slew of effects on attention, behavior, alertness, and reactivity. Chronic sleep deprivation is one of the major causes of human errors that lead to accidents. The comparison is often made between drowsy driving and driving under the influence of alcohol: the National Sleep Foundation declares that driving after being awake for twenty-four hours is the same as driving with a blood alcohol level of 0.1—or 1%—well above the legal limit, which in most countries is set between 0.5 and 0.8. A 2018 study in the journal *SLEEP*, for example, reported that drivers who had slept less than the recommended seven hours were much more likely to cause an accident. This is a bleak picture, and should serve as a wake-up call for us to go back to bed—pun intended.

Depending on which source you turn to, the picture of how much sleep we are getting is either bad or very bad. Somewhere between one-third and one-half of all Americans are not sleeping enough. This means that they do not get the recommended seven to nine hours of sleep a night. The state of affairs in the United States does not seem far off from what is happening in other parts of the world. A study of over 11,000 respondents in twelve countries, commissioned by the electronics company Phillips, showed that the average person gets approximately 6.8 hours of sleep, with four in ten saying the quality of their sleep had declined over the past five years, and 80% saying they would like to improve the quality of their sleep.

The upside to this chilling look at the effects of even partial sleep deprivation is that there exists a solution—more sleep. Or rather just the right amount of sleep, which is somewhere between seven and nine hours for most adults.

MAKING SLEEP SACRED AGAIN

For most of my life, I have been quick to rise and quick to hit the hay. I am fortunate to be a very good sleeper and in all my years as a businessman, although I had to travel constantly, change time zones, and so on, it only rarely happened that I could not get a good night's sleep. This has astonished many and drives my wife crazy because she, unfortunately, has a more difficult time falling asleep. She often complains that she will try to talk to me as we get into bed for the night, only to find that I am already sleeping. Although I do consider myself lucky in this regard, I have also always been disciplined about my sleep habits, what the researchers call "sleep hygiene." Every night, with few exceptions, I am in bed and falling asleep by 11:00 p.m. The next morning at 7:00 a.m., I am up again, like clockwork.

The only time I really lost significant amounts of sleep was when my first business was struggling in its early stages. Mostly due to factors outside my control, I was having trouble aligning the requirements of the various actors involved in supply, storage, working capital, finance, and sales. I was fully absorbed by the struggle to stave off bankruptcy, which I eventually managed to do. But for months, my mind could not quiet down. I was constantly required to come up with creative solutions to an endless string of problems. Throughout this whole process, my routine was upset and I spent hours unable to sleep at night. This lack of sleep only hindered my efforts to save my business, and, as the weeks went by, it gradually wore me down further. If you're ever in a similar situation, let me tell you that the ability to make clear-headed decisions is essential, and whittling yourself away with worries will do little to help your case.

It happened that I was recommended a sophrologist by a friend of mine, and although I was somewhat skeptical, I decided that there would be no harm in trying it out. Sophrology is a secular practice inspired by Eastern and Western wisdom, and focuses on relaxing both the body and the mind. To my surprise, I found that it helped enormously. I essentially learned relaxation techniques to put my body to sleep one piece at a time. The method I learned made use of visualization and breathing in order to slow down the body and bring calm from the feet, to the knees, all the way up to the chest and shoulders and the brain until, finally, you just fall asleep.

Anxiety can be a huge barrier to wellbeing, health, and good sleep. It's important therefore to know how and when to simply stop worrying. What I learned in my sophrology experiment was a simple technique to alleviate this anxiety, and relax both my body and my mind. On a basic level, the way to do this is to think about something other than whatever you are preoccupied with. The strategy I used was to visualize the Japanese flag, which has always fascinated me because of its simplicity. A solid red circle encompassed by a white rectangle. The color red focuses all of your attention, which is then effectively dissipated by the surrounding white. Everything else disappears. You let it go. All that is left is quiet, calm.

At the time, I had only recently returned from Japan, and had bought a Japanese flag during my trip. When I finished my course with the sophrologist, I was so pleased with the results that I gave her the flag as a token of appreciation. I learned later that she would sometimes use it with her students who needed help finding something on which they could channel their focus.

I have found that allowing yourself the chance to focus inwards and find the right way of relaxing, and releasing any tensions you may have, is a practice that is within everyone's reach. Finding a way to your own inner peace and tranquility is a life changer. No matter how many the problems or anxieties, or how much work you may have—nothing justifies ruining your health over it. And this is what will happen if you deprive your body of the sleep which it needs. What you want to do is to clear your mind and evacuate the stresses of your day. Whatever the method you choose, it's the results that count. It need not be sophrology, and you might consider any range of peaceful activities that take your mind off of your daily life.

GOOD SLEEP HYGIENE MAKES

A BIG DIFFERENCE

In addition to what is happening inside, it is also important to create an environment around you that is conducive to sleep. Preserving a bastion of serenity each night within which we can properly recover from the wear and tear of the day is a cornerstone of good health. If you find it hard to wind down, you may want to consider taking the time to create better sleeping conditions. You could do this internally, as we have just seen; there are many different mindfulness practices that are worth looking into. The method is secondary to the objective.

Whereas we once were limited by how much light was available in our environments, we now live in an age where life has been thoroughly electrified and as a result business is conducted 24/7, 365 days a year. Information is practically infinite, networks are operating nonstop, communication is immediate, and entertainment abounds. There is no shortage of problems to solve, and there are distractions enough at our fingertips to keep anyone awake for as long as the body will allow before it shuts off in exhaustion.

In order to get a good night's sleep, you have to create the time and environment to do so. Everything surrounding the way we sleep is referred to as sleep hygiene, and this is an aspect of our lives that we can all strive to improve. While some of the conditions and factors keeping you awake may require medical attention, such as sleep apnea, insomnia, prostate problems, or incontinence, there are also a number of things you can do to improve the conditions in which you are trying to get some shut-eye. If you feel you are not sleeping as well as you could be, here a few tips you can try.

Leave your stress outside. Anxiety, as illustrated by my own experience, is a big factor. Any problems you have can wait, work related or otherwise. I know how counterintuitive this can seem when something pressing is on your mind. I'm a *doer* by nature, and will only tolerate so much deliberation before I decide to take action on any given problem. That said, there is a lot of wisdom in the old saying that you should sleep on it. You will not be any wiser for pulling an all-nighter, only more exhausted and less able to focus. Be strict with yourself, and build yourself a safe space where peace of mind is not only possible, but necessary.

Keep regular hours. Our learning is bolstered by repetition, no matter what the skill is, and sleeping is no exception. We all have what are called circadian rhythms, meaning cycles in the body that roughly equal a twenty-four hour period. Regularizing your sleep schedule will have deep-reaching effects on a whole range of hormonal triggers and processes. If you condition yourself to sleep at the same time every day, your body will begin to anticipate bedtime through a whole range of these internal processes, and you will become better at it.

Minimize screen time before bed. Shutting off electronics at least an hour before bedtime has at least two major effects. The first is to avoid the excitement of entertainment and communication with the outside world. Your emotional response to this information is a form of stimulation that can affect your ability to sleep. The second effect has to do with the light of the screen itself. This sends strong signals to the brain that it should be staying awake. By avoiding exposure to the particularly stimulating blue light on screens, your body will naturally produce more melatonin, one of the hormones most directly involved in sleep.

Darken the lights in the house. If this is not something you are in the habit of doing, you may be surprised by how well it actually works. Try to dim or even turn off the lights in the house, and if possible block out any lights coming in from the outside. As mentioned above, blue lights from screens are particularly effective at keeping the brain stimulated, and suppress melatonin levels. Don't forget all the blinking lights from electrical appliances and gadgets. These also have an effect. We are hardwired to respond to darkness, and you may find yourself nodding off as soon as the lights go out.

Lower the temperature. Try turning down the heating, wearing less clothes, or opening a window. Lower temperatures are conducive to good sleep, and the body responds almost immediately, making it easier to fall asleep. Since the objective is to lower the body's temperature slightly, something which happens naturally during sleep anyway, another good strategy that many people employ is taking a warm bath before bed. It is a little counterintuitive, but once you leave the hot tub you have been soaking in, your body swiftly responds to this situation by lowering the thermostat.

Get enough exercise. Of course I *would* say that. Yet, the research is clear: people who get enough daily exercise sleep better. As mentioned repeatedly throughout this book, exercise naturally regulates metabolism, and this includes the hormonal processes involved in sleep. I.don't usually exercise in the evening, but some people like to take an evening walk, which you may want to try.

Pay attention to pain. This is something which can keep you awake, and even wake you up if it occurs acutely during the night. Take measures to address any physical issues that may be ailing you. You may also want to think about the quality of your mattress, pillow, and bed itself, especially if you wake up with aches and pains first thing in the morning. Firm mattresses tend to be better for your posture during sleep. Quality sleeping materials might be a worthwhile investment.

Time your meals appropriately. Do not go to sleep with a full stomach, but try not to go to bed hungry either. Too much food to digest will take up energy and detract from other sleep-related healing processes, whereas going to bed hungry may trigger survival hormones that tell your body to stay awake so you can go looking for food. You should experiment a little and try to find the sweet spot, which for most people is eating somewhere between two and four hours before bedtime. You may also find that getting this right will help you manage your weight, since improving sleep quality also improves hormone levels that are related to weight gain.

Avoid stimulants and sedatives. The substances we ingest have an effect on our ability to sleep. This includes stimulants such as caffeine, but also sedatives such as alcohol. If you drink too much within a close time frame of going to sleep, the alcohol in your system will seriously affect your ability to go into REM sleep, and therefore block your ability to get the proper restorative sleep necessary to keep the body healthy. Try leaving a few hours between your last drink and your bedtime, and you may notice a big difference.

Ask someone about your snoring. If you are prone to excessive snoring, or tend to wake up in the morning feeling tired and unrefreshed, you might want to further investigate the quality of your sleep. A number of people suffer from a condition—often accompanied by heavy snoring—known as sleep apnea, during which natural breathing is interrupted for short periods, causing gasping or heavy breathing. Over time, the stress this condition puts on your cardiovascular system can cause a range of metabolic complications including heart problems and high blood pressure.

Check your medication. Any medication you are taking could be negatively impacting your sleep patterns, particularly as regards your ability to get enough REM sleep. It's important to note that most sleeping pills, like alcohol, fall into the sedative category, which is very different from natural sleep. Sedatives restrict the type of sleep you are getting, and although they may alleviate conditions such as insomnia, they may also have negative effects in the long term that are on par with partial chronic sleep deprivation.

Beyond this, all strategies are worth a try. It depends on your tastes and preferences. Remember that routine does not merely serve productivity, it can also help you relax and find some internal peace. Try to figure out what makes you feel good, and simply do it every day. Make it a nightly ritual.

15
TOGETHER IS BETTER

Strong, healthy relationships are elixirs of health and can benefit your fitness. Although we live in an era of radical individualism, the fact remains that we are highly susceptible to—and dependent upon—the social environments we live in. Our social life has a very deep effect on everything we are and everything we do. When it comes to leading an active lifestyle, much of my focus has been to appeal to some form of individual agency, because ultimately we all bear responsibility for the choices we make and the lives we lead. Nevertheless, we should not neglect the deep, powerful social dimension at work too. In the face of a challenge, you could sit back, throw your arms up in defeat, and accept inactivity as the norm. Or, you could lean on those you know and love, those you appreciate, and those you meet along the way, to continue onward on your journey to an active lifestyle *together*.

RELATIONSHIPS ARE KEY TO GOOD HEALTH

For as long as I can remember, I have felt it necessary to maintain contact with all kinds of people of all ages. I feel this has a positive influence on my psychology and general wellbeing, in addition to keeping me in touch with the world. I have never found it particularly difficult to maintain a social life, as relationships have always come naturally, but looking back on it now, I do realize that I have always made this something of a priority. I find myself constantly reminded how much of our lives we owe to the companionship, generosity, and mere presence, even, of others in our lives and, as a result of this, of how essential it is to be surrounded by people that we respect and care for.

A now-famous longitudinal study carried out by Harvard Medical School over a period of eighty years, from the late 1930s and early 1940s until today, sought to assess the factors that influence healthy aging and wellbeing. It was able to highlight and, to some degree, quantify the crucial importance of social connection. The Harvard Study of Adult Development, as it is known, followed over 700 men from the Boston area over the course of their lifetime, with regular checkups to monitor their physical and mental health, and perceptions of wellbeing. The results were clear: our relationships directly impact our health. They prevent mental and physical decline and, in this study, they were found to be among the very best predictors of whether someone would lead a happy and healthy life.

Conclusions from the data presented by Dr. George Vaillant, who ran the study between 1972 and 2004, included the observation that while physical health and joyful living themselves depend on a variety of distinct contributing factors, both are needed in tandem in order to age well. Alongside factors such as smoking, which was the greatest killer; alcoholism, which was the cause of much devastation to existing relationships; education levels, which accounted for great differences in behaviors and self-care; and weight, which leads to more non-communicable disease; the importance of deep, healthy, meaningful relationships was at the top of the list. One fascinating detail highlighted by Vaillant is that it doesn't matter so much that people care for you or that you care for them, as whether or not you are able to let those feelings truly land and sink in—he highlights gratitude, forgiveness, the ability to accept compliments, and the ability to receive and deeply feel affection.

As a kid, I was lucky to have plenty of opportunities to hang around my parents' friends, a lot of whom were colleagues or acquaintances of my father. He was a relatively modest pipeline contractor who laid down lines that carried natural gas, crude oil, and water, mostly within the state of California. My parents were solidly in the middle class and although it wasn't a particularly intellectual crowd, it was full of interesting and friendly people. My parents led a very active social life and I guess this got me used to it early on. I was interested in the adults I came across and often got to talk to them extensively, though I suppose now that this was mainly because they were interested in me. I remember the parties held at our home as well as local social events, including an old style dance club that had its own orchestra which my mother was particularly fond of. She loved to dance, and although my father had two left feet, he would put on a tuxedo and stoically go along with it.

These early experiences were positive for me and meant that I became used to being surrounded by others. I had a lot of friends my own age and among older kids, but I also appreciated being around my elders. I learned early that these exchanges could enrich my life. I would listen to their stories and advice, and I still retain fond memories of them to this day. The impact of these stories on my childhood imagination was considerable. I vividly remember my uncle Elmer, with his hoarse laugh and wry smile, who was something of an early hippie and very much a product of the 1930s. He loved animals, the outdoors, fishing, gardening, and basically everything to do with the natural world. He loved the swap meets where people would gather to exchange possessions and stories. Eventually, he became well known locally for the curiosities that he collected in three Quonset huts that he had purchased from the army. He had thousands of oil lamps, hundreds of traps for catching foxes and "vermin" that crept in during the night and killed farm animals, electric wire insulators made of glass, and other knickknacks.

As I grew up, staying social was always relatively easy, and I never had to go too much out of my way to make friends among my peers. As I entered the business world, it became clear that this was an asset, but one which deserves some qualification. Much is said nowadays about the value and necessity of networking, as well as the importance of *who* you know. There is certainly truth to this statement, but it should be said further that the quality of these relationships is what matters most. As a general rule, you cannot build lasting relationships from false premises. Whether inside or outside of a professional environment, most people have a good radar for insincerity and contrivance. You may *know* everyone, but it won't get you anywhere if there's no substance to the relationship. It's important to understand that human interactions require authenticity to be of real value.

It doesn't take much to build some form of connection with people. And even when these relationships remain superficial or are not nurtured over time, they are an important source of learning, experience, and enjoyment—they contribute to making life interesting and full. I am of the opinion that directness and courtesy are essential on some level. You have to be straightforward, coherent, and respectful in the way you treat—and interact with—others. Even within a business relationship, and despite the fact that you may be seeking to further your own interests, you cannot be purely self-serving. This will raise red flags every step of the way, and ultimately it won't get you very far. Opportunities for real, sincere exchanges are everywhere; you just have to be a little open, ready to listen, and able to ask the right questions. Showing good will and good faith will serve you well. Only then can you begin to establish some sense of another person's character and personality, and begin to cultivate some form of meaningful relationship.

As I now find myself squarely in what gerontologist Louise Aronson terms "elderhood," I find that I benefit from surrounding myself with people from all walks of life and all generations. The joys of being around children are immense and will allow you to reexamine your own perspective in light of their youth, the freshness of their perspective, and the wonder they experience on a daily basis. I also find it very rewarding to spend time with adults who are my juniors. This makes for rewarding interactions and allows me to keep abreast of the pace at which society at large is advancing. One way I have found to do this has been to surround myself in my office with young entrepreneurs whom I interact with on a daily basis during my work week. I find these occasional conversations to be stimulating and informative. They keep me privy to the goings on in their world, and I am able to contribute my own two cents as a veteran of the rearguard. While contributing to satisfy my deep curiosity for what's going outside my own spheres of interest and activity, they also contribute to keep me functioning at a decent level of mental acuity.

Even the more casual forms of social interaction that occur in one's day-to-day life can be gratifying and make an important contribution to one's sense of belonging. The street I have my office on, for example, is full of small businesses and bustling with life. There are a number of hairdressers, a funeral parlor, a chocolate shop, a café, a sign maker's store, a butcher's shop, and several other places too. My work weeks are peppered with the small interactions I have with these neighbors. A good sense of humor helps, but I wouldn't say you need to have much chutzpah to engage in conversation, because people are always ready to talk. My barber, who is next door to my office, has a stock one-liner he uses on me when we meet, exclaiming that such long hair doesn't look good on me, and that I should really get a decent barber. There is a good deal of banter, and once and a while we might share a coffee or a drink at the café on the corner, sometimes we might even exchange favors and help each other out, but above all there is a lot of waving as we walk past each other's windows or pass each other on the street. This fluid network of relationships and interactions is deeply pleasing yet does not require much effort or commitment. Over time, it creates an unmistakable sense of community and wellbeing.

THE IMPORTANCE OF FAMILY

Over the years, despite a busy schedule, I have always made it one of my first priorities to spend quality time with my family. As a husband, a father, and now a grandfather, it is hard to understate the importance of maintaining strong links within the family. Claire-Lise and I have just celebrated our fifty-second wedding anniversary, and what a ride it has been. Having children—and grandchildren—and being able to spend time with them is rewarding in itself. Simply being present for the little things that come up at every stage of life is indescribably important. Seeing how children grow and, gradually, outpace us, how life moves on from generation to generation, and how we have to give up our control over their education and development, with the tutelage slowly reversing as they begin to accompany us into old age. It's no wonder we want to be around for longer, live better, and have the affection of our children and grandchildren for as long as possible, for this is truly among life's greatest joys.

I have always tried to strike the balance as best I could between the requirements of my job, and the desire and need I have always had to spend time with my family. That said, I have not always been able to fulfill this aspiration as I would have liked. Starting and building businesses from the ground up, as I have done for much of my life, is an undertaking that requires an enormous commitment. Time, energy, resources, attention, thoughts—everything you have is susceptible to being swallowed up in this process if you are not careful. There was a bad year, for example, when the U.S. dollar dropped like a stone against the Swiss franc. The fact that my company's expenses were in Swiss francs but its income was in dollars almost bankrupted the business overnight. In terms of our financial numbers, it was a disaster, and the only solution was to work harder, and sell more. At that time, I was traveling all over the world, and the Middle-East in particular. I managed to save the business, but because I was gone all the time, my relationships at home took a hit, for sure. Things came back to an even keel after that, but I became very aware of the give-and-take nature of things, and made sure from then on not to live an impossible lifestyle, and do my utmost to give priority to my family. Even after this close call, there have been times when my work required every single spare hour of my time. But during these trying moments I did everything I could to be at home with my children for breakfast in the morning, and there also for evening playtime and dinner, after which I would be back at work until the early hours of the morning.

And then, of course, there were the times when we could all get away as a family. One of the ways we ritualized our time together was through our many family vacations. We didn't have to go far, though we sometimes did travel to exotic destinations—Turkey, Egypt, Japan, Australia, the Philippines, among others—the important thing was that we were together and expanding our horizons by experiencing new places, new activities, new cultures, and so on. Winters, we would—and still do—go to the mountains on the weekends to ski. Over time, this has become something of a ritual, with the grandkids continuing to join us even as they are beginning to come of age. These are invaluable experiences for us as parents and grandparents.

One of the great shared memories we have are the family vacations we used to take in Maine. For many years, we would spend our summers visiting my mother-in-law's family property on the Kennebec River. There was a large house there that had been passed down through several generations and had become a gathering place for the extended family. As a result, there were often six or seven families there at once, all piling into the many rooms of the main house together or into one of the three bungalows built on the property. Where anyone was housed mattered little, however, because the kids were everywhere and they quickly broke down any barriers, making it clear we were all in this together. One great advantage for my wife and myself was getting to better know the parents of the other kids, for although they were relatives, we had few occasions to see them. This was a unique opportunity to socialize and further develop relationships in the midst of this large family spread out over several continents and states.

These vacations in Maine were like being at camp. The place teemed with friends and relatives, and all were delighted to share the experience. Meals were taken together as a kind of free-for-all, and the property was big and remote enough so that we did not have to worry about giving the kids free rein. There was a natural pond on the property that functioned as a swimming hole. We installed a rope swing that hung down from the branch of a tall tree so the kids—and us adults—could launch into the water. We went for hikes up the river, bike rides on the forest trails, there was tree climbing, and an endless succession of games that kept everyone happily busy for days on end. And the fun didn't stop outdoors. Inside the house, the atmosphere was very special because of the number of people, and especially the children that were there. They never missed an opportunity to make the experience interesting. There was a dress-up trunk full of old clothing worn decades earlier by people who had stayed in the house. The girls in particular would instigate dress-up shenanigans, wearing old shoes, women's hats, and scarves of all shapes, sizes, and colors. These sessions were not only hilarious, they were contagious. It didn't take long before the boys were dressing up as well, using the fur-lined topcoats, coattails, and top-hats of bygone generations. No need for music for this carnival, the *oohs* and *aahs* of the parents and the cacophony of the performers were entertainment enough as they paraded around in their historic garb.

The most popular sporting activity was one in which all three generations present could participate in. This was canoeing. Something about canoeing always had a powerful draw on my family. There's something democratic about it. In a canoe, you're all in it together and whatever you do, you have to do it as a unit. Everyone gets a chance to paddle, but you need patience, endurance, strength, and a certain amount of finesse for steering.

If you're on a slow moving river, or a lake, the silence is imposing and offers opportunity for contemplation. It's exciting and you move through scenery you would never see from the road. Most of rural Maine is filled with a river network that flows in and out of lakes, and this is a fantastic way to see the countryside. Many people take their canoes around on the roof of their cars and will spend a day here and there going around a lake or a pond. If you plan it right though, you can go for days and camp along the way without having to use a motorized vehicle. The children learn quickly that their participation is essential and that being unhelpful will reflect poorly on them. They also learn synchronized paddling, which is not an easy skill to pick up, and requires you to tune into the movement of the canoe and its other paddler. It was a bucolic experience, with picnics in the fields, surrounded by cows. To this day, our middle-aged children still talk about the experience.

Some years later, when the children were a bit older, my wife and I held our twenty-fifth wedding anniversary there and invited our friends and family from around the world. People came from Paris, Tokyo, London, and Geneva, and a number of American cities too. They all learned how to canoe, how to do reel dancing, and the fun of charades. We had a great time. A party with good friends and family is hard to beat.

STRENGTH IN NUMBERS

What does all this have to do with exercise? One of the fundamental tricks to successfully adopting an active lifestyle is learning to find pleasure in the process. And yet, all pleasures in life are so much sweeter when shared with those we care for, or whose friendship and company we value. How better to enjoy the moment than to live through it with others that are having the same experience? Sharing these physical experiences is invigorating, and it also is the greatest enhancement of pleasure there can be. It creates a sense of intimacy with people you do not know well, and deepens your connection with—and the affection you have for—those you already know and love. We're hardwired for empathy and deep connections and it doesn't take much to benefit from the effects these have upon our wellbeing. Find others who are already active or find a way to get others interested in joining your efforts, because there's no reason to go at it alone.

Exercising alongside others

Although physical activity may be a struggle, it is not one that we face alone. Everybody needs exercise, and you should find solace and encouragement in the fact that we all face the same uphill struggle. This means there are probably lots of people around you who are also looking for ways to get more active. The need for exercise is deeply human, and this gives all physical activities a highly social dynamic.

Physical activity is much more fun when you're doing it with others. The camaraderie fostered by shared exercise creates strong emotional bonds. Taking on challenges or adventures, facing the highs and lows that come with, and succeeding—these are powerful experiences. Having other people to go through these experiences with makes them all the more interesting and stimulating.

An active lifestyle does not have to be a lonely pursuit. On the contrary, it's the perfect opportunity to get more social. You might try to find members of your family who also are looking to get fit, and try to get them interested in an activity that you can do together. This is a great way to get your exercise while also spending quality time with your loved ones. As I will discuss later in the chapter, committing to exercise with friends will also help keep you committed. You might, for example, want to join a club, or try taking a class of some kind. Remember, anything that gets you moving is good for you! It doesn't have to be a marathon, it can be as simple as a walk in the woods.

Don't be afraid to go further afield, ask your friends if they want to join you. Be creative and don't hesitate to ask around. What you will find is that most people are grappling with similar issues as you are, in one way or another. More likely than not, they will welcome the opportunity to discuss, if not join you to partake in physical activity.

Furthermore, you may want to step out of your comfort zone and try new things or meet new people. You'd be surprised how little it takes to develop a sense of camaraderie with a stranger. It can be as simple as a look exchanged with someone at the right moment in a gym or out on a walk. There's no harm in having short conversations with someone you've never met. Whether it is a conversation in the garden with your neighbors or the chance meeting halfway up the hiking trail, there's no need for you to spend time with people you don't like, but you may just find that there are new friends to be made.

Making new friends

One of the most difficult aspects of living a long life is losing your friends. This is tragic, but inevitable. A true friend is irreplaceable, but as harsh as it might sound to put this down in writing, that's why it's also important to continue to meet new people and make new friends. You're not disrespecting those you have lost, forgetting them, or even replacing them. As human beings, we need the stimulation of social interaction. Even at an advanced age, maintaining a social life should continue to be among our top priorities. The world is full of interesting people, so this really shouldn't be too much of a problem if you are open and curious about others.

One way you can do this is by getting out more and finding places where your peers tend to gather: clubs, associations, and so on. In our own village where we live in Switzerland, there are regular events which are fun and tend to attract new people. Church and other religious gatherings are one option, as are fitness centers, clubs, organizations, and associations of all kinds. Volunteering is another great way to get out and meet people outside your usual circle and walk of life. And if you don't mind going beyond your own generation, I highly recommend cultivating friendships with younger people. You can make these friendships through mutual acquaintances, through your own family's social circles, or out in public. Don't worry about age difference, this tends to matter less and less as you get older.

At time of writing, in the summer of 2020, the lockdown measures taken around the world to control the COVID-19 pandemic have highlighted the seriously deleterious effects that an absence of meaningful social interaction and activity can have both on our physical and mental health. We are social animals and derive a great many benefits merely from being surrounded by others with whom we maintain deep relationships. After the lockdown relaxed here in Switzerland, Claire-Lise and I started to invite friends and couples over, one by one. We have avoided parties and big groups and always meet outside as a precaution. We do feel, however, that maintaining our social life is as important as anything else we do to stay healthy, and by inviting friends over, we are also combating the negative psychological impact of the lockdown mentality that everyone has been experiencing for several months now. I am not questioning the official measures or governmental decisions, but only pointing out that a lack of regular social activity is having a noticeable effect on many people, and I do believe that it is important to try to do what we can to stay positive, healthy, and active—without neglecting hygiene and safety measures. Loneliness is a terrible problem, and there are many people—especially the elderly—who are feeling increasingly isolated. This in itself can increase the risk of infection and disease.

Keeping you accountable

Once you start talking to your friends and family about your efforts to become more active, you begin to make it real in a way that it is not when the project remains inside your head. By talking to those around you, you create expectations in others that you will then experience as a form of reality check. It will keep you honest and working hard to live up to the objectives that you set for yourself. Whether it is on your own or in the company of others—exercise will be much harder to blow off when other people know about it.

Including others into your fitness plans means that you have to show up when and where you say you will. For those days where you have trouble getting yourself off the couch, or you just don't feel like putting on your shoes and leaving the house, it is much easier to stay disciplined if there is another person involved in the effort who is expecting you to show up and with whom you can share the experience and its challenges. There's nothing like the positive reinforcement of others to help you stick with an exercise routine or hold yourself to your commitments.

The social dimension of physical activity does not merely serve to get you going. It can also be very beneficial for your performance. No matter what your level of fitness is, it is likely to benefit from the outside influence of a sporting partner. I, for one, have always found surrounding myself with others that are better than me at whatever sport or activity we're doing will improve my own abilities. When we're around others that have more proficiency and skill, or even fitness, this will tend to positively influence us. In French, we refer to this as the process, literally, of pulling upwards, or *tirer vers le haut.*

You might be one of those, like me, who enjoys the experience of a clear head during a long bike ride or run. If you decide to go at it alone, that's absolutely fine too. Nevertheless, you may still be able to draw some benefit from simply telling someone about your efforts to get active, if not inviting them along. Getting other people involved in our journey into an active lifestyle will reinforce these efforts.

Whether it is telling people about the progress you are making, sharing the challenges that you face and those you have already overcome, relating the adventures that have happened to you along the way, or even simply opening up about your aspirations or motivations, all of these things anchor your efforts in the world and strengthen your commitment to them. You can share your efforts in person, or, you can do so by joining one of the many online communities forming around fitness thanks to the many fitness tracking apps now available on the market. By getting other people involved, you externalize what may otherwise be a mostly personal process, and make it much more likely to become a regular fixture of your life.

The way we identify with others has a significant influence on the way we see ourselves. We sometimes can benefit from verbalizing the things we want to do, and while too much talk can forever delay taking action—I have met a few experts at this in my time—sometimes a little conversation is the perfect catalyst to get started, or it provides the right encouragement to keep going. Similarly, getting even a brief outside view on ourselves is sometimes enough to shift our own perspective. And, finally, there is also the non-negligible issue of self-respect and reputation: no-one wants to feel—or be seen as—unreliable, and by sharing your intentions and aspirations you put pressure on yourself to live up to these claims. Bringing a social dimension to your physical activities can be a powerful motivating force, because it is akin to publicly presenting the version of yourself that you want to become, and this will contribute strongly to turning these aspirations into reality. This in itself can be a game changer.

In any case, we all need a nudge now and then, and it may be that the smartest thing to do is to surround yourself with people willing and able to do the nudging. Ultimately, the need for exercise is a universal challenge that concerns us all. Tapping into this shared predicament is a goldmine for your fitness and your general wellbeing. Exercise can be an enjoyable bonding experience, and this social aspect of exercise can become a powerful motivating force, both for the pleasure it provides and the incentive it generates to keep at it when the going gets tough. There is health, and strength, in numbers—we can only benefit from framing our exercise and adventures in a social context.

16
LIFE GETS US IN THE END

It is hard to accept the eventuality of death, but doing so may positively affect your life. Everything in our being is programmed against the recognition of our own mortality. But the long and short of it is that one day we are all going to die. And what is more, life in this world will go on after we depart. This ought to give us pause. The fact that we are reluctant to face our own finitude does not make it less real. A lack of preparation and foresight does not make the possible effects of one's disappearance less of a problem or in any way diminish the impact on those we leave behind. I want to address this very hard topic head-on, precisely because it is something that people too often suppress from their thoughts and, whether consciously or subconsciously, refrain from acting upon. Many times, this omission persists until it is too late, to the detriment of the people we love most. I want to suggest that preparing for the eventuality of death is the ethical thing to do. You may well find that taking the necessary steps will lift a considerable burden of anxiety off of your shoulders.

A CELEBRATION OF LIFE

I was introduced to the notion of death very early on in my life, and the memory of it remains strong. It was not an accident, or a tragedy, but a calculated move by my grandfather. He had started out as a house painter, but worked his way up in the world. At the time, he was an undertaker in California and for a few months in between moves, my family lived in his big house, which was situated above his funeral parlor. For a period, my older brother Don and I had a brief but intense fascination with the notion of death. We would try to catch a glimpse of the bodies entering the premises in my grandfather's big black Packard custom-built hearse. We also invented a game in that house which we called *playing dead*. This was essentially a somewhat morbid version of hide and seek, but appropriate for a funeral home. Many times we came close to giving my grandmother a heart attack when she discovered us, unmoving and holding our breath, in the closet behind the coats, or underneath the sink. My grandfather got a real kick out of this, but was adamant about keeping his office off limits.

One day, when I was about five years old, he called my brother and me into his office and declared that it was time we saw a dead body. He marched us into the refrigeration room and pulled out a drawer from the wall upon which was laid out a man whose funeral was planned for the next day. The body had been cleaned, embalmed, made up, and dressed for the occasion. He declared that this was a fine man who had "done good" and died happily after a fulfilling life. I lost all mystical apprehension of death from that day. In my mind, death became simply a concrete fact of life. One which I had witnessed, literally, in the flesh. And although I have lived with a keen awareness of what lies in wait for us, I have done so without fear. The approval I felt my grandfather express toward this man who had "done good" has stayed with me throughout my life. Over time, it turned into a desire to meet those standards and do good, whatever that means, just like the man my grandfather had praised on the eve of his funeral. This feeling has been a source of motivation that has kept—and continues to keep—me going, and I try not to waste a single moment of my life worrying about how or when it will end.

Unfortunately, we live in a time when death is mostly neglected and ignored. Out of sight out of mind, as they say. It happens, of course, but for the most part we try to keep it out of our daily lives. It is relegated to the margins of consciousness and or wrapped up in euphemisms. While many among us still have rituals in place to honor the dead in one way or another, death is often considered more of an inconvenience than a tragedy for those not directly affected, not least because it upsets schedules, plans, and the sense of order which our daily lives rely upon. When a death occurs, more often than not, the body of the departed is whisked off and physical contact with it is avoided. I often wonder whether the trauma of not having to confront any material evidence of death is worse than its alternative, and I often think we should probably cultivate a more wholesome approach, which would at least have the benefit of allowing us to prepare both physically and mentally for the inevitable.

I once attended a wake in Ireland for a former colleague of mine, and it was a lively—dare I say, almost a *fun*—affair. All his friends and family were present, and it was very touching. To my surprise, however, the wake began in the man's bedroom, rather than at a funeral parlor. The body had been prepared by a mortician and respects were paid to him by his friends and family as he lay in his own bed. This is also where the service was held by the attending priest. We were then ushered down into the living room where the festivities took place. Here we were sitting around, drinking beer, with everyone sharing their special moments and telling stories, laughing at the jokes my colleague used to tell, as well as those told about him. There was singing, and a good deal of lively tunes played by some wonderful local musicians on fiddle, guitar, accordion, and tin whistle. People would periodically take their leave of the party to pay short visits to the departed who lay upstairs. The hosts heartily encouraged all of us to stay all night. I complied. I remember leaving around dawn as people lingered, some still feasting, drinking, and smoking. This experience remains with me as an uplifting celebration of life rather than merely a lamentation of death. I would venture that this is the way to say goodbye.

BEING MORTAL

Throughout my seventies, as I negotiated a slew of physical challenges that have taken a toll on my fitness and health, I was forced to stop and take stock of my situation. The realization gradually dawned upon me that, although I intend to live as long and as fully as possible, preparing for my death is also of utmost importance. I began asking myself a series of difficult questions, both philosophical and practical. I asked myself what exactly would happen if I disappeared from the face of the earth? What would happen to my family? What would happen if I or my wife were to get sick? What if we were to have an accident and it was serious, or fatal? What do our adult children have as instructions?

Dr. Atul Gawande, whose wonderful book *Being Mortal* I often recommend to friends, speaks in great length about what he perceives as the need to accept death as an inevitable outcome. He advocates in favor of this "act of acceptance," and a reconciliation with the implications it has for your life. Recognizing the emotional, philosophical, and metaphysical dimensions that crop up in the face of one's own mortality is not easy, and it requires us to face some difficult truths. These may include all of those things we've pushed out of our mind either because we didn't know what to do with them, or because we couldn't bring ourselves to do what was necessary at the time. Taking the time to think through these matters, discussing them with one's friends and relatives, seeking counsel from those in a position to help, these are just some of the ways we can kick-start this important psychological process. It can be very therapeutic to try to reconcile one's beliefs, fears, desires, and questions regarding the end of one's life. Forgiveness and reconciliation—with others as well as with yourself—are important elements in this process. And although we may not have the same challenges or needs in the face of death, it is nevertheless a reality that concerns us all. As long as you have time left to live, you have the opportunity to implement changes and make things happen.

I have no intention of going deep into a conversation about religion, but I will mention the fact that I consider myself a moderate Christian. By this I mean that I aspire to the basic moral principles of the Christian tradition, understood in the broadest sense. I take significant metaphysical comfort in my faith, which has also helped guide my decision-making in the face of these difficult questions concerning the end of one's life. That said, the polarization surrounding the religious question today requires me to state further that I am critical of the blind dogmatism rampant in some circles. My faith does not prevent me from otherwise taking a thoroughly empirical and scientific orientation in life. Furthermore, I hold the highest regard for the political tradition of secular government prevalent in the West and despite my Christian beliefs, firmly believe in the importance of separating the realms of church and state.

The main reason I am addressing, if only summarily, the question of my faith here is that I trace to it my conviction that we have an ethical duty to give back to the world. Whether it is out of affection or gratitude, or a sense of civic responsibility, I have always been taken by the question of what our obligations are to society, community, friends, and family. When we've had the benefit of living a good life, marked by successes that, while brought about in part by hard work, *savoir-faire* and diligence, are also largely due to fate and circumstance, is it not our obligation to share this bounty with others? I believe these questions ultimately deserve much closer attention than I can give here. Nevertheless, it is my observation that we have such duties, and in my case I feel indebted to all those listed above for their contributions in enabling my journey through life.

My reasoning goes as follows: it is one thing to posit the idea of this kind of social responsibility in the abstract, and it is another to take action upon it. Whenever I get caught up in the dilemmas of the former, I keep my rudder oriented toward how I can come to a resolution that satisfies the latter. I am and have always been a doer, and at some point you have to make a decision, decide to the best of your ability what is the appropriate action, and put things in motion to simply get it done.

WHERE THERE'S A WILL

As I pondered these questions with increasing frequency and intensity, I realized that even though I had left a one-page will, I had not organized my business interests to make it easy for the people I would be leaving behind. I also had not restructured my affairs in a way that would satisfy my desire to give back to society. I strongly felt there was a cluster of issues nagging at me that I needed to resolve in order to find some kind of interior peace and tranquility. I decided to make a plan. To do so, I needed some time for solitude and reflection during which I could turn everything over in my mind. What I needed was a chance to think through all the variables, draw up a detailed list of outstanding problems and tasks, and decide upon the best ways to complete them. It was only natural for me to gravitate towards cycling as a way of creating the necessary time and headspace. After some deliberation, I chose to complete the Compostela pilgrimage route—known in English as the Way of St. James—a trip that I had been drawn to because of its spiritual and historical significance, its appeal as a physical adventure, its exercise value, and its natural beauty. The route would take me from Geneva, Switzerland, to Santiago de Compostela in Galicia, Spain. Whereas most people complete the journey on foot, something about being on the road with my bicycle has always been a great source of calm and has provided me with the perfect opportunity for peaceful contemplation and undisturbed thought.

When a person dies without putting their affairs in order, those affected by their death often face a series of ordeals as a consequence. The practical steps that need to be taken after a person's passing are often relegated to third parties, with varying levels of success. Not infrequently, there is a fair amount of grief and turmoil that could otherwise be avoided. Hard as it may be to face the idea of our disappearing, there are important steps we can take to better prepare, both in terms of how we live with the thought and with regards to how those around us will be affected by our death. As I have said, it is the ethical thing to do, and can also bring great peace of mind. My belief is that by recognizing and planning for death, an event which is unforeseeable yet inevitable, we can minimize its negative effects on our family and friends and, by extension, better enjoy and profit from the time we have left.

One crucial issue that many of us shy away from addressing is what we want done if, due to accident or illness, we lose our autonomy and decision-making abilities. This is, unfortunately, a relatively common scenario, forcing family members to make heart-wrenching life-or-death decisions on behalf of loved ones who are no longer able to communicate or, even, survive unassisted. Many doctors advise older patients who are starting to show signs of physical or mental decline to write out instructions for their children if they become *non compos mentis* or lose their ability to speak. Should that happen, the family member or friend with legal decision-making power will have to urgently answer a number of questions, often with considerable distress. Should the person be kept alive on a ventilator? If not, are they willing to donate their organs? Putting these issues on the table can be painful, but any discomfort you may experience in discussing them with your loved ones pales in comparison to the agony of a family member having to make these decisions alone and without any clear idea of your desires.

Very often, we fail to anticipate all the problems that will arise after our passing. Writing a will goes a long way toward simplifying all decisions concerning what ought to happen to one's possessions and assets after death, and ensuring this happens in an equitable manner, with minimal conflict. What does the family keep and what do they sell to improve their financial position? What about any paintings, jewelry, tableware, artwork, books, clothes, and other prized possessions you may have accumulated over time? What objects have sentimental value for your children and what would they want to hold on to? These questions can range from the highly problematic to the merely tedious. The very notion of dealing with these issues creates discomfort in many people's minds, but it is essential that you pluck up courage and sort them out. To some, this may appear terribly materialistic. To them I would say that this is also an opportunity both to deepen their emotional bond with their heirs and to prepare themselves psychologically for the inevitable.

I myself have been the executor for four different estates, none of which had instructions like those I describe above. I am convinced that this is because most of us have an ingrained psychological aversion to confront the possibility of our dying. The role of the executor is to take responsibility for fairly distributing assets and belongs after a person's death. The executor is often a lawyer, a notary, a relative, or a trusted business associate. In one particular case, a friend of mine chose me as his executor because, I suppose, he believed no one else would take the succession issue as seriously as me. I have no idea how he arrived at this conclusion, but I accepted. I made the mistake, however, of not asking him to prepare the appropriate papers and directions. When he passed, I asked his wife for his will. She did not know anything about it, or even whether he had one. We went into his safe deposit box and found nothing useful for the task I had been assigned. After working through all the papers we could find, I was able to pull together bank statements and enough information to officiate the succession. But the lack of any instructions made it hard work. His children were dismayed, but luckily they accepted the authority their father had invested in me, and in the end we were able to execute a fair and equal distribution of his assets. Things went well given the circumstances, and I suppose everyone was grateful for this, myself included. It wasn't easy though, not by a long shot.

It would not be right to discuss this situation in greater detail here, but based on my experience, I would like to strongly urge anyone at risk of creating a similar situation to take stock and consider the broader implications. The process of managing an unplanned succession can be a difficult, painful endeavor. Not taking the time to formulate your wishes and instructions in writing creates a vacuum of intent and the burden of decision is transferred onto others. Those who see themselves invested with power of executor, as well as the natural beneficiaries, may end up having to expend a great deal of energy, make imperfect decisions, and may even sometimes end up fighting bitterly over who gets what, and over what to do with the estate. Depending on the country you live in, if no will exists, a notary or judge may even step in and decide how the inheritance should be distributed, according to his or her own interpretation of the law.

Ultimately, it is my belief that much confusion, frustration, and even conflict can be avoided with a few simple provisions. Take the time to write down your wishes in a will. Clearly state what you would like to happen with your belongings and assets, and also touch upon the topic of your own person and what should be done in the case that medical decisions have to be made on your behalf. Don't be afraid to specify whether you would like to be put on life support, or whether you would prefer such measures be avoided, should the day come. Make sure this document is kept somewhere safe and that your family members and executors know about it. You might, for example, consider leaving it with a notary or lawyer. These few simple measures could make what is already a painful situation much less likely to cause unnecessary grief and conflict.

PEACE OF MIND

I spent many hours mulling over the question of how best to prepare for my eventual death as I cycled the Compostela trail in three stages, one every summer over three consecutive years. This time of contemplation on the road for me was, somewhat paradoxically, a deeply life-affirming event. It's a long trip, and a feat to accomplish at any age—exactly my kind of challenge. In addition, it would be both a head-clearing experience and a very focused exercise in pragmatic decision-making. As a general rule, I have found that establishing clear paths of action is the best way for me to create meaning both in my life and in the world around me. In this case, I needed to look hard, ruthlessly even, at the past in order to discern the direction I wanted to take for the future. I questioned everything and listed all the things I didn't need in my life anymore, as well as many of the things I was lacking, and those things I still wanted to do or make happen. The writing process I adopted during this trip helped me organize things with surprising clarity and efficiency. I successively went through the stages of noting down first my reflections, then the alternatives I figured were available, followed by working hypotheses and, finally, what decisions I could settle upon.

I decided, for example, that owning companies with many employees and far-flung locations—which requires lots of travel—was becoming an untenable situation. If anything happened to me, little to no instructions were available to anyone among my family, friends, or colleagues on how to take over or operate any of the businesses, and the outcomes in such a scenario would be left largely to chance and accident. Thus, I set out to sell various assets, a process which took the better part of two years. It was also clear that of all my priorities, my responsibility to my family was at the very top of the list. I resolved to spend as much time as possible with them and to make sure I would not burden them after my death. The bigger picture was also brought into better focus. I reevaluated priorities, decided how I wanted to attribute my time, attention, and resources. I established a strategy to bring a new order into my affairs, slim down my business responsibilities, redesign my schedule and occupations, and establish the details of my succession. The decisions I took during that journey have been foundational for what has become a whole new chapter of my life.

The preparation of a will need not happen by decree. It can be the object of a discussion. I thus made a point of meeting with my family to talk through the relevant details and procedures, make them aware of the various options before I moved forward, and discuss any issues that might arise. Soliciting the opinions of your family members and friends can be very helpful and also gives you the opportunity to take into consideration their desires and concerns. Not only will it avoid conflicts of interest, which often spill into the legal domain when beneficiaries cannot agree, but it also can be a chance to come together as a family. When I met with my wife and children to discuss these matters, we also concluded a pact that spelled out what would happen in the eventuality that either my wife or myself get sick, suffer a major accident, or become in any way incapacitated to the point where our ability to make decisions or express ourselves is compromised. We decided which of our children would be legally responsible for taking any medical decisions on our behalf in such a case, and put it all down in writing with everyone's consent.

Few people want to take the time to properly think through and take action to prepare for the time when they are no longer there. While it's true that there are more enjoyable things to occupy your thoughts with, the bottom line is that it's important to do so, for two reasons. First, it will save your loved ones a lot of trouble, both emotional and administrative. Second, it may go a long way toward improving your wellbeing during the remaining years of life––I, for one, have found it a surprisingly rewarding experience. Facing the eventuality of one's death does not mean checking out. On the contrary, in my case, I am still very much alive, working on projects that are important to me, spending time with friends and family, and planning my next adventure.

Life gets us in the end, and that is unavoidable, but it has given me considerable satisfaction and peace of mind to know that I've done my due diligence, so to speak. There is enough to worry about with all that is not within our control. It feels good, therefore, to create order for those things that are. The main outcome of my resolutions was to create an action plan that I have, since then, been working to implement. These resolutions have implications not only for the distant future which I will not be around for, but for the foreseeable future too, during which I intend to continue living my life to the fullest.

Epilogue
THERE IS ALWAYS A WAY

M y age does not prevent me from doing, it enables my doing. Things take a little more time for me than they once did, and I don't try to fool myself into thinking that I am as strong, agile, or physically fit as I was in my youth. Nevertheless, I still take just as much, if not more, pleasure in the experience of being active as I did when I was younger, and I feel the need to continue making my way forward. It doesn't matter whether you are winning or losing, you won't be able to change the future unless you are able to accept things as they are and work from there. "No excuses," is what my father always used to say to me. And this lesson has served me well.

As I wait out the current COVID-19 pandemic, I am working myself back into shape with local bike rides so I can undertake the final leg of my Compostela journey. So far, I have completed two thirds of the way, and will begin again from Roncevalles, just inside the northern border of Spain, for the final, most historic stretch of the trail. I was prevented from doing this earlier due to the shoulder injury I suffered in 2019, which kept me off my bicycle for several months. Now that I am on the mend and able to ride again, however, my hope is to be back on the road as soon as possible. Despite the magnitude of the challenge, and the occasional protest from concerned friends or relatives, the truth is that I can't wait to get going again.

The pilgrim's trail I have been following in stages over several years ends in Santiago de Compostela, capital of the Galicia region in northwestern Spain. Throughout the centuries, the constant popularity of this historic pilgrimage led to the development of a thriving network of trails that reach far and wide across Europe before connecting to the original routes down from France and across northern Spain. Depending on where you are traveling from, there are now hundreds of ways you can reach the city built in honor of the apostle James, whose remains are said to have been discovered at the location where the cathedral now stands. There are official itineraries from Amsterdam, Arthus, Gdansk, Budapest, Zagreb, and Bari, to name but a few, some stretching for several thousand kilometers as they wind their way to Santiago. The route I am following is about 2,300 kilometers long, and even though I split it into three parts, that still means riding for close to 800 kilometers at a time. The itinerary in question is an overlap of the Compostela route and the French Grande Randonnée trail number 65, or GR65, and is part of a trans-European network of long-distance hiking trails.

Also known as the *Via Gebennensis*, or *Chemin de Genève*, the GR65 leads travelers from Germany, Austria, and Central Europe through Switzerland and on to Le Puy-en-Velay in southern France, a picturesque medieval town perched atop volcanic rocks, which is a historic gateway to the Compostela trail and a famous stopover for weary pilgrims. Following the GR65, I left Geneva and rode along the Rhône River into France, which winds between the pre-alpine Vuache hills and the Jura mountains via Frangy, just south of Bellegarde. From there, the trail leads down through the Savoie through deep gorges dug out by the Rhône, before turning west at the Lac de Bourget as the river meanders up and around towards the city of Lyon. At Condrieu, a small region famous for its excellent Viognier wine and where I shared a bottle with fellow travelers during my stay overnight, the GR65 crosses the Rhône again, heading southwest this time, towards the Loire River. This stretch of the journey traverses the Massif Central mountain range, in central France, a region full of eerily evocative abandoned villages and mills from the early era of industrialization, and finishes in the high plateaux of the Haute-Loire department.

From Le Puy-en-Velay, the trail continues on what is known as the *Via Podensis* through the mountainous terrain of the Lozère region, and crosses three rivers—the Allier, the Truyère, and the Bès—before dipping in and out of the limestone valley of the river Lot and heading west. Cahors, Condom, Aire-sur-l'Adour, Mourenx, Saint-Jean-Pied-de-Port—you pass through all of these medieval towns on your way to the Spanish border, and each is more magnificent than the last. After several days of riding—or walking, for most pilgrims—with nothing to do but go forward, you almost feel as though you are moving not only across the country but back through time as well. When I saw my first Romanesque church on the river Rhône, it was a real thrill. Every church you pass thereafter compounds the effect. These medieval places of worship are like little jewels, lovingly maintained and restored over the centuries, but seemingly untouched by time. There is a magical sense of being almost able to touch history when you follow this ancient road. You find your thoughts wandering back to all the people who have followed the same trail since the Middle Ages, criss-crossing the French countryside, in and out of these old, walled cities that are still standing today. And you cross paths with other travelers who have their own stories and reasons for embarking on this journey, some of which you may share. In my experience, you could sum it up by saying that there are those looking for redemption or new beginnings, those seeking to pay their respects or fulfill a religious duty, and those who are simply looking for an adventure. As I reflect on the experience today, I can relate to something in all of these motivations.

During all the twenty-two bike tours I participated in over the years, I was the one in charge of organizing and taking care of everybody. I set up the itinerary and the logistics, served as translator, and dealt with any glitches along the way. If anyone wanted or needed anything, if there was an issue to negotiate with a driver or hotel, I was the one taking care of things, and making it happen on behalf of the group. I took pleasure in this responsibility, and saw myself as more of a facilitator and an ambassador than a leader. Everyone else was happy with the arrangement, so it all worked out for the best. The Compostela trail marked a departure for me: this was the first time I embarked on such a journey alone. Setting out with only my bike and what I could carry upon it was a very different feeling. For the first time, I was unburdened by anyone else's problems and free to reflect on life in general and on the questions I had about my future and that of my family. I was able to contemplate my situation, and all the potential outcomes. As I have said, this is not an easy task, but one which can nevertheless bring great peace of mind. This, at least, has been my experience. Whatever the unknowns are that hang over our head, it is worth facing up to them, and figuring out what—if anything—can be done to prepare.

At the end of the day, my philosophy is pretty straightforward. I am drawn to the nuts and bolts of solving problems in the real world, and I happen to be good at finding new problems to solve along the way. This has been my *modus operandi* through the years, and it continues to be what I am drawn to, even in my elderhood. As I rode along the Compostela trail, I spent a good portion of my time thinking about the future, about how to reorient myself in life, and how to plan my succession and related affairs. This also meant thinking about how I would prefer to be spending my time, which implied making concrete changes in the present moment. The hidden benefit for me of planning for tomorrow, in other words, was that it helped me anchor my purpose for today.

This kind of concrete problem-solving has always been a stimulating and intellectually demanding exercise from which I can gain a lot of satisfaction. It is at the core of what it means to be in business, it's how I've dealt with the setbacks—be they business or health related—that have occurred in my life, and it is pretty much the only way I know how to act, no matter what situation lies ahead of me. More than just a way of coping, however, it is my way of facing what is ahead and meeting every new day with enthusiasm and gusto. Whenever I feel like I am standing still, I find a way to articulate a new project. It can be a new business, a trek, a bike ride, or a family reunion. This, to me, seems essential. It is a source of vitality and much-needed energy. It is my way of avoiding complacency, and I am a firm believer in the need for action, even if it means making mistakes. There will always be risk involved, but that only means that we need to evaluate the risk and figure out how to mitigate it. Once you have done that, it's time to make a decision and act. We may make mistakes, but as long as we learn from them, we keep moving forward.

Some people are able to withdraw to a mountain cabin to meditate in isolation and reflect on their lives. This just isn't me. I would be incapable of staying put. I need to be active and on the move. That is my safe haven, my way of retreating within myself to think and collect myself, even as I am covering large distances and happily expending energy every day. The challenge of a journey such as the Compostela trail is mental and physical, but also logistic. You need to be able to eat, sleep, and—in my case—manage your bicycle and gear. A typical day for me on the road usually involves waking up at 6:30 a.m. in a bed and breakfast or small hotel and doing my normal exercise routine to loosen up. I have a good breakfast of muesli, fresh fruit, as well as a croissant. Usually, I will also have a chat with the innkeeper or host to find out what's going on in the area and glean any useful tips that might help orient me on the road. I then fill my water bottles, check my gear, which consists mainly of a small toolbox for the bike and two spare inner tubes, load up my saddle bags, and be on my way. For the first few minutes, I have to take it a little slower to give my body time to adapt, but after three or four kilometers I begin to feel warmed up, and I naturally slip into a steady rhythm. I rarely book accommodation ahead of time in order to have the flexibility to go longer, or stop off earlier if I feel like it. This adds an element of uncertainty, and although I have occasionally struggled to find a place to stay, it also means I am free to go at my own pace.

Most of the day plots out along the actual trail, which is meant mostly for hikers, meaning it gets pretty rough in certain spots. I can manage this because I ride a hybrid bike that is versatile enough to take on rugged, mountainous terrain, yet slick and light enough to be easy to handle on the road. I carry a map to stay oriented and will sometimes take a detour if there are sights worth seeing. I might climb a hill or cycle a little off the trail to visit a nearby town. Having the possibility to do this at a relatively low cost, energetically speaking, is another great advantage of being on a bicycle. Lunch is usually light so it doesn't slow me down, and in the evening I try to eat a big meal. I do my washing after dinner, and while it doesn't always dry, this is not usually a problem. I'm happy to be in the company of any pilgrims that are around, and I have met many interesting people along the way. I take a moment in the evening to check my emails, messages, and calls, since I leave my phone in the bag throughout the day. I also spend about an hour writing down all my reflections in a notebook. Sleeping conditions are usually good along the trail, though often very rudimentary, and I always carry a lightweight linen sleeping bag with me as a precaution against the presence of bedbugs, which I've come across before.

Riding a bicycle is the perfect way to travel in my opinion. It is about five times faster than walking, so you cover that much more ground, but it is still a lot slower than a car, so you have time to observe and really let the scenery sink in, which creates a feeling of connection with the environment. For these reasons and more, I've always loved long bike trips. One of the chief features for me is the thrill of confronting and moving through the unknown. The sensation of being on the move and in full control of your speed and your exertions, makes you feel fully alive. Once the planning and logistics are in place and you set out propelled only by the motor force of your pedaling and the spinning of the wheels, it's just you, the road, and the landscape you are moving through. You embark on these journeys as you would on an adventure, a voyage of discovery. Covering long distances on a bike is a feeling like none other. Maybe it's the increase in oxygenation from the sustained effort, the stimulation from the increase in blood flow to muscles, brain, and cells throughout my body, but whatever it is, the rhythm I get into is somehow relaxing rather than tiring. Even when I am on the road for up to nine hours every day.

Much of the time, I find myself slipping into a state of flow, and I sometimes feel as though I am gliding along in a sort of bubble. There is something about cycling, especially over long periods and distances, which has mind-cleansing qualities. Your perceptions change and slow down, you get into what I might call a second state, in which you are both very focused and very free. You are not easily provoked or disturbed by anything coming from outside or inside yourself, whether problems to solve or obstacles to avoid. It's a wonderful feeling. You become like a metronome, and with your legs going pretty much at a regular rate, it's almost as if you are asleep on the bike. You might do 20 or 30 kilometers on the same trail and you're observing everything, taking in the scenery, having thoughts about what your body perceives and senses, but only halfway, as if consciousness were taking a back seat to the experience. Everything is aligned and you feel good about yourself, the world, life, pretty much everything, really. There are no errant thoughts, no nagging feelings of dissatisfaction or urges to have anything be different, you simply feel at peace. From what I have read and heard about meditation from friends who practice it, I would compare the experience to a meditative state.

There is an auditory component as well: the sound of the wind as you are going at between 22 and 26 kilometers per hour has a hypnotic quality, and I find myself drawing a comparison to the stories about ashrams in India where they chant mantras and make use of droning sounds that have a physical effect upon the human body. There is a visual component, where you witness the scenery, but with a certain amount of detachment. You might be observing a beautiful forest and marvel at the intricacy of these ecological systems, their historical timespan—all the while, your mind takes it in but without dwelling on it. You might go over an old bridge made of stone, and you wonder in what century it was built, but there's no sign around, so you simply register the fact that it is probably several hundred years old, still standing and being used every day by large trucks that rumble precariously across it. These thoughts flit in and out of your mind, and while they do not have any real function——it's not like you're going to do anything with them——they produce a lasting feeling of wellbeing that is in deep contrast with the stressful hustle of everyday life, with all its requirements and interruptions. Your mind wanders, and you are in a state where this is exactly what it needs to be doing. Your mind and body are alive with activity and working together, but problem solving comes later. For now, in the moment, for as long as it lasts, it is therapeutic. These episodes leave a memorable imprint that accompanies you daily, even months after the fact.

Our relation to physical activity changes throughout life, just as we change too. From the time I defied my doctor's orders to stay off my feet at age fourteen, to the pursuit of high-altitude summit climbs and long-distance trips on a bicycle, to simply making sure that I do my exercises every morning, physically demanding activities have always been a source of pleasure, adventure, stability, strength, and inspiration for me. Most importantly, exercise has always been one of my most fundamental sources of vitality. As I see it, the essential question is not how long I have left to live, so much as how well I am able to live in the time I have left. There will always be doubt about our projected outcomes and our ability to succeed. Sometimes we meet our objectives, and sometimes we don't. We get delayed, waylaid, and the possibility of failure is always looming somewhere around the corner. Sometimes, we may have to quit. But we cannot take this as a reason not to try. We cannot afford to stay on the bench as life goes on around us. Ultimately, what we do doesn't matter so much as the fact that we actually *do* it.

We all tell ourselves stories, and have our own complex reasons for taking *this* path, or *that* path. Some strategies work better than others, just as some paths are more fruitful than others. It's all part of the process, and everything about these efforts is what makes life beautiful, interesting, and worth living. Behind all of this, however, is the same simple, elegant, undeniable imperative—we need to keep *doing*. All it takes is turning that little switch in your mind on—that little *click* that signals your decision to start up again. If nothing else, I hope this message will come across loud and clear. No matter what you may have come to believe, it is still possible for you to move beyond your age and develop your fitness. Despite the heavy breathing you may be in for when you get that heart of yours pumping again, despite the exhaustion and disillusionment that may arise when you realize how far your *real* fitness level is from what you thought it was, we all have the capacity within ourselves not only to get active and healthy again, but to find enjoyment as we do so. Whether it is doing more of the things you find the most pleasure in, learning new activities, making new friends, or simply carrying out those tasks you decide *have* to get done, there is always a way. Sometimes this way will be hard, sometimes it will be fun, but it will always be necessary.

REFERENCES

FURTHER READING

Aronson, Louise. *Elderhood: Redefining Age, Transforming Medicine, Reimagining Life*. BloomsburyPublishing, 2019.

Gawande, Atul. *Being Mortal: Medicine and What Matters in the End*. Picador, 2017.

James Levine, James A. *Get up! Why Your Chair Is Killing You and What You Can Do about It*. St. Martin's, 2014.

Lyon, Daniel. *The Complete Book of Pilates for Men*. Harper Collins, 2005.

Ornish, Dean. *UnDo It! How Simple Lifestyle Changes Can Reverse Most Chronic Diseases*. Ballantine Books, 2019.

Walker, Matthew P. *Why We Sleep: The New Science of Sleep and Dreams*. Penguin Books, 2018.

CHAPTER 1: LIFESTYLE PREVENTS DISEASE

Buttroff, Christine, et al. "Multiple Chronic Conditions in the United States." *RAND Corporation*, 2017, https://www.rand.org/pubs/tools/TL221.html.

Global Cancer Data by Country. World Cancer Research Fund, 2018, World Cancer Research Fund, https://www.wcrf.org/dietandcancer/cancer-trends/data-cancer-frequency-country.

Johnson, Johanna L., et al. "Ten-Year Legacy Effects of Three Eight-Month Exercise Training Programs on Cardiometabolic Health Parameters." *Frontiers in Physiology*, vol. 10, no. 452, 16 April 2019, www.frontiersin.org/articles/10.3389/fphys.2019.00452/full.

Key Findings from the Global Burden of Disease Study 2017. Institute for Health Metrics and Evaluation, 2018, http://www.healthdata.org/sites/default/files/files/policy_report/2019/GBD_2017_Booklet.pdf.

Key Findings of the World Population Prospects 2019. United Nations Department of Economic and Social Affairs, June 2019, https://population.un.org/wpp/Publications/Files/WPP2019_10Key Findings.pdf.

"NCD Countdown 2030: Worldwide Trends in Non-Communicable Disease Mortality and Progress Towards Sustainable Development Goal Target 3.4" *Health Policy,* vol. 392, no. 10152, 22 September 2018, https://www.thelancet.com/pdfs/journals/lancet/PII S0140-6736(18)31992-5.pdf.

Pratt, Michael, et al. "The Cost of Physical Inactivity: Moving Into the 21st Century." *British Journal of Sports Medicine*, vol. 48, no. 3, 2014, https://bjsm.bmj.com/content/48/3/171.

Reynolds, Gretchen. "10 Years After an Exercise Study, Benefits Persist." *The New York Times.* 19 April 2019, https://www.nytimes.com/2019/04/17/well/move/10-years-after-an-exercise-study-benefits-ersist.html.

Rosser, Max, and Hannah Ritchie. "Cancer." *Our World in Data*, November 2019, https://ourworldindata.org/cancer.

CHAPTER 3: AGE IS RELATIVE

Christinaz, Caroline. "Marcel Remy, patriarche des cimes." *Le Temps*, 19 February 2018,https://www.letemps.ch/societe/marcel-remy-patriarche-cimes

"Diabetes." *World Health Organization*, 8 June 2020, https://www.who.int/news-room/fact-sheets/detail/diabetes.

Gisi, Christian. *Marcel Remey - 94 Years Old and Back to the Summit*. MAMMUT, 31 March 2020, https://www.youtube.com/watch?v=sqnDztcwKLc.

"Non-Communicable Diseases." *World Health Organization*, 1 June 2018, https://www.who.int/news-room/fact-sheets/detail/noncommunicable-diseases.

CHAPTER 4: ACTIVITY IS EVERYWHERE

Levine, James A. "Non-Exercise Activity Thermogenesis (NEAT)." *Best Practice & Research Clinical Endocrinology & Metabolism*, vol. 16, no. 4, December 2002, pp. 679 - 702, https://doi.org/10.1053/beem.2002.0227.

"Mayo Clinic Discovers a Key to 'Low Metabolism' – and Major Factor in Obesity." *ScienceDaily*, 31 January 2005, https://www.sciencedaily.com/releases/2005/01/050128224400.htm.

CHAPTER 5: EXERCISE IS INDISPENSABLE

Our need for exercise

"Physical Activity Factsheet for the 28 European Union Member States of the WHO European Region. Overview 2018." *World Health Organization*, 2018, http://www.euro.who.int/en/health-topics/disease-prevention/physical-activity/data-and-statistics/physical-activity-fact-sheets/factsheets-on-health-enhancing-physical-activity-in-the-28-eu-member-states-of-the-who-european-region.

"Physical Inactivity a Leading Cause of Disease and Disability, Warns WHO." *World Health Organization*, 4 April 2002, https://www.who.int/mediacentre/news/releases/release23/en/.

"Regular Exercise Reduces Large Number of Health Risks
    Including Dementia and Some Cancers, Study Finds."
    ScienceDaily, 16 November 2010, www.sciencedaily.com/
    releases/2010/11/101115074040.htm.

Shaw, Jonathan. "The Deadliest Sin." *Harvard Magazine*, March
    2004,https://harvardmagazine.com/2004/03/the-power-of-
    exercise.

Exercise guidelines
"Key Facts on Physical Activity." *World Health Organization*, 23
    February 2018, https://www.who.int/news-room/fact-sheets/
    detail/physical-activity.

Strength training and sarcopenia
Santilli, Valter, et al. "Clinical Definition of Sarcopenia." *Clinical Cases in
    Mineral and Bone Metabolism*, vol. 11, no. 3, 3 September 2014,
    https://www.ncbi.nlm.nih.gov/pmc/articles/PMC4269139/.

Volpi, Elena, et al. "Muscle Tissue Changes with Aging." *Current
    Opinion in Clinical Nutrition and Metabolic Care*, vol. 7, no.
    4, July 2004, https://www.ncbi.nlm.nih.gov/pmc/articles/
    PMC2804956/#:~:text=One%20of%20the%20most%20
    striking,60%20%5B4%2C5%5D.

Westcott, Wayne L. "Resistance Training Is Medicine: Effects of Strength
    Training on Health." *Current Sports Medicine Reports*, vol.
    11, no. 4, July 2012, https://journals.lww.com/acsm-csmr/
    fulltext/2012/07000/resistance_training_is_medicine___
    effects_of.13.aspx#:~:text=Resistance%20trainig%20may%20
    promote%20bone,aging%20factors%20in%20skeletal%20
    muscle.

Lung capacity
"Oxygen Consumption - VO2." *Sports Medicine Program*, University
    of California Davis, 2020, https://health.ucdavis.edu/
    sportsmedicine/resources/vo2description.html.

"Your Lungs and Exercise." *Breathe*, vol. 12, 2016, https://breathe.
    ersjournals.com/content/12/1/97.

Cardiovascular effects of exercise

"Exercise and Your Arteries." *Harvard Health Men's Watch*, Harvard Health Publishing, 21 June 2019, https://www.health.harvard.edu/heart-health/exercise-and-your-arteries.

"The Many Ways Exercise Helps Your Heart." *Harvard Heart Letter*, Harvard Health Publishing, March 2018, https://www.health.harvard.edu/heart-health/the-many-ways-exercise-helps-your-heart.

Hormonal effects of exercise

"Cardio Exercise and Strength Training Affect Hormones Differently." *ScienceDaily*, 24 August 2018, www.sciencedaily.com/releases/2018/08/180824101138.htm.

"Exercising to Relax." *Harvard Health Men's Watch*, Harvard Health Publishing, 07 July 2020, https://www.health.harvard.edu/staying-healthy/exercising-to-relax.

Cellular effects of exercise

Reynolds, Gretchen. "How Exercise Changes Our DNA." *The New York Times*, 17 December 2014, https://well.blogs.nytimes.com/2014/12/17/how-exercise-changes-our-dna.

Sandoiu, Ana. "How Exercise Rejuvenates Cells, Extending Lifespan." *Medical News Today*, 25 September 2017,https://www.medicalnewstoday.com/articles/319532#:~:text=According%20to%20the%20new%20study,food%20we%20eat%20into%20energy.

Effects of exercise on bones

"Facts and Statistics." *International Osteoporosis Foundation*, 2017, https://www.iofbonehealth.org/facts-statistics.

Effects on the brain

Chekroud, Sammi R., et al. "Association Between Physical Exercise and Mental Health in 1·2 million Individuals in the USA Between 2011 and 2015: A Cross-Sectional Study." *THE LANCET Psychiatry*, vol. 5, no. 9, 1 September 2018, https://www.thelancet.com/journals/lanpsy/article/PIIS2215-0366(18)30227-X/fulltext.

Gingell, Sarah. "How Your Mental Health Reaps the Benefits of Exercise." *Psychology Today*, 22 March 2018, https://www.psychologytoday.com/us/blog/what-works-and-why/201803/how-your-mental-health-reaps-the-benefits-exercise.

Godman, Heidi. "Regular Exercise Changes the Brain to Improve Memory, Thinking Skills." *Harvard Health Blog*, Harvard Health Publishing, 09 April 2014, https://www.health.harvard.edu/blog/regular-exercise-changes-brain-improve-memory-thinking-skills-201404097110.

"Physical Exercise and Dementia." *Alzheimer's Society*, 2020, https://www.alzheimers.org.uk/about-dementia/risk-factors-and-prevention/physical-exercise.

The U-curve of exercise benefits

Merghani, Ahmed, et al. "The U-Shaped Relationship Between Exercise and Cardiac Morbidity." *Trends in Cardiovascular Medicine*, vol. 26, no. 3, 2015, https://www.researchgate.net/publication/280135702_The_U-shaped_relationship_between_exercise_and_cardiac_morbidity.

Simon, Harvey B. "Exercise and Health: Dose and Response, Considering Both Ends of the Curve." *The American Journal of Medicine*, vol. 128, no. 11, 29 May 2015, https://www.amjmed.com/article/S0002-9343(15)00455-6/fulltext.

6: A WORKOUT WILL MAKE YOUR DAY

"Physical Activity Guidelines for Americans." U.S. Department of Health and Human Services, 20 January 2020, https://health.gov/our-work/physical-activity/current-guidelines.

"Physical Activity Guidelines for Older Adults." UK National Health Service, 8 October 2019, https://www.nhs.uk/live-well/exercise/physical-activity-guidelines-older-adults/.

"The 4 Mmost Important Types of Exercise." Harvard Health Letter, Harvard Health Publishing, 20 August 2019, https://www.health.harvard.edu/exercise-and-fitness/the-4-most-important-types-of-exercise.

8: SITTING IS THE ENEMY

Dunstan, D.W., et al. "Television Viewing Time and Mortality." Circulation, vol.121, no. 3, 11 January 2010, https://www.ahajournals.org/doi/10.1161/CIRCULATIONAHA.109.894824.

Hinde, Natasha. "What Sitting All Day Does to Your Body – and How to Counteract It." Huffington Post, 26 March 2019, https://www.huffingtonpost.co.uk/entry/how-sitting-all-day-affects-the-body_uk_5930184de4b0540ffc84d81c?guccounter=1&guce_referrer=aHR0cHM6Ly93d3cuZ29vZ2xlLmNvbvbS8&guce_referrer_sig=AQAAAKaZ2ZnIDJnO_qFNn0V-n5Go tDQLcsbkreNEmDRAQhGjI4NVoPbEiyZSWns6MC QLdAXpKa6sWGz71FVKNzvlkpfc7JTNTQrMkPnF9 WRi8re_ydCoch6ojwKoxTRgJ8mq5PntYGYoRIpa-1Oz4N3QPOwQXQEMJq_GpbpRi1GMVov.

Katzmarzyk, Peter T., et al. "Sitting Time and Mortality from All Causes, Cardiovascular Disease, and Cancer." Medicine and Science in Sports Exercise, vol. 41, no. 5, 2009, http://citeseerx.ist.psu.edu/viewdoc/download?doi=10.1.1.460.5833&rep=rep1&type=pdf.

Laskowski, Edward R. "What Are the Risks of Sitting Too Much?" Adult Health, Mayo Clinic, 21 August 2020, https://www.mayoclinic.org/healthy-lifestyle/adult-health/expert-answers/sitting/faq-20058005.

Lavie, Carl, et al. "Sedentary Behavior, Exercise, and Cardiovascular Health." Circulation Research, vol. 124, no. 5, March 2019, https://www.ahajournals.org/doi/pdf/10.1161/CIRCRESAHA.118.312669.

Michos, Erin Donnelly. "Sitting Disease: How a Sedentary Lifestyle Affects Heart Health." John Hopkins Medicine, https://www.hopkinsmedicine.org/health/wellness-and-prevention/sitting-disease-how-a-sedentary-lifestyle-affects-heart-health.

"New WHO-Led Study Says Majority of Adolescents Worldwide Are Not Sufficiently Active." World Health Organization, 22 November 2019, https://www.who.int/news-room/detail/22-11-2019-new-who-led-study-says-majority-of-adolescents-worldwide-are-not-sufficiently-physically-active-putting-teir-current-and-future--health-at-risk.

Owen, Neville, et al. "Sedentary Behavior: Emerging Evidence for a New Health Risk." Mayo Clinic Proceedings, vol. 85, no. 12, 1138–1141, 01 December 2010, https://www.ncbi.nlm.nih.gov/pmc/articles/PMC2996155/.

Owen, Neville, et al. "Too Much Sitting: The Population Health Science of Sedentary Behavior. Exercise and Sport Sciences Reviews, vol. 38, no. 3, July 2010, https://journals.lww.com/acsm-essr/Fulltext/2010/07000/Too_Much_Sitting__The_Population_Health_Science_of.3.aspx.

9: WEIGHT MATTERS

"Adult Obesity Facts." United States Centers for Disease Control and Prevention, 29 June 2020, www.cdc.gov/obesity/data/adult.html.

Albright, Anne L, Judith S. Stern. "Adipose Tissue." Encyclopedia of Sports Medicine and Science, 10 July 1998, http://www.sportsci.org/encyc/adipose/adipose.html.

"Obesity and Overweight." World Health Organization, 1 April 2020, https://www.who.int/news-room/fact-sheets/detail/obesity-and-overweight.

Szalay, Jessie. "What Are Calories?" LiveScience, 14 November 2015, https://www.livescience.com/52802-what-is-a-calorie.html.

"Taking Aim at Belly Fat." Harvard Women's Health Watch, Harvard Health Publishing, August 2010, https://www.health.harvard.edu/staying-healthy/taking-aim-at-belly-fat.

Tello, Monique. "Intermittent Fasting: Surprising Update." Harvard Health Blog, Harvard Health Publishing, 29 June 2018, https://www.health.harvard.edu/blog/intermittent-fasting-surprising-update-2018062914156.

"The Glycemic Index and International GI Database." University of Sydney, 26 November 2019, https://www.glycemicindex.com/.

13: REST IS OVERRATED

"Aren't Sure? Brain Is Primed for Learning." Yale News, 19 July 2018, https://news.yale.edu/2018/07/19/arent-sure-brain-primed-learning.

"Exercise and Aging: Can You Walk Away from Father Time." Harvard Health Publishing, March 2014, https://www.health.harvard.edu/staying-healthy/exercise-and-aging-can-you-walk-away-from-fater-time.

Freene, Nicole, et al. "Objectively Measured Changes in Physical Activity and Sedentary Behavior in Cardiac Rehabilitation." Journal of Cardiopulmonary Rehabilitation and Prevention, vol. 38, no. 6, November 2018, https://journals.lww.com/jcrjournal/Citation/2018/11000/Objectively_Measured_Changes_in_Physical_Activity.17.aspx.

Hirsch, James G., et al. "A Study Comparing the Effects of Bed Rest and Physical Activity on Recovery from Pulmonary Tuberculosis." American Review of Tuberculosis and Pulmonary Diseases, vol. 75, no. 3, March 1957, https://www.atsjournals.org/doi/abs/10.1164/artpd.1957.75.3.359.

"Low-intensity Exercise Reduces Fatigue Symptoms by 65 Percent, Study Finds." ScienceDaily, 2 March 2008, www.sciencedaily.com/releases/2008/02/080228112008.htm.

Mahler, Beatrice, and Alina Croitoru. "Pulmonary Rehabilitation and Tuberculosis: A New Approach for an Old Disease." Pneumologia, vol. 68, no. 3, 09 Dec 2019, https://content.sciendo.com/configurable/contentpage/journals$002fpneum$002f68$002f3$002farticle-p107.xml.

McGavock, Johnathan M., et al. "A Forty-Year Follow-Up of the Dallas Bed Rest and Training Study: The Effect of Age on the Cardiovascular Response to Exercise in Men." The Journals of Gerontology, vol. 64A, no. 2, https://www.ncbi.nlm.nih.gov/pmc/articles/PMC2655009/.

Murray, John F. "Bill Dock and the Location of Pulmonary Tuberculosis." American Journal of Respiratory and Critical Care Medicine, vol. 168, no. 9, 4 September 2003, https://www.atsjournals.org/doi/abs/10.1164/rccm.200307-1016OE.

"Recovering from Heart Surgery." Harvard Health Publishing, January 2019, https://www.health.harvard.edu/heart-health/recovering-from-heart-surgery.

14: SLEEP IS SACRED

"Brain Basics: Understanding Sleep." National Institute of Neurological Disorders and Stroke, 13 August 2019, https://www.ninds.nih.gov/Disorders/Patient-Caregiver-Education/Understanding-Sleep.

Brueck, Hillary. "You Are Probably Not Getting Enough Sleep, and It Is Killing You." Business Insider, 27 April 2018, https://www.businessinsider.com/how-much-sleep-is-enough-health-risks-dangers-of-sleep-deprivation-2017-11?r=US&IR=T.

"Drowsy Driving vs. Drunk Driving: How Similar Are They?" The National Sleep Foundation, 28 July 2020, https://www.sleepfoundation.org/articles/drowsy-driving-vs-drunk-driving-how-similar-are-they.

Shepard, John W., et al. "History of the Development of Sleep Medicine in the United States." Journal of Clinical Sleep Medicine, vol. 1, no. 1, 15 January 2005, https://www.ncbi.nlm.nih.gov/pmc/articles/PMC2413168/.

"Sleep Apnea." Patient Care and Health Information, Mayo Clinic, 28 July 2020, https://www.mayoclinic.org/diseases-conditions/sleep-apnea/symptoms-causes/syc-20377631.

"Sleep Deprivation Increases Alzheimer's Protein." National Institutes of Health, 24 April 2018, https://www.nih.gov/news-events/nih-research-matters/sleep-deprivation-increases-alzheimers-protein.

Tefft, Brian C. "Acute Sleep Deprivation and Culpable Motor Vehicle Crash Involvement." Sleep, vol. 41, no. 10, October 2018, https://academic.oup.com/sleep/article/41/10/zsy144/5067408.

"The Global Pursuit of Better Sleep Health." Phillips Global Sleep Survey, 2019, https://www.usa.philips.com/c-dam/b2c/master/experience/smartsleep/world-sleep-day/2019/2019-philips-world-sleep-dy-survey-results.pdf.

15: TOGETHER IS BETTER

Lambert, Craig. "From the Archives: The Talent for Aging Well." Harvard Magazine, 08.09.2019, https://harvardmagazine.com/2019/08/the-talent-for-aging-well.

Mineo, Liz. "Good Genes Are Nice, but Joy Is Better." The Harvard Gazette, 11 April 2017, https://news.harvard.edu/gazette/story/2017/04/over-nearly-80-years-harvard-study-has-been-showing-how-to-live-a-healthy-and-happy-life/.

Solan, Matthew. "The Secret to Happiness? Here's Some Advice from the Longest-Running Study on Happiness." Harvard Health Blog, Harvard Health Publishing, 05 October 2017, https://www.health.harvard.edu/blog/the-secret-to-happiness-heres-some-advice-from-the-longest-running-study-on-happiness-2017100512543.

ACKNOWLEDGEMENTS

No book is complete without acknowledgements, particularly if you are a first-time author like myself. Fresh out of the box, it is terribly difficult to write a good book, no matter how much knowledge and study go into it. You need good advice, time, and concentration.

The greatest help for me was to have time allotted to me by my family. My wife, Claire-Lise, has been used to having an ultra-busy husband all of her married life. But a book? She could have seen it as another one of my over-the-top ambitions, or just a way of filling the time I suddenly had on my hands after selling a business, not being one to ever sit still. But, no, she embraced the idea of this book, and also of creating a foundation to address what I have come to see as one of the most crucial challenges facing our rapidly aging and increasingly sedentary world, namely, the importance of physical fitness for remaining healthy and active into old age. I thank her from the bottom of my heart for her understanding and patience with the late nights and weekends of writing, editing, phone calls, and interminable corrections. Thank you, my dear Claire-Lise.

I also want to thank our three children, Viviane, Justin, and Christian, for their encouragement when the book project was only a dream, and for all their help, advice, and time in bringing the Fit For Life Foundation into existence. They stepped into the breach while I was recovering from a serious shoulder injury and gave me a morale boost when things looked pretty scary. Our daughter, Viviane, an editor and translator by profession, contributed many useful suggestions and corrections to the final draft.

Sincere thanks to my colleague Andrew Gordon, who spent months helping me craft the text of the book. He helped give my prose a more vibrant tone, assisted me in researching the science behind the insights I present, and was able to draw out of me many anecdotes from my life that would not otherwise have been included here.

Thanks also go to Marty Saunders for his editorial support through the final stages of the project, and Rachel Gimbert for her role in designing the cover and bringing the book to print.

Last, but not least, I would like to thank Nicola Crosta, Antonella Notari, Michael Lindenmayer, and Thomas Baskett for their helpful comments on the draft. After reading about my experiences and adventures, most of them commented that I must have been out of breath for most of my life! But they were kind enough also to say that this gave them a better understanding of who I am, what makes me tick, and why I am so determined to spread the message about the importance of physical activity for a happy, active old age.

I hope this book will inspire you, too, to *get fit for life*!

ABOUT THE AUTHOR

A successful entrepreneur and all-round athlete, Jack Lowe has been involved in amateur and professional sports for decades. He has climbed the highest peaks in Europe, Africa, and South America, and traveled twenty-two countries by bike. He has sponsored cycling teams and helped lead basketball camps for youth in Switzerland. He has also participated for many years in a Geneva-based study on how aging athletes perform physically over time.

Over the past fifty years, Jack has created half a dozen businesses in as many industries, from restaurants to private equity and microfinance. In 2020, at the age of 78, he championed the creation of the Fit for Life Foundation in order to translate into actions the philosophy of active aging he explores at length in this book. The foundation aims to promote active lifestyles, fitness and independent mobility among middle-aged and older people worldwide, and supports innovative, high-impact projects through its annual Fit for Life Awards.

Jack holds an MBA from Stanford University and is fluent in English, French, Japanese, and Spanish. He lives with his wife in near Geneva, Switzerland, and has three adult children and seven grandchildren who regularly join him on hiking, skiing, and cycling adventures.

Printed in Poland
by Amazon Fulfillment
Poland Sp. z o.o., Wrocław

66762394R00130